TESI GREGORIANA
Serie Teologia

—————————————— 123 ——————————————

MERVYN DUFFY

HOW LANGUAGE, RITUAL AND SACRAMENTS WORK

According to John Austin, Jürgen Habermas and Louis-Marie Chauvet

EDITRICE PONTIFICIA UNIVERSITÀ GREGORIANA
Roma 2005

Vidimus et approbamus ad normam Statutorum Universitatis

Romae, ex Pontificia Universitate Gregoriana
die 14 mensis apriliis anni 2005

R.P. Prof. GERALD O'COLLINS, S.J.
Mons. Prof. LIAM BERGIN

ISBN 88-7839-038-0

GREGORIAN UNIVERSITY PRESS
Piazza della Pilotta, 35 - 00187 Rome, Italy

A corporeal or material element
set before the external senses,
representing by similitude,
signifying by institution
and containing by sanctification,
some invisible and spiritual grace.

Hugh of St Victor (1096-1141),
De Sacramentis Christianae Fidei,
P. IX, c.2; *PL* 176, 317b.

ACKNOWLEDGEMENTS

In presenting this work I acknowledge with gratitude the people who have helped bring it to term:

- Professor **Philip Rosato, SJ** who proposed the topic for my tesina and then led me into this area of doctoral research;
- Professor **Gerald O'Collins, SJ** who took over the role of supervisor and who has been consistently approachable and encouraging;
- My congregation, the **Society of Mary,** the New Zealand Province of which gave me this opportunity and the Italian Province which has hosted me and treated me as a member of the family;
- My fellow students of the Gregorian University for their support, especially **Fr Michael Shortall** who has willingly discussed the topics herein over innumerable cappuccini;
- Those who have proofread the text, especially **Jenny Clark**, for their help with scrambled ideas and errant punctuation.

INTRODUCTION

The central mystery of sacramental theology is the efficacy of the sacraments. The Catechism teaches that «the seven sacraments are the signs and instruments by which the Holy Spirit spreads the grace of Christ the head throughout the Church which is his Body»[1]. This notion of «sign» (*signum - semeion - 'ôth*) is a rich biblical concept. The Hebrew word was used of the «mark» of Cain[2], of the rainbow as sign of the covenant with Noah[3], and of the sign-actions of the prophets[4]. Its usual translation in the Septuagint – *semeion* – is, in the New Testament, used of: the sign given to the shepherds[5], the sign of Jonah[6], the sign demanded from Jesus[7], the sign of the Son of Man[8], the wonderful works of Jesus in John's gospel[9], and the kiss of Judas as a sign to those ordered to arrest Jesus[10]. In the fifth century Augustine linked the concepts of sacrament and sign: «*sacramentum, id est sacrum*

---

[1] *CCC* §774.

[2] Gen 4:15.

[3] Gen 9:12.

[4] For example: Isaiah's giving of a name in Isa 8:1-18; Isaiah's going naked in Isa 20:3, and Ezekiel's representing the siege of Jerusalem with the aid of a tile, Ezek. 4:1-3.

[5] Luke 2:12.

[6] Matt 12:39-40; 16:4; Luke 11:29-30.

[7] Matt 12:38; Luke 11:16; 11:29.

[8] Matt 24:30.

[9] John is the NT work that uses *semeion* most frequently, 17 times. Sign is a major theme in the gospel, as evidenced by verses like John 2:11 «This was the first of the signs given by Jesus: it was given at Cana in Galilee». (*JB*)

[10] Matt 26:48.

signum»[11]. This was taken up by Hugh of St Victor, Peter Lombard and Thomas Aquinas in the great medieval systematisation of theology[12].

The efficacy of the sacraments is, therefore, a question about how a sign can sanctify or «contain grace». Aquinas developed an answer according to instrumental causality. However, he also made the intriguing assertion that a sacrament contains grace «*in the same way as the human voice contains the spiritual power to arouse the mind of the hearer*»[13]. This thesis explores a philosophy about the power of the human voice to influence a hearer and endeavours to connect this notion to the efficacy of the liturgical celebrations of the seven sacraments.

The scholastic theory of the efficacy of sacraments is based on classical metaphysics. The present generation is not well attuned to metaphysics. Modern and post-modern philosophies have introduced multiple alternative world-views and terminologies. They have had a subtle and pervasive influence on the cultures of the world. It is plausible to suggest that this phenomenon has had a negative impact on sacramental catechesis. While ontology is out of vogue, phenomenology and communication theories are, at present, very influential in sociology, psychology, pedagogy and the social sciences in general. Approaching sacramental efficacy from this perspective offers the hope of refreshing the catechesis on sacraments with insights that resonate with the concerns of contemporary culture. As the Congregation for the Doctrine of the Faith advises: «It is the theologian's task [...] to draw from the surrounding culture those elements which will allow him better to illumine one or other aspect of the mysteries of faith»[14]. It mentions the use of philosophy to gain «a solid and correct understanding of man, the world, and God»[15]. The perennial task of theology is to speak of divine

---

[11] AUGUSTINE, *De civitate Dei*, 10.5: *PL* 41, 282.

[12] Hugh of St Victor (d. 1141) «sacramenta sunt signa rei sacrae» *De Sacramentis Christianae Fidei*: Peter Lombard (d. 1164) «Sacramentum proprie dicitur quod ita signum est gratiae Dei, ei invisibilis gratiae forma, ut ipsius imaginem gerat et causa existat» IV *Sent.*, d.I, n.2; St Thomas Aquinas (d. 1274) «Signum rei sacrae in quantum est sanctificans homines» *ST* III, q.60, a.2.

[13] *ST.* III, q. 62, a.4, ad 1; «sicut etiam in ipsa voce sensibili est quaedam vis spiritualis ad excitandum intellectum hominis, inquantum procedit a conceptione mentis. Et hoc modo vis spiritualis est in sacramentis, inquantum ordinantur a Deo ad effectum spiritualem».

[14] CDF, *Instruction on the Ecclesial Vocation*, 10.

[15] CDF, *Instruction on the Ecclesial Vocation*, 10, citing *Optatam Totius*, 15.

revelation to each generation of the human family, and, as for Paul at the Areopagus (Acts 17:22-33) so today, the language and concepts of philosophy assist in this task.

The twentieth century experienced a «turn to language» by philosophers. One aspect of this was the work of «ordinary language» philosophers. As opposed to synthetic approaches, these philosophers endeavoured to use everyday language as their source of information and useful distinctions. Religious language is one part of ordinary language, thus the relevance of this approach to theology. Theology about everyday language is accessible to ordinary believers and therefore useful in catechesis.

1. The Aim and the Limits

The question that focuses this study is «How do the sacraments work?» The contention is that speech act theory, initially proposed by John Austin, can provide *an* answer. Speech act theory, therefore, holds this thesis together and defines its boundaries. We start from Austin who showed how language works – how it *does* things. The impact of Austin's ideas on various fields is considered as speech act theory found progressively wider application, including within the areas of religious language and ritual. Habermas's development of speech act theory into the theory of communicative action is dealt with as providing a more elaborated philosophical theory of how all types of communication are efficacious. The link to theology is provided by Chauvet, who applied speech act theory to sacramental theology with his theory of symbolic efficacy. In brief, the path followed is: from how utterances do things, via how rituals provide a setting for performative utterances, to how sacraments work. Only those parts of the work of Habermas and Chauvet related to the development of Austin's ideas are considered. Chauvet's theory of sacramental efficacy does not depend on Habermas's theory of communicative action, yet they share common ground in using Austin's speech act theory. This provides the mix of diversity and commonality that comparison and critique require.

Habermas develops speech act theory into his theory of communicative action which is central in the third chapter, rather than, for example, his political philosophy on the modern liberal state. Similarly Chauvet's theory of symbolic efficacy, again explicitly indebted to speech act theory is the focus of that chapter rather than his concern for the connection between scripture and ethical praxis.

With respect to the scope of the thesis, «sacraments» are understood as referring to the seven ritual sacraments of the Roman Catholic Church. Wider senses of the term – Christ as sacrament of God, the Church as sacrament of Christ – are not addressed. While it is hoped the approach outlined will have benefits for an ecumenical understanding of the sacraments, the chosen point of view is from within the Roman Catholic faith community.

1.1 *John Austin: Speech Act Theory*

The first chapter focuses on the work of John Langshaw Austin (1911-1960). In addressing «the turn to language» Austin is located in terms of the philosophical currents of his day. A biographical sketch gives an historical context. Austin's view of philosophy is touched on as background for his innovative method of concerning himself with the minutiae of ordinary language. The method itself is explored according to the concern for what can and cannot be said, the importance of the etymological origins of language, the sources of novelty, and the evolutionary processes that produce and conserve distinctions within ordinary speech. Following this consideration of his method we detail his results. He derided the long-standing view of language as «the Descriptive Fallacy», and he advanced the contrary position by which some utterances are seen as performative – as *doing* something. Given that he addressed functions of language other than the descriptive, he required an attribute distinct from «truth»; hence Austin introduced the notion of a «happy» outcome to a speech act. The thesis investigates his «doctrine of infelicities» and the many ways in which the outcome of a speech transaction can be unhappy.

While exploring ordinary language Austin invented new terminology to communicate his findings. These terms will be introduced and illustrated. Austin adverted to the obvious fact that things are said to influence people, thus that communication is not always transparent. His distinctions about the type of act being done are spelled out and his theory of the forces at work in utterances explained. Some of the implications for the place of truth in communication and philosophy are explored. Austin's positive view of the self-expression involved in communication is briefly addressed. All of this leads to a presentation of Austin's most highly regarded contribution, his analysis of the priority of the performative over the descriptive.

Austin argued that an utterance can only achieve a happy outcome when there is uptake by the hearer. The final section of the first chapter deals with the «uptake» of Austin's ideas in various fields: philosophy, linguistics, anthropology, literature, and theology. The crucial role of Austin's disciples – his students from Oxford – is described. Connections are made between speech act theory and ritual, text, religious language, parables, prophecy, gospel dialogue, liturgy and sacraments.

The method used in presenting the work of Austin and Habermas in the first two chapters is discursive. The aim is to explain their approach and achievements, using their vocabulary and frame of reference. Attention is focussed on what will have application in showing how sacraments work, but that application is made in the last chapter.

1.2 Jürgen Habermas: Theory of Communicative Action

The protagonist of this second chapter is a very different philosopher operating in a radically different context. However, one of the features that distinguishes Jürgen Habermas (b. 1929) from other members of the Frankfurt School was precisely his use of the philosophical ideas of John Austin. The treatment of Habermas parallels that of Austin: he is located philosophically and historically, his view of philosophy explored, his method outlined and then his relevant contribution detailed. Habermas is a prolific writer across a great range of philosophical, sociological, ethical and political issues. There is no attempt to outline the full range of his thought. The thesis addresses only his use of speech act theory and his development of it into the theory of communicative action. Attention is paid to his concept of «lifeworld» and to his three «worlds of discourse», plus his analysis of what an «act» involves. His theory of «Universal Pragmatics», wherein he attempted to generalize speech act theory into universal conditions of possible understanding, is of particular interest.

One of Habermas's major philosophical preoccupations has been the identification of systematically distorted communication and its role in dysfunctional societies. This is addressed in this thesis as a guard against any naïve optimism about communication theory and the power of symbols. In his «ideal speech situation» Habermas outlined his criteria for distortion-free communication. He identified in the validity claims made in utterances what he considered to be the basis for Austin's performative force. He also connected these claims to his three «worlds».

Another philosophical point addressed by Habermas which is of theological importance is the role of freedom in communication, in particular, the freedom to refuse to accept what is being said. He connected this idea with the structure and formation of the human personality. Communication is also the foundation of Habermas's contribution to ethical theory – his «discourse ethics». While this connection is acknowledged, it is not explored in depth. For Habermas his theory of communicative action explained the progressive rationalization (and secularisation) of society. To be authentic to Habermas and his «methodological atheism», it is necessary that these applications of the theory which evaluate religion as transient be acknowledged in an attempt to appropriate his theory for theological ends.

1.3 *Louis-Marie Chauvet: Symbolic Efficacy*

The third chapter treats of the sacramental theology presented by Louis-Marie Chauvet (b. 1942) in *Symbol and Sacrament* and *The Sacraments*. Chauvet explicitly rejected traditional explanations of sacramental efficacy and the entire ontological metaphysics underlying them. He attributed various negative features of Catholic life, liturgy and self-understanding (triumphalism, sacramental minimalism, the metaphor of production) to the effects of «onto-theology». Chauvet's critique is examined and commented upon. In the place of onto-theology Chauvet offered a language-centred «symbolic order». He, like Habermas, presented a phenomenological worldview where reality is only accessed via the mediation of language.

Chauvet's direct use of speech act theory is considered, in particular his understanding of the constative-performative relationship. Then it is shown how Chauvet sought to supplement Austin's theory of the performative force of utterances by drawing on the insights of the sociologist Pierre Bourdieu. Significant for the argument of the thesis is Chauvet's identification of the force underlying rituals with the performative force of utterances. This enables applications of speech act theory to be considerably widened and clarifies the role of convention in performative utterances. It is used to throw light on the role of the spokesperson of a group, the authorised representative of the social consensus.

An indirect connection between Chauvet and Austin is explored: the theories of the self-implicative nature of religious language developed by Donald Evans and Jean Ladrière on the basis of Austin's ideas. This includes a consideration of how religious language operates efficaciously in liturgy in general and in sacraments in particular. Words are not the only symbols used in sacraments; therefore consideration is given to a major theme of Chauvet's, that of «symbolic exchange». Chauvet applied this notion to speech transactions as well as gift exchanges. Chauvet's schema of the act of symbolization will be addressed as will the issues of corporality and particularity which he stressed as a counter to the abstraction and a-historical tendencies of onto-theology. The culmination of this chapter is a presentation of Chauvet's model of how sacraments simultaneously operate as revealers and reveal as operators.

1.4 *Sacraments within a Catholic Lifeworld*

The methodology of this final chapter is different from those that precede it. Rather than describing the ideas of others it develops a synthesis which is applied to sacramental topics and tested against established dogmas. Since both Habermas and Chauvet have already incorporated the thought of Austin, the challenge lies in making connections and corrections between Habermas and Chauvet. Perceived strengths of Habermas's theory of communicative action are identified in ways that show their applicability to Chauvet's model of symbolic efficacy.

Habermas's sociological lens and terminology are applied to the Roman Catholic Church, thereby envisioning it as a distinct culture, a communicative community in its own right. Considering the Church from this perspective enables the application of the already discussed communication theories to the rituals of the Church, in particular to the liturgy and to the seven sacraments. The contention is that the Church culture not only hands on the sacramental tradition, but also forms in its members the competencies the sacraments require. The ways the sacramental signs refer to the word, past events, present relationships, and eschatological future is linked to Habermas's fundamental three-fold structure of communication. His notions of lifeworld and worlds of reference are recapitulated and applied to the central utterances of a sacramental rite.

The role of the Church in the utterance of the minister of the sacrament is addressed in terms of Habermas's taxonomy of speech acts. This leads to a consideration of how the Church both defines and guarantees the sacraments. The strength of this formal theory is in how it reveals subjectivity. Therefore we focus on the subjects involved in a sacramental rite and test the communicative model against traditional teachings on the intention of the minister, the holiness of the minister, and the subjective requirements of the recipient of the sacrament. Limit cases for a communicative model are those where the recipient is unable to respond, so the cases of the baptism of a baby and the anointing of a person *in extremis* are discussed in terms of the actual communications involved. The communication model is also tested against teachings relating to the character conferred by some sacraments, the continuity of the sacraments in history, and their institution by Jesus Christ. Particular attention is paid to the performative-constative relationship identified by Austin and partially assimilated by Chauvet. Both divine revelation and sacraments are considered in light of the implications of Austin's assertion of the priority of the performative. Finally, a vision of salvation history in terms of communicative action is sketched out to provide a context for the proposed interpretation of sacraments.

2. Toward a Formal Communicative Theory of Sacraments

Classical scholastic theology drew upon Aristotelian metaphysics and its categories, for example substance and accident. This philosophy, whose great exponent was Thomas Aquinas, affirms the reality of the external world and the objectivity and accessibility of truth. Pope John Paul II wrote of Aquinas that:

> Looking unreservedly to truth, the realism of Thomas could recognize the objectivity of truth and produce not merely a philosophy of «what seems to be» but a philosophy of «what is»[16].

However, despite the praise of Thomas, the Pope goes on to declare: «The Church has no philosophy of her own nor does she canonize any one particular philosophy in preference to others»[17]. He also notes that one characteristic of today is «the proliferation of systems, method, concepts and philosophical theses»[18].

Chauvet, writing before *Fides et Ratio*, strongly critiques and rejects Thomistic philosophy; describing his task as «overcoming metaphysics»[19]. Chauvet goes on to outline a philosophy based not on objectiv-

---

[16] *FR* 44.
[17] *FR* 49.
[18] *FR* 51.
[19] For example L-M. CHAUVET, *Symbol and Sacrament*, 48: «Overcoming metaphysics then is no simple matter of crossing it out with one stroke of the pen as if it were an opinion, doctrine, or system to be refuted; rather to do so one must re-ascend

ity, but on subjectivity and inter-subjectivity. Habermas similarly rejects metaphysics. Paul Lakeland characterizes Habermas's position in these terms:

> Habermas wants to pass beyond the instrumentality of reality that takes place when my starting point is that I am a subject and everything else is for me an object. On the contrary, says Habermas, I am constituted as a self in my intersubjective communicative praxis. Habermas's linguistic turn, like that of so many twentieth century philosophers, carries him away from the philosophy of consciousness to the philosophy of language. But for Habermas there is a difference. The linguistic unit upon which the philosopher must concentrate, and that forms whatever foundation there is to human subjectivity, is the speech act. The act of communication rests upon certain fundamental characteristics and so is in a sense foundational, but the foundation is only formal, not substantive[20].

In following Habermas and Chauvet this thesis presents a formal communicative theory of the seven sacraments. Unlike Habermas and Chauvet we do not take this as implying a rejection of metaphysics. In an age characterized by a plurality of philosophies, a single monolithic philosophical-theological system may not be the best, or even a possible, response. A formal theory which talks of how sacraments work and emphasizes the perceptions of the subjects who participate in them is a useful complement to a substantive theory that addresses the objective realities involved. As will be discussed below[21], metaphysical approaches deliver a sharp focus on the validity of sacraments, while a formal communicative approach throws light on their fruitfulness. The formal-substantive distinction is one that comes from scholastic theology and may suggest an avenue for integrating the philosophical underpinnings of the two theological approaches. This thesis follows the formal path without denying the importance or effectiveness of what has been developed via the more well-trodden substantive way.

---

to the very source of its life, that is to the "truth of Being" which is its *ignored* "foundation"».

[20] P. LAKELAND, *Postmodernity*, 22.

[21] See Ch. IV 2.8 below.

Figure 1: John Austin, 1951

CHAPTER I

John Austin and Speech Act Theory

1. The Contribution of Communication Theory

The most elaborate and important human creation in the field of signs and symbols is language itself. Each human language is a marvel of complexity and brilliance, the heritage of many generations of human ingenuity. Language coordinates and enables all human endeavours. Sacraments and liturgy are activities embedded in language and dependent on it for their performance. There are non-linguistic signs and symbols involved in sacramental rites but they are introduced and accompanied by linguistic utterances. Given that speech provides the context and much of the content of sacramental celebration, an investigation into how speech does things is a good place to begin a study of how sacraments do what they do.

2. The Turn to Language

At the start of the twentieth century two linked groups with a common agenda were prominent in European philosophy. They were the Vienna Circle[1], also known as the Logical Positivists, and the English Analytic School. These two groups did not want to base their systems of thought on anything prone to romanticism and bias. They wished to avoid any field with the taint of irrationality. Language, history and sociology were seen by them as potentially corrupting fields of investigation. Mathematics and the science of logic were their paradigms for ra-

---

[1] A group of scientifically minded philosophers working in Vienna under the loose leadership of Moritz Schlick, Otto Neurath and Rudolf Carnap.

tional thought. Collective entities, like nations, or peoples, were especially suspect for the Vienna Circle. They saw the popular conception
of these as being the fanciful constructions of demagogues. Instead,
their model was the individual, scientific observer.

G. E. Moore and Bertrand Russell were the acknowledged leaders of
the English Analytic movement. Russell's masterpieces, *The Principles
of Mathematics*[2] and what was originally conceived as its second volume but which instead became the three volumes of *Principia
Mathematica*[3], made significant strides in the science of logic and attempted to lay out the foundations of mathematics in an entirely logical
form. Russell viewed logic as conceptually prior to mathematics and
began the task of showing how all of mathematics could be derived
from a set of logical axioms. Russell and Moore expected mathematics
to be just the first discipline of many to be conquered by logic. With the
rules for inference and argumentation clearly defined, any body of
knowledge could potentially be shown to be built up through strictly
valid logical processes from a denumerable list of true propositions.

In the Logical Positivist view language is used only in the most careful and univocal senses to *describe* propositions precisely. Preferable
by far was the use of logical notation, the predicate calculus introduced
by Russell and Whitehead[4]. Truth was seen as an *attribute* of propositions which, preserved in valid argument, is transmitted to the conclusion. The ordinary use of language in day-to-day speech was to be
avoided as imprecise and largely irrational.

Russell's most brilliant pupil, Ludwig Wittgenstein, demonstrated
the limits of the logical positivism of the Vienna Circle and changed
the direction of philosophical thought. Wittgenstein's first book the
Tractatus Logico-Philosophicus[5] was a masterly expression of the programme of logical positivism, and received a very positive reception.
Yet his second major work *Philosophical Investigations*[6] retracted
many of his own assertions and argued the contrary. The later Wittgenstein expressed dissatisfaction with the bases of logical positivism. He

---

[2] B. RUSSELL, *The Principles of Mathematics*, London 1903, 1937[2].
[3] A.N. WHITEHEAD – B. RUSSELL, *Principia Mathematica*, London 1910, 1925[2].
[4] Alfred North Whitehead (1861-1947), mathematician and philosopher of science.
He taught mathematics at Trinity College, Cambridge, and Bertrand Russell was one
of his students.
[5] First published in 1921 in *Annalen der Naturphilosophie*. English edition 1922.
[6] Published posthumously – L.WITTGENSTEIN, *Philosophical Investigations*,
Blackwell, Oxford 1953.

went away from the use of symbolic logic and argued for a focus on language. He pointedly redefined truth from «correspondence to objective fact» to «agreement between persons». Wittgenstein understood truth to be contextual, conventional and relative, produced by a particular «language game». Logic was only one language game among many. This change in philosophical direction was the «turn to language».

The glorious quest to rebuild all thought on a structure of strict logic encountered a fundamental difficulty in the field that was meant to be most amenable to that process. In 1931 the Czech-born mathematician, Kurt Gödel, published an ingenious proof which showed that, no matter what set of axioms – even a denumerably infinite one – was to be constructed, there would still be mathematical truths that were not derivable from those axioms. Gödel's Incompleteness Theorem showed, once and for all, that mathematics, and hence all science, would never be reducible to a construction of pure logic. Symbolic logic had been hoist with its own petard. Logic had been used to show that propositional logic could not be the ultimate basis of critical thought. Truth is thus a stronger and more fundamental concept than «provability».

While Wittgenstein exercised a great intellectual influence at Cambridge, Oxford, as ever, followed a different path. Oxford's philosopher, John Austin, turned to language, not as one of many types of game, but language as it is ordinarily spoken.

3. John Langshaw Austin

When the allied troops landed on the Normandy beaches on D-Day, they had with them a volume about the German dispositions, coastal defences, formations and transport systems. This «guidebook» was entitled *Invade Mecum*. The co-ordination of the vast amount of intelligence information it represented, and the word-play of the title[7], were the work of Lieutenant-Colonel John Langshaw Austin. His achievement as the man who «more than anybody was responsible for the life-saving accuracy of the D-Day Intelligence»[8] was acknowledged by the United Kingdom with an OBE, by the French with the *Croix de*

---

[7] A *Vade-mecum* is a guidebook, or a small reference manual, carried on one's person. The title translates as «go with me». By entitling his work *Invade mecum* (Invade with me) Austin is offering it as the indispensable ready-reference for an invasion.

[8] Quoted by G. Warnock in «John Langshaw Austin, A Biographical Sketch», *SJL*, 9.

Guerre, and by the Americans with appointment as an Officer of the Legion of Merit.

Before the war, Austin had been a Fellow at All Souls College of Oxford (1933-35) and then a Fellow and tutor at Magdalen College (1935-40). He was himself an alumnus of Oxford, having studied classics there. In his pre-war philosophical work he was concerned with the investigation of the history of philosophy. He edited H.W.B. Joseph's lectures on Leibniz (published 1949)[9] and translated Frege's *Grundlagen* (published 1950)[10]. Austin's very first publication «Are There *A Priori* Concepts?»[11] reveals such interest by its many explicit historical references – something that is far less frequent in his post-war work.

Austin returned to Oxford after his distinguished military career. He devoted most of his energies to teaching in the tumultuous environment of that period – the large university classes with many mature students. His publications are all based on symposia presentations, public lectures and university courses. His priority was his students not his reading public. In 1952 Oxford appointed him as White's Professor of Moral Philosophy. In February 1960, after a short battle with cancer, he died at the age of 49 to the shock and grief of his colleagues and students.

The books through which Austin are best known, *Sense and Sensibilia* and *How to Do Things with Words*, were both produced posthumously on the basis of his lecture notes. *Sense and Sensibilia* is based on a course he had taught regularly since 1947 and which had come to be known by that wonderful title. *How to Do Things with Words* is from his 1955 William James Lectures at Harvard which he himself had been attempting to get into publishable form up until his death.

4. Austin's View of Philosophy

One of the scholars that Austin delighted in attacking was his contemporary and colleague Alfred J. Ayer, then lecturer in philosophy at Oxford. Ayer was the leading British exponent of logical positivism,

---

[9] H.W.B. JOSEPH, *Lectures on the philosophy of Leibniz*, Oxford 1949.

[10] G. FREGE, *Die Grundlagen der Arithmetik, eine logisch-mathematische Untersuchung über den Begriff der Zahl*, Darmstadt 1961; English trans., *The Foundations of Arithmetic: A logico-mathematical enquiry into the concept of number*, tr. J.L. Austin, Oxford 1959[2].

[11] *PhP*, 1-22.

with his reputation established by the publication, in 1936, of his work, *Language, Truth and Logic*. An indication of Ayer's approach to philosophy is given in this assertion from that work:

> The propositions of philosophy are not factual, but linguistic in character – that is, they do not describe the behaviour of physical, or even mental, objects; they express definitions, or the formal consequences of definitions. Accordingly, we may say that philosophy is a department of logic[12].

Austin's position could scarcely have been more different. Where Ayer and the Logical Positivists saw philosophy as part of the greater discipline of logic, Austin considered it as the «sun-source» of all organized thought. Far from being a subset, it is the universal set that contains all else. Where Ayer used *formal logic* as the tool for providing *certain truth* Austin took up *ordinary language* as a guide to *useful truths*.

Austin did not see himself as offering a vast new vision of philosophy, (he once entitled an unpublished talk «One Way of Possibly Doing One Part of Philosophy»[13]), yet his modest approach conceals a radical novelty. He hoped to be part of a co-operative effort to bring structure to one little corner of the field. Perhaps influenced by his war experience of organizing a division of intelligence experts whose dogged efforts sifted the truth from multifarious sources, Austin desired to be part of a team enterprise. He envisaged that the problems of philosophy could be solved, not in a flash of insight by a single genius, but by the hard work and co-operation of numerous intelligent thinkers. If philosophers were to follow his example of striving to achieve limited goals such as the meaning of relatively simple parts of life, for example the function of excuses, then the great philosophical goals of understanding truth, goodness and meaning might be brought incrementally closer. He summed up this vision in a paper to the British Academy, subsequently published as «Ifs and Cans»:

> In the history of human inquiry, philosophy has the place of the initial central sun, seminal and tumultuous: from time to time it throws off some portion of itself to take station as a science, a planet, cool and well regulated, progressing steadily towards a distant final stage. This happened long ago at the birth of mathematics, and again at the birth of physics: only in the last century we have witness the same process once again, slow and at the time almost imperceptible, in the birth of the science of mathematical logic,

---

[12] A.J. AYER, *Language, Truth and Logic*, 57.
[13] According to J.O. URMSON, «Austin, John Langshaw», 572.

through the joint labours of philosophers and mathematicians. Is it not possible that the next century may see the birth, through the joint labours of philosophers, grammarians, and numerous other students of language, of a true and comprehensive science of language? Then we shall have rid ourselves of one more part of philosophy (there will still be plenty left) in the only way we ever get rid of philosophy, by kicking it upstairs[14].

Austin claimed a centrality for philosophy. His earlier work on the history of philosophy shows itself in this perspective. He recalled how mathematics was once considered a sub-discipline of philosophy, and astronomy a further specialization. Instead of viewing the developments of the science of logic as supplanting philosophy or giving it a new and certain basis, he presented that field as evidence of the ongoing fruitfulness of the parent discipline. Rather than reject other fields of study as infected with the irrational, Austin proposed a collaboration of philosophers with grammarians and students of language. The precise discipline that the logical positivists had avoided as tainted by unreason was embraced by Austin as an avenue forward for the philosophy of the twentieth century.

5. Austin's Method

5.1 What is it that we say?

«"What is truth?" said jesting Pilate, and would not stay for an answer. Pilate was in advance of his time»[15]. This is how Austin began a 1950 presentation to the Mind Association and the Aristotelian Society. As he attempted an answer to the jesting demand, he shifted into his characteristic mode for seeking to understand a concept: «What is it that we say is true or is false? Or how does the phrase "is true" occur in English sentences?»[16] Austin gave a name to his approach only once in print. That he did not persist in its use suggests he found it unsatisfactory, yet he never actually rejected it:

In view of the prevalence of the slogan «ordinary language» and of such names as «linguistic» or «analytic» philosophy or «the analysis of language», one thing needs specially emphasizing to counter misunderstandings. When we examine what we should say when, what words we should use in what situations, we are looking again not *merely* at words (or «mean-

---

[14] J.L. AUSTIN, «Ifs and Cans», 180.
[15] J.L. AUSTIN, «Truth», 85.
[16] J.L. AUSTIN, «Truth», 85.

ings», whatever they may be) but also at the realities we use the words to talk about: we are using a sharpened awareness of words to sharpen our perception of, though not as the final arbiter of, the phenomena. For this reason I think it might be better to use, for this way of doing philosophy, some less misleading name than those given above – for instance, «linguistic phenomenology», only that is rather a mouthful[17].

To call upon an authority much admired by Austin, the *Oxford English Dictionary*[18] defines «phenomenology» as «the science of phenomena as distinct from that of being (ontology)»[19], which puts Austin in the philosophical tradition of Edmund Husserl. Yet by appending «linguistic», Austin has given a turn of phrase that is, at least, paradoxical. The phenomenological movement tended to oppose concern with language and urged knowledge based on the intuiting, or seeing, the matters that thought is about[20].

Austin, by modifying «phenomenology» with «linguistic» shifted the focus back to language and suggested that words and phrases – *«what we should say when»*[21] – provide a perception of the phenomena. Austin clearly used words as his tools, not unlike a microscope, to look through them at the world with a sharper vision. He claimed to look «at the realities we use the words to talk about»[22]. But by entitling his approach «phenomenology», he implied that his is not an ontological philosophy; there is no claim to speak of an underlying reality beneath the phenomena.

Philosophers have long found merit in carefully distinguishing closely allied ideas. Austin's claim was that his approach reveals a rich source of useful and subtle distinctions.

First, words are our tools, and as a minimum, we should use clean tools: we should know what we mean and what we do not, and we must forearm ourselves against the traps that language sets us. Secondly, words are not (except in their own little corner) facts or things: we need therefore to prise them off the world, to hold them apart from and against it, so that we can realize their inadequacies and arbitrariness, and can re-look at the world

---

[17] J.L. AUSTIN, «A Plea for Excuses», 130.

[18] J.L AUSTIN, «Unfair to Facts», 111-13 provides an example of Austin's use of the *OED* as a tool of philosophical discourse. He analyzes list of uses of the word «fact» in the dictionary.

[19] «Phenomenology», *OED*, 1989², XI, 673.

[20] See L. EMBREE, «Phenomenological Movement», 334.

[21] J.L. AUSTIN, «A Plea for Excuses», 129 (emphasis his).

[22] J.L. AUSTIN, «A Plea for Excuses», 130.

without blinkers. Thirdly, and more hopefully, our common stock of words embodies all the distinctions men have found worth drawing, and the connexions they have found worth marking, in the lifetimes of many generations: these surely are likely to be more numerous, more sound, since they have stood up to the long test of the survival of the fittest, and more subtle, at least in all ordinary and reasonably practical matters, than any that you or I are likely to think up in our arm-chairs of an afternoon – the most favoured alternative method[23].

All philosophizing is done with words. Austin recommended that close attention be paid to ordinary language so that philosophers can argue with precision and clarity. If words are «our tools», then they should be treated with care. Austin also acknowledged that words can conceal as well as reveal. Attention ought be paid to how language can blind us to some aspects of reality. Again this will not be obvious without careful attention to the language we actually use. A recurring question for Austin was «what can we not say?» in a particular situation. For example «You are prohibited from saying "I know it is so, but I may be wrong", just as you are prohibited from saying "I promise I will, but I may fail"».[24] When there is a turn of phrase that is not usual or somehow prohibited in the language, Austin would examine if there were good reason for this, or, if the words are false-to-the-facts.

In sharp contrast to the classic picture of a solitary introspective phenomenologist intuiting his own mental processes, Austin proposed a concerted attack on everyday language by a team of experts in language and philosophy. He wanted an open, scholarly endeavour. The secrets of the phenomena he sought were not, at least directly, those hidden in the deep recesses of the mind, but those already in the very public domain of ordinary language. Austin's approach to linguistic phenomenology is comparable to the work of Linnaeus[25] in botany. Austin was attempting the first grand taxonomy of words, but he hoped to be followed by a horde of fellow professionals who would fill in, expand and correct his initial tentative model.

---

[23] J.L. AUSTIN, «A Plea for Excuses», 129.

[24] J.L. AUSTIN, «Other Minds», 66.

[25] Carl Von Linné (*Carolus Linnaeus* in Latin), 1707-1778, a Swedish botanist and explorer who was the first to frame principles for defining genera and species of organisms and to create a uniform system for naming them.

5.2 *What can we not say?*

«What we say» and, often more importantly, «what we cannot say» in ordinary language reflects the collective experience of our culture. Our language has evolved[26] over millennia, and the words and turns of phrase which have endured have done so because they are useful to people in relating to the world and to each other. It contains «the inherited experience and acumen of many generations of men»[27].

Mark Twain observed that «Truth is more of a stranger than fiction»[28]. Everyday life throws up innumerable events and problems requiring precise communication and subtle distinction:

> If a distinction works well for practical purposes in ordinary life (no mean feat, for even ordinary life is full of hard cases), then there is sure to be something in it, it will not mark nothing[29].

Austin did not *restrict* himself to ordinary language, nor thought that common parlance is always right or that it contains the ultimate insights. He acknowledged the recent contributions of science («the resources of the microscope and its successors»[30]) and the fallibility of language:

> It must be added too, that superstition and error and fantasy of all kinds do become incorporated in ordinary language and even sometimes stand up to the survival test (only, when they do, why should we not detect it?). Certainly, then, ordinary language is not the last word: in principle it can everywhere be supplemented and improved upon and superseded. Only remember, it *is* the *first* word[31].

By claiming language as the first word, Austin asserted that ordinary language is our starting point. It is through language that we experience and understand the world. Before anyone philosophizes they live in and interact with the world – using language. When they begin to philoso-

---

[26] Since the early 1970s various authors have tried to adopt the principle of evolution by selection to understand the continuous change in cultural behaviours. Richard Dawkins in *The Selfish Gene*, Oxford 1976, coined the term «meme» as the cultural/mental equivalent of the biological «gene». Dawkins seems much less convinced than Austin of the accuracy of the grasp that language and culture have on the world.

[27] J.L. AUSTIN, «A Plea for Excuses», 133.

[28] *Following the Equator*, Pudd'nhead Wilson's New Calendar, 1897.

[29] J.L. AUSTIN, «A Plea for Excuses», 133.

[30] J.L. AUSTIN, «A Plea for Excuses», 133.

[31] J.L. AUSTIN, «A Plea for Excuses», 133 (emphases his).

phize the words and ideas that first come to mind are those of ordinary language. They can, and should, be improved on, but they cannot be *bypassed* because they are embedded in all of us.

5.3 *Look to the Past*

Austin's preference as a classically trained scholar was to look into the deep history of words. As he put it, words come «trailing clouds of etymology»[32] and his first step was to call on «that goddess fair and free (fairly fair, frailly free), divinest Etymology»[33]:

> A word never – well, hardly ever – shakes off its etymology and its formation. In spite of all changes in and extensions of and additions to its meanings, and indeed rather pervading and governing these, there will still persist the old idea. In an *accident* something befalls: by *mistake* you take the wrong one: in *error* you stray: when you act *deliberately* you act after weighing it up (not after thinking out ways and means)[34].

Implicit in his method is that words carry their history with them. Language is conservative. It carries its past embedded in it. The evolutionary analogy Austin uses in describing language as evolving can be extended. Encoded in the genes of language is the DNA of its earlier forms. Just as our genetic code is 95 percent identical to that of the great apes, so our language carries much that belonged to the Roman Empire. Specially bleached togas are no longer worn by those seeking high political office, but we still call them «candidates»[35].

5.4 *But Attend to the New*

Along with this attention to the «old» within language is a concern for the sources of novelty and change. Austin stated that modern science has yet had little opportunity to make its impact on language[36].

---

[32] J.L. AUSTIN, «A Plea for Excuses», 149.

[33] J.L. AUSTIN, «Pretending», 208.

[34] J.L. AUSTIN, «A Plea for Excuses», 149.

[35] The Latin term *candidatus* means «clothed in white».

[36] An example in support of Austin's thesis that ordinary language is slow to adopt concepts from science: We still speak of «full-blooded» individuals of a particular race thereby reflecting Darwin's erroneous notion of blood as the *mechanism* of inheritance. The terminology of Crick and Watson (the discoverers of the structure of DNA, which *is* the mechanism of inheritance) has not yet made the same impact.

However modifying this assertion, he elsewhere identified two major sources of precision and distinction that impact on language:

> For this problem too the field of Excuses is a fruitful one. Here is matter both contentious and practically important for everybody, so that ordinary language is on its toes: yet also, on its back it has long had a bigger flea to bite it, in the shape of the Law, and both again have lately attracted the attentions of yet another, and at least a healthily growing, flea, in the shape of psychology. In the law a constant stream of actual cases, more novel and more tortuous than the mere imagination could contrive, are brought up for decision – that is, formulae for docketing them must somehow be found. Hence it is necessary first to be careful with, but also to be brutal with, to torture, to fake and to override, ordinary language; we cannot here evade or forget the whole affair. (In ordinary life we dismiss the puzzles that crop up about time, but we cannot do that indefinitely in physics.) Psychology likewise produces novel cases, but it also produces new methods for bringing phenomena under observation and study: moreover, unlike the law, it has an unbiased interest in the totality of them and is unpressed for decision. Hence its own special and constant need to supplement, to revise and to supersede the classifications of both ordinary life and the law[37].

Ordinary language is «on its toes» – it contains a wealth of different turns of phrase containing many subtle nuances – when it deals with matters of import to a great many people. The legal profession and the judiciary use language and influence language. Legal parlance is largely drawn from the common stock of words but they are given greater precision or even a completely new twist and backed with case law in the courtroom. Moreover this language of the courts filters back out into the streets.

In his «Plea for Excuses», Austin gave, as an example of both correct and incorrect usage of language, part of the transcript of the tragic case of *Regina vs. Finney*[38] in which Finney, a nurse in a psychological ward carelessly (accidentally? negligently?) scalded a patient to death. The Law literally has to deal with «hard cases» and its decisions have to be written up in ways that will be understood by those who come after. It uses language and adds to its development in the process.

---

[37] J.L. AUSTIN, «A Plea for Excuses», 133-134.

[38] J.L. AUSTIN, «A Plea for Excuses», 143-145. Finney bathed the patient, let the water out, then, distracted by a question, started the bath refilling with very hot water, without having removed the patient. If it were judged to be *carelessness* then he would have been guilty of manslaughter. It was deemed to be an *accident* and he was found not guilty.

Austin's affirmation of psychology shows he considered at least one modern science had made an impact on language. He characterized psychology as a «healthily growing flea»[39], and implied that it contributes valuable insights into human perception and the understanding of what motivates us. The nature of psychology is such that it looks beyond commonplace explanations; so everyday language does not suffice to express psychological explanations and theories. Hence psychology will be a constant source of neologisms, some of which will eventually make their way into ordinary discourse[40].

5.5 When «what we say» Fails

Austin was particularly interested in communication breakdowns, because the things that can go wrong throw light on the processes involved in successful communication:

> Typically we distinguish different abstracted «acts» by means of the possible slips between cup and lip, that is, in this case, the different types of nonsense which may be engendered in performing them[41].

The ways in which communication can fail are revelatory of the inner workings of the speech act, even when the distinctions between the «different parts» are only abstractions.

Austin identified ways in which communication could fail apart from truth and falsity. He called these «infelicities» meaning the communication was not «happily» accomplished. A significant class of «infelicities» are those related to the inner world of the speaker. These are not directly evident to the addressee. They can arise in the areas of feelings, thoughts and intentions. Austin gave examples of each:

> «I congratulate you», said when I did not feel at all pleased, perhaps even was annoyed. [...]

---

[39] Austin is not disparaging psychology, but alluding to the verse beloved by logicians: «So, naturalists observe, a flea / Hath smaller fleas that on him prey, / And these have smaller still to bite 'em, / And so proceed *ad infinitum*». Jonathan Swift, *Poetry, a Rhapsody* (1733).

[40] There seems to be a natural lag between when theories have their scientific vogue and when they impact on everyday speech. Freudian terminology is now commonplace, for example «Freudian slip», but that of the thinkers presently held in high academic regard has yet to «filter down».

[41] J.L. AUSTIN, *How to Do Things with Words*, 147.

«I advise you to», said when I do not think it would be the course most expedient for you. [...]

«I declare war», said when I do not intend to fight[42].

Each of these statements is somehow awry, despite being grammatically well formed and virtually identical to the sincere form of the same. The «unhappiness» is not to be found in the words. Exactly the same thing could be said by a different person, or even by the same person in different circumstances to quite different effect. The man, who insincerely congratulates a co-worker in being promoted over him, could then use the same phraseology to warmly congratulate a friend from another firm who has also been promoted.

The wrongness is not simply that the acts fail to be what they purport to be. When someone maliciously gives bad advice they are still giving advice. Their statement «I advise you to ...» is still a true statement. In making it, they *are* offering advice. As Austin concluded:

> We see that in order to explain what can go wrong with statements we cannot just concentrate on the proposition involved (whatever that is) as has been done traditionally. We must consider the total situation in which the utterance is issued – the total speech-act[43].

His study of when and how communication can fail shows that utterances cannot be taken out of context, without sense and reference changing. For a happy outcome to be achieved requires far more than a true proposition and a valid argument. Understanding utterances demands understanding something of the inner world of the speaker, the addressee, and the social world that they share.

5.6 *The Distinctions within Ordinary Language*

According to Austin, one key to that social world and to the human perception of the real world is found in common parlance:

> We must pay attention to the facts of *actual* language, what we can and cannot say, and *precisely* why, another and converse point takes shape. Although it will not do to force actual language to accord with some preconceived model: it *equally* will not do, having discovered the facts about «ordinary usage» *to rest content* with that, as though there were nothing more to be discussed and discovered. There may be plenty that might happen and

---

[42] J.L. AUSTIN, *How to Do Things with Words*, 40.
[43] J.L. AUSTIN, *How to Do Things with Words*, 52.

does happen which would need new and better language to describe it in. [...] There may be extraordinary facts, even about our every-day experience, which plain men and plain language overlook[44].

Austin ferreted out the subtleties of language as the base data to build philosophical theory upon. He invented new terminology to describe his discoveries[45], yet he warned against the philosophical practice of redefining words:

> It is advisable always to bear in mind (a) that the distinctions embodied in our vast and, for the most part, relatively ancient stock of ordinary words are neither few nor always very obvious, and never just arbitrary; (b) that in any case, before indulging in any tampering on our own account, we need to find out what it is that we have to deal with; and (c) that tampering with words in what we take to be one little corner of the field is always liable to have unforeseen repercussions in the adjoining territory. Tampering, in fact, is not so easy as is often supposed, is not justified or not needed so often as is often supposed, and is often thought to be necessary just because what we've got already has been misrepresented[46].

Stylistically, Austin preferred plain language and he deprecated the pretentious use of elaborate terminology when adequate plain terms were available.

Austin saw himself as exploring familiar, common territory in his attention to «actual» language. The expressions he adverted to are known to all accomplished speakers of English. The power of his argument comes from the accessibility of the matter it is based on. He did not claim any extraordinary experience or insight, simply that he paid attention to the ways in which we all speak. He expected to win agreement from students of the language in his classification of the distinctions contained in common speech.

> There is a singular difference between the two forms of the challenge: «*How* do you know?» and «*Why* do you believe?» We seem never to ask «*Why* do you know?» or «*How* do you believe?» And in this, as well as in other respects to be noticed later, not merely such other words as «suppose»

---

[44] J.L. AUSTIN, «The Meaning of a Word», 37.

[45] «Illocution», «illocutionary», «performative» and «perlocutionary» are inventions by Austin which have gained such widespread currency that they feature in the *OED*.

[46] J.L. AUSTIN, *Sense and Sensibilia*, 63.

«assume», &c., but also the expressions «be sure» and «be certain», follow the example of «believe», not that of «know»[47].

When we read phrases like those Austin invokes in his argument above, we naturally try to sound them out. «Why do you know?» is subtly amiss for those who speak English as their mother-tongue. We ourselves verify his base data and are therefore open to the arguments that he develops on this foundation. Austin did not argue for some grand theory. He had a profound distrust of anything styled «important»[48], and he attempted to thoroughly establish apparently minor points, like the difference between believing and knowing:

> The «existence» of your alleged belief is not challenged, but the «existence» of your alleged knowledge is challenged. If we like to say that «I believe», and likewise «I am sure» and «I am certain», are descriptions of subjective mental or cognitive states or attitudes, or what not, then «I know» is not that, or at least not merely that: it functions differently in talking[49].

Note that the basis of his argument is how the words «function in talking». He establishes that the English language uses the two words in different ways, and his assumption is that language does not make a distinction when none is required. Accepting this assumption means that definitions of knowledge as «a justified belief» are no longer tenable.

This careful, modest, methodical approach, often involving a specially selected team of students who helped gather and test the language data, bore all the hallmarks of Lieutenant-Colonel Austin of British Intelligence at work on the German order of battle. However, his opponent had changed. He assembled his arguments for battle against the logical positivist position.

6. Austin's Results

6.1 *The Descriptive Fallacy*

Principia Mathematica is one of the triumphs of the logical positivist approach. Its ingenious blend of philosophy and mathematics revolutionized the science of logic. Consistent with the method they propose,

---

[47] J.L. AUSTIN, «Other Minds», 46.

[48] «I am not sure importance is important», J.L. AUSTIN, «Pretending», 219.

[49] J.L. AUSTIN, «Other Minds», 46.

Russell and Whitehead begin from extremely simple propositions, and construct their edifice of reason upon that certain foundation:

> By an «elementary» proposition we mean one which does not involve any variables, or, in other language, one which does not involve such words as «all», «some», «the» or equivalents for such words. A proposition such as «this is red», where «this» is something given in sensation, will be elementary.[50]

It is this foundation which Austin attacked. He denied the primacy this approach gives to that type of proposition. He identified a danger in taking this very abstract model and assuming that all propositions function in this restricted sense.

> The principle of Logic that «Every proposition must be true or false», has too long operated as the simplest, most persuasive and most pervasive form of the descriptive fallacy. Philosophers under its influence have forcibly interpreted all «propositions» on the model of the statement that a certain thing is red, as made when the thing concerned is currently under observation.[51]

The term «descriptive fallacy» was coined by Austin and is still in current use in linguistic philosophy. In an unscripted talk delivered on the Third Programme of the BBC in 1956, he described the behaviour he considered fallacious thus:

> We have not got to go very far back in the history of philosophy to find philosophers assuming more or less as a matter of course that the sole business, the sole interesting business, of any utterance – that is, of anything we say – is to be true or at least false. Of course they had always known that there are other kinds of things which we say – things like imperatives, the expressions of wishes, and exclamations – some of which had even been classified by grammarians, though it wasn't perhaps too easy to tell always which was which. But still philosophers have assumed that the only things that they are interested in are utterances which report facts or which describe situations truly or falsely.[52]

Truth or falsity was a preoccupation of the logical positivists and, with predicate calculus, they constructed a way of analyzing arguments that consisted of descriptive propositions. Because this method proved so powerful, and interesting, there was a temptation to consider that de-

---

[50] A.N. WHITEHEAD – B. RUSSELL, *Principia Mathematica*, 91.
[51] J.L. AUSTIN, «Truth», 99.
[52] J.L. AUSTIN, «Performative Utterances», 220.

scriptions (which Austin termed «constative utterances»[53]) were *all* that language and communication is about.

This appealingly simple model of communication is: a speaker generates a proposition about their internal state or about the external world, a report of a fact or the description of a situation. The proposition is coded into language and spoken (transmitted). The addressee decodes the language, recovers the proposition and as a result achieves the same internal state as the speaker. This can be represented, following a diagram by Anne Reboul, as follows:[54]

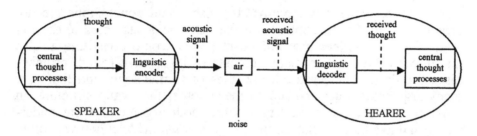

Figure 2: The Code Model of Communication

According to Reboul's account, this model involves two significant hypotheses:

a) The only possibility for miscommunication is a misunderstanding due to noise in the communication channel;

b) Communication is successful in as much as the message recovered is the same as the message sent, i.e. if both communicative devices share the same internal representation as a consequence of the communication process.[55]

This second assumption she refers to as the «hypothesis of semantic transparency».

Austin pointed out that much of language does not work in anything like this fashion.

It was for too long the assumption of philosophers that the business of a «statement» can only be to «describe» some state of affairs, or to «state

---

[53] J.L. AUSTIN, *How to Do Things with Words*, 3.

[54] A. REBOUL, «Semantic Transparency », 47.

[55] A. REBOUL, «Semantic Transparency », 47.

some fact», which it must do either truly or falsely. Grammarians, indeed, have regularly pointed out that not all «sentences» are (used in making) statements; there are, traditionally, besides (grammarians') statements, also questions and exclamations, and sentences expressing commands or wishes or concessions. And doubtless philosophers have not intended to deny this, despite some loose use of «sentence» for «statement». Doubtless, too, both grammarians and philosophers have been aware that it is by no means easy to distinguish even questions, commands, and so on from statements by means of the few and jejune grammatical marks available, such as word order, mood, and the like[56]:

Questions, exclamations, commands, wishes and concessions are not propositions of the descriptive sort that logic is accustomed to dealing with. They are neither true nor false. (What would constitute a false question?) Moreover, as many students of logic have found, ordinary discourse does not operate on the rules of formal logic and there are many arguments that persuade by means other than valid structure. In those primitive days in education when both arguments were understood, and available to the teacher, *argumentum ad baculum* was often far more convincing than the syllogisms encoded in «Barbara Celarent»[57].

If language is not fundamentally description of the world, what is it? Austin's key insight was that many utterances *do* something. In inter-*acting* we are *acting* upon the world. A common assertion based on the code model of communication is that to say «I believe *x*» is a description of the speaker's inner state, and that to say «I know *x*» is essentially a similar statement backed with evidential support. In a 1940 symposium with John Wisdom[58], who advocated such a view, Austin responded as follows:

---

[56] J.L. AUSTIN, *How to Do Things with Words*, 1.

[57] *Argumentum ad baculum* is «*argument to the cudgel*» which, in an earlier academic context, was a coded reference to the threat of caning. The full form of the famous scholastic mnemonic for the forms of the logical syllogisms is: «*Barbara celarent sarii ferio baralipton / Celantes dabitis fapesmo frisesomorum; / Cesare campestres festino baroco; darapti / Felapton disamis datisi bocardo ferison*». It first appeared in print in the *Introductiones in Logicam* or *Summulae* of William of Shyreswood (about 1225).

[58] Wisdom, (Arthur) John, 1904-1993, British philosopher. He studied at Cambridge, and became professor there (1952-68) and at the University of Oregon (1968-72). He developed a distinctive mode and style of philosophising which represented philosophical paradoxes as revealing partial truths rather than linguistic confusions.

To suppose that «I know» is a descriptive phrase, is only one example of the *descriptive fallacy*, so common in philosophy. Even if some language is now purely descriptive, language was not in origin so, and much of it is still not so. Utterance of obvious ritual phrases, in the appropriate circumstances, is not *describing* the action we are doing, but *doing* it («I do»): in other cases it functions, like tone and expression, or again like punctuation and mood, as an intimation that we are employing language in some special way («I warn», «I ask», «I define»). Such phrases cannot, strictly, be lies, though they can «imply» lies, as «I promise» implies that I fully intend, which may be untrue.

Austin agreed that language can and does describe. He rejected the descriptive function as primary to language and, in particular, denied it with respect to the affirmation «I know *x*».

To sustain this denial, Austin introduced various obviously performative utterances, which will be considered in more detail. For now, notice how «I promise *x*» functions according to Austin. We do not speak of true promises and false ones. We do speak of insincere promises and promises that are not kept. To promise involves establishing a relationship and future obligations. The social world of the speaker and the hearer is different after a promise is uttered. Austin claimed that «I know» functions far more like «I promise» than it does like «I believe».

> You are prohibited from saying «I know it is so, but I may be wrong», just as you are prohibited from saying «I promise I will, but I may fail». If you are aware you may be mistaken, you ought not to say you know, just as, if you are aware you may break your word, you have no business to promise[59].

Austin was not unconscious of human fallibility, nor is ordinary language unequipped to deal with it, but he claimed that it is so taken for granted that reference to it is only introduced when there is special reason for doing so. Adding «but I am a weak human being» to every assertion, would, according to Austin «be no more exciting than adding "D.V."»[60]. Every human person knows human frailty and it is an im-

---

His most important works are *Other Minds* (1952), *Philosophy and Psychoanalysis* (1953), and *Paradox and Discovery* (1965).

[59] J.L. AUSTIN, «Other Minds», 66.

[60] J.L. AUSTIN, «Other Minds», 66. «D.V.» is the abbreviated form of the expression «*Deo volente*» or «God willing» which, as a pious expression, can be used after any statement about the future. That this practice, never universal, is no longer in

plicit assumption in every conversation. However, this does not prevent us using both «I promise» and «I know» in the ways that we do.

There is no reason in formal logic why we cannot say «I promise I will, but I may fail»; yet native-speakers of English detect a «wrongness» in this phrase as they utter it. This is one place where the structure of ordinary language carries a signal about reality. Promises are to be made only when you have the capacity and the intention of fulfilling them:

> When I say «I promise», a new plunge is taken: I have not merely announced my intention, but, by using this formula (performing this ritual), I have bound myself to others, and staked my reputation, in a new way. Similarly, saying «I know» is taking a new plunge. But it is *not* saying «I have performed a specially striking feat of cognition, superior, in the same scale as believing and being sure, even to being merely quite sure»: for there is nothing in that scale superior to being quite sure. Just as promising is not something superior, in the same scale as hoping and intending, even to merely fully intending: for there is nothing in that scale superior to fully intending. When I say «I know», I *give others my word*: I *give others my authority for saying* that «S is P»[61].

Thus an apparently simple and fundamental assertion about the world, «I know this is red», does far more than the logical positivists advert to. It clearly has a larger and more relational function. It involves the future as well as the present, relies on the authority of the speaker, and is void without uptake on the part of the hearer.

Austin strongly distinguished «knowledge» from «belief» – the latter being held with different levels of certitude.

> We all *feel* the very great difference between saying «I'm *absolutely* sure» and saying «I know»: it is like the difference between saying «I firmly and irrevocably intend» and «I promise». If someone has promised me to do A, then I am entitled to rely on it, and can make promises on the strength of it: and so, where someone has said to me «I know», I am entitled to say *I know too*, at second hand. The right to say «I know» is transmissible, in the sort of way that other authority is transmissible. Hence, if I say it lightly, I may be *responsible* for getting *you* into trouble[62].

---

vogue may partly be because anything which can be said about *everything* is effectively meaningless.

[61] J.L. AUSTIN, «Other Minds», 67.
[62] J.L. AUSTIN, «Other Minds», 68.

Our utterances do more than encode facts. They establish and maintain relationships. When knowledge is conveyed, it carries with it authority. We place trust in the one who uttered the item of information, thereby making ourselves dependent in a sense. When we pass this item on we extend this web-work of relationships. In trusting, we are trusted and we are responsible for accurately conveying knowledge to others.

When we say that we know something we assert our grasp on reality. Without denying our frailty we are pledging something of ourselves along with our assertion about the way that world is. Identifying, naming and attacking the descriptive fallacy is one of Austin's recognized contributions to philosophy and to communication theory. His key linguistic evidence for the inadequacy of the code model of communication, which is one manifestation of the fallacy, is the existence of expressions which Austin dubbed «performative utterances».

6.2 *Performative Utterances*

In his 1956 talk on the Third Programme of the BBC Austin began by saying:

> You are more than entitled not to know what the word «performative» means. It is a new word and an ugly word, and perhaps it does not mean anything very much. But there is one thing in its favour, it is not a profound word[63].

Profound or not, famous or not, much turns on «performative» for Austin. Contrary to the code model and the descriptive fallacy Austin demonstrated that a large part of language does not function as statements.

> I want to discuss a kind of utterance which looks like a statement and grammatically, I suppose, would be classed as a statement, which is not nonsensical, and yet is not true or false. [...] Suppose, for example, that in the course of the marriage ceremony I say, as people will, «I do» – (sc. take this woman to be my lawful wedded wife). Or again, suppose that I tread on your toe and say «I apologize». Or again, suppose that I have a bottle of champagne in my hand and say «I name this ship the *Queen Elizabeth*». Or suppose I say «I bet you sixpence it will rain tomorrow». In all these cases it would be absurd to regard the thing I say as a report of the performance of the action which is undoubtedly done – the action of betting, or christening, or apologizing. We should say rather that, in saying what I do, I actually perform that action. When I say «I name this ship the *Queen Eliza-*

---

[63] J.L. AUSTIN, «Performative Utterances», 220.

beth» I do not describe the christening ceremony, I actually perform the christening; and when I say «I do» (sc. take this woman to be my lawful wedded wife), I am not reporting on a marriage, I am indulging in it. Now these kinds of utterance are the ones we call performative utterances. This is rather an ugly word, and a new word, but there seems to be no word already in existence to do the job[64].

Logical positivists had seized on «statements» as the key to language and had assumed they were descriptions that were either true or false. Statements that were not were classed as «nonsense». They could be dangerous if irrational or irrelevant if merely conventional «phatic» communication. Austin directed attention to common phrases which look like statements but have quite a different set of characteristics.

One thing Austin's phrases are not is nonsense. They make perfect sense to us. Marrying, christening, apologizing and betting are part of everyday life. Yet they appear quite distinct from descriptions. When a ship is being formally named there is no other process going on which this statement could be describing. Significantly, the naming is usually a ritual act involving other conventional features like the bottle of champagne. The act is not simply notional, it has real world consequences. Subsequent documentation will refer to the ship by the given name. Referring to it by any other name will be inappropriate.

When one party to a marriage declares «I do» they are not describing the action of God at that moment, *they* are doing the marrying and that speech act is an essential part of the ritual. We could propose the utterance as a description of an internal commitment being made at that point, but the commitment has usually been made earlier and marriage is, in part, the *public declaration* of it. Their relationship has changed with the public words. Their social status is altered and they will be treated differently. An apology can be insincere or perfunctory but we do not call it «true» or «false». When one says «I apologize», however grudgingly, an apology has in that very utterance been *made*. A New Zealander had a dispute with the Totalisator Agency Board over a telephone bet on a horse race. When they played him a recording of his own voice, he conceded the argument because he heard himself *make the bet*. In all these cases the utterance *is the deed*.

The examples Austin gave on the BBC (marrying, christening, apologizing and betting) do not exhaust the field. In his famous lecture

---

64 J.L. AUSTIN, «Performative Utterances», 222.

series at Harvard, he identified a wide range of verbs as being used in performative utterances and classified them:

> I distinguish five very general classes [...]
> The first, verdictives, are typified by the giving of a verdict, as the name implies, by a jury, arbitrator or umpire. But they need not be final; they may be, for example, an estimate, reckoning, or appraisal. It is essentially giving a finding as to something – fact, or value – which is for different reasons hard to be certain about.
> The second, exercitives, are the exercising of powers, rights, or influence. Examples are appointing, voting, ordering, urging, advising, warning, &c.
> The third, commissives, are typified by promising or otherwise undertaking; they *commit* you to doing something, but also include declarations or announcements of intention, which are not promises, and also rather vague things which we may call espousals, as for example siding with. They have obvious connexions with verdictives and exercitives.
> The fourth, behabitives, are a very miscellaneous group, and have to do with attitudes and *social behaviour*. Examples are apologizing, congratulating, commending, condoling, cursing, and challenging.
> The fifth, expositives, are difficult to define. They make plain how our utterances fit into the course of an argument of conversation, how we are using words, or, in general, are expository. Examples are «I reply», «I argue», «I concede», «I illustrate», «I assume», «I postulate». We should be clear from the start that there are still wide possibilities of marginal or awkward cases, or of overlaps[65].

When the foreperson of the jury declares «We find the defendant guilty», a verdict *is given*. It may be a wrong decision but it cannot be a false statement, because in stating it they *make it so*. When a department head appoints someone to a position in the department, it may be unwise but it cannot be a lie.

> «I promise that» [...] is not a description, because (1) it could not be false, nor, therefore, true; (2) saying «I promise that» (if happy, of course) *makes it* a promise, and *makes it* unambiguously a promise[66].

The overwhelming impression that Austin conveyed was that performative utterances are in very common use in our world. A significant proportion of everyday utterances fall into these categories.

---

[65] J.L. AUSTIN, *How to Do Things with Words*, 151-152.
[66] J.L. AUSTIN, «Other Minds», 70.

At this point in the development of his argument, Austin was suggesting a model like this:

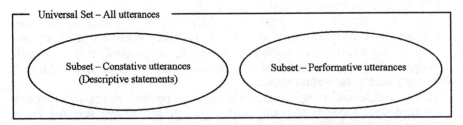

Universal Set – All utterances

Subset – Constative utterances
(Descriptive statements)

Subset – Performative utterances

Figure 3 : Initial Constative-Peformative Relationship

The relative size of these two subsets of language has not been established. Neither is insignificant. The above diagram separates them because in identifying performative utterances, Austin aimed to discover and categorise an entirely distinct class of speech act.

Austin did not claim that, because these utterances do not have truth value like the descriptive statements, they are therefore infallible; he showed that the English language has many expressions to cover the various failings and foibles of humanity. At one point he asserted that we share «the birthright of all speakers, that of speaking unclearly and untruly»[67]. All utterances can fail and Austin was very interested in the reasons why.

6.3 *The Doctrine of Infelicities*

Austin called all communicative utterances «speech acts» using the term «act» interchangeably with «action» and taking it in its broad philosophical sense.

> The beginning of sense, not to say wisdom, is to realize that «doing an action» as used in philosophy, is a highly abstract expression – it is used in the place of any (or almost any?) verb with a personal subject, in the same sort of way that «thing» is a stand-in for any (or when we remember, almost any) noun substantive, and «quality» a stand-in for the adjective[68].

Now there are the normal ways that any action can fail, but speech actions have further ways of coming unstuck which Austin detailed in his

---

[67] J.L. AUSTIN, «Other Minds», 65.
[68] J.L. AUSTIN, «A Plea for Excuses», 126.

doctrine of infelicities. Firstly he eliminated the cases of what he calls «aetiolations»:

> For example, there are insinuating (and other *non-literal* uses of language), joking (and other *non-serious* uses of language), and swearing and showing off (which are perhaps expressive uses of language). We can say «In saying *x* I was joking» (insinuating ... , expressing my feelings, &c.)[69].

He considered non-literal and non-serious uses of the language as secondary and derivative of the literal, serious uses: It is not by examining the secondary forms that we gain an appreciation of the full power of the utterance[70].

> If the poet says «Go and catch a falling star» or whatever it may be, he doesn't seriously issue an order. Considerations of this kind apply to any utterance at all, not merely to performatives[71].

These aetiolations show the significance of the context of the utterance, which Austin repeatedly referred to as essential in understanding the meaning of what is said[72]. However, given a context that is serious and an utterance that is literal, there are still many things that need to be in place for everything involved in the action to come off «happily»:

> Some at least of the things which are necessary for the smooth or «happy» functioning of a performative [...]
>
> (A. 1)   There must exist an accepted conventional procedure having a certain conventional effect, that procedure to include the uttering of certain words by certain persons in certain circumstances, and further,
>
> (A. 2)   the particular persons and circumstances in a given case must be appropriate for the invocation of the particular procedure invoked.
>
> (B. 1)   The procedure must be executed by all participants both correctly and
>
> (B. 2)   completely.

---

[69] J.L. AUSTIN, *How to Do Things with Words*, 122.

[70] Jacques Derrida strongly criticised this step by Austin. See his «Signature Event Context» article in *Glyph* 1 (1977). He felt that excluding the «non-serious» was just one more example of the standard and problematic philosophical privileging of the straightforward case when in real life there never is a straightforward case.

[71] J.L. AUSTIN, *How to Do Things with Words*, 228.

[72] See *PhP*, 32, 57, 87-88, 138, 198, 232-233, *Sense and Sensibilia*, 53, 118, *How to Do Things with Words*, 5, 6, 8, 16, 52, 100, 107, 137-139, 143, 145, 148.

(Γ. 1)   Where, as often, the procedure is designed for use by persons having certain thoughts or feelings, or for the inauguration of certain consequential conduct on the part of any participant, then a person participating in and so invoking the procedure must in fact have those thoughts and feelings, and the participants must intend so to conduct themselves, and further
(Γ. 2)   must actually so conduct themselves subsequently.

Now if we sin against any one (or more) of these six rules, our performative utterance will be (in one way or another) unhappy[73].

This insight into criteria other than «truth» or «noise in the communication channel» that determine the effectiveness of communication is considered to be one of Austin's greatest contributions to linguistic philosophy. Given that he used the speaking of marriage vows as an example of a performative utterance, it may be helpful to unpack his conditions and apply them to that example. Austin's «I do» could be referring to a range of different types of wedding services, but for this explication we will restrict ourselves to marriage as understood by the Roman Catholic Church where we can call on canon law as evidence for Austin's rules. Obviously custom is far broader and more influential than law, and many performative utterances occur in situations which law does not concern itself with. Yet, Austin claimed:

Writers on jurisprudence have constantly shown themselves aware of the varieties of infelicity and even at times of the peculiarities of the performative utterance[74].

Thus it seems reasonable to look to the law for confirmation of Austin's criteria for a «happy» performative utterance. Austin's categories may be applied as follows:

(A. 1.) *Conventional procedure* – «those rites are to be observed which are prescribed in the liturgical books»[75].

Having a certain conventional effect – the legal consequences of marriage are spelled out in the *Code of Canon Law*, canons 1134-1140, in a section entitled «The Effects of Marriage». For example they include the legitimacy of any children who are conceived[76].

---

[73] J.L. AUSTIN, *How to Do Things with Words*, 14-15.
[74] J.L. AUSTIN, *How to Do Things with Words*, 19.
[75] *CIC* 1119.
[76] See *CIC* 1137.

Certain words – «A necessary condition, however, is that, in the rite the priest assisting at such marriages must ask for and receive the consent of the contracting parties and the nuptial blessing should always be given»[77]. There are adaptations permitted in the wording of the consent but it must be a consent – taking the other as spouse, exclusively and permanently. The consent can consist of an affirmation by each party to marriage: «I, N., take you, N., for my lawful ...», or by a response (Austin's «I do») to a question «N., do you take N. to be your ...». The consent is a key focus of canon law with respect to marriage.

Certain persons – Canons 1073-1094 spell out those who are impeded from marrying, by, for example, consanguinity. Canon 1108 specifies some of the persons who must be present: Bishop, priest or deacon to assist and two witnesses. Canon 1104 is worth quoting in full:

§1 To contract marriage validly it is necessary that the contracting parties be present together, either personally or by proxy.

§2 The spouses are to express their matrimonial consent in words; if however, they cannot speak, then by equivalent signs.

The subsequent canon spells out in detail what is involved in such a proxy. The acceptability in law of «equivalent signs» supports an assertion by Austin: «many conventional acts, such as betting or conveyance of property, can be performed in non-verbal ways»[78].

Certain circumstances – Canon 1115 specifies the ordinary place of marriage. There are days in the Church year on which marriages cannot be performed. Canons 1083-1094 detail some circumstances, such as abduction, which invalidate marriage.

(A. 2.) *the particular persons and circumstances in a given case must be appropriate for the invocation of the particular procedure invoked* – Given that all the above conventions do exist we now have a particular concrete case that must conform to those conditions: a couple that wish to marry and are free to marry; a cleric to assist; a pair of witnesses; a place and a time that are appropriate; and pre-nuptial preparation and paper-work completed. Now all that is required is for their consent to be uttered.

---

[77] *The Rites of the Catholic Church*, I, 724.
[78] J.L. AUSTIN, *How to Do Things with Words*, 19.

Canon 1057 §1 A marriage is brought into being by the lawfully mani-
fested consent of persons who are legally capable.

(B. 1) *The procedure must be executed by all participants both correctly* – the couple must express their consent. The assistant and witnesses must hear both expressions of consent. The nuptial blessing is to
be given. Despite the clarity of the law and Austin's rules, this is not a
magical rite which will only function if every syllable is correctly pronounced. In a complicated ceremony, with the nervousness of those
who are conscious that they are in the process of one of the most important acts of their life, it is easy for mistakes to happen and *usually
this does not matter*. The bride omits part of her husband's name (as
Princess Diana did) or gets her own wrong, but the clear intention and
the momentum of the rite overrides such flaws and hitches.

Austin suggested that such mis-executions *vitiate* the act rather than
disallow it[79]. We can imagine a mother-in-law saying: «It is such a
shame that she stumbled in the vows, they both wanted everything *to
go right* today». The hypothetical mother-in-law would be conscious of
a performative act that was *marred* but not *invalidated*. Canon law supports this interpretation:

Canon 1060 Marriage enjoys the favour of law. Consequently, in doubt the
validity of a marriage must be upheld until the contrary is proven.

(B. 2) *completely* – the consent needs to be completed by both parties
and the nuptial blessing pronounced by the assisting priest for the marriage to be valid. An interrupted wedding ceremony is disastrous, but
the caveats expressed above again apply.

(Γ. 1) *must in fact have those thoughts or feelings* – it is difficult to
legislate for thoughts and feelings, hence the wisdom of this edict:

Canon 1101 §1 The internal consent of the mind is presumed to conform to
the words or the signs used in the celebration of a marriage.

The law of the Church operates as we all do in respect to communication – we trust that expressions of thoughts and feelings are sincere
unless there is evidence to the contrary.

(Γ. 2) *must actually so conduct themselves subsequently* – The con-
summation of the marriage is one piece of subsequent behaviour that is
legislated about[80]. Canons 1151 – 1155 deal with «Separation while the

---

[79] J.L. AUSTIN, *How to Do Things with Words*, 18.
[80] For example *CIC* 1061.

Bond Remains», which involves situations where the subsequent behaviour does not correspond to the ideal expressed in the marriage
vows.

Note the distinction Austin insisted on between the first four rules
and the last two. He deliberately uses the Latin alphabet for the «external world» cases and the Greek alphabet for the last to indicate that the
root of the infelicity in those cases is to be found in the inner consciousness of the speaker. This is even clearer when Austin laid out the
possible types of «unhappiness»:

We get then the following scheme[81]:

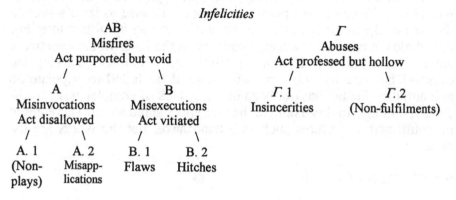

Figure 4: The Types of Infelicity

The Γ. 2 cases are particularly interesting. Many performative acts involve the future, marrying, betting and promising among others, and
they will be hollow if they are not fulfilled. The fulfilment is an external world phenomenon («Here is the five Euro I promised you»), but by
classing it with insincerities Austin suggested that the root of non-
fulfilment is an internal world reality – «I should not have promised
what I knew I could not deliver».

It is clear that Austin's «infelicities» apply to the overall act of which
the utterance may be only one, albeit crucial, part. In the example
elaborated the context of ritual and the customary behaviours that sur-

---

[81] J.L. AUSTIN, *How to Do Things with Words*, 18. In his Harvard lecture Austin
did not name A.1 and Γ. 2, I have used here the titles that, according to J.O. Urmson,
he applied on different occasions. Grimes, in «Infelicitous Performances and Ritual
Criticism» 111, points out that most of the different kinds of infelicity don't *necessarily* involve words and he applies them to rituals.

round the exchange of consent often loom larger in the consciousness of the participants than the words of the vows.

It may be helpful to contrast a simpler example of a performative:

> Tim: «I bet you five dollars that New Zealand beats Australia in the Rugby World Cup semi-final».
> Paul: «Done!»

The conventional procedure of betting exists in antipodean culture. A pair of sporting enthusiasts of modest means could appropriately engage in such a private bet. Tim must be clear as to which sporting fixture is intended. Paul must accept the challenge before the bet comes into effect. Witnesses are not required, but it is wise to have some. At the time of the bet they must both be willing to pay up if they lose. For the whole act to achieve a happy conclusion the loser would eventually hand over the money. If Tim were interrupted before specifying the event «I bet you five dollars that ...» or if he failed to stipulate an amount, then the bet has not been made. A lack of completeness invalidates it entirely. In this example the utterances stand alone. There might be confirmatory gestures such as a handshake, but the words are the deed.

6.4 *The Parts of Speech*

Having attempted and failed to come up with a clear test for distinguishing performative utterances from descriptive statements, Austin started anew. He intended to establish a theory of communication in which the two classes of utterance are clearly separable. He started by defining «utterance»:

> It is time to refine upon the circumstances of «issuing an utterance». To begin with there is a whole group of senses, which I shall label (A), in which to say anything must always be to do something, the group of senses which together add up to «saying» something, in the full sense of «say». We may agree, without insisting on formulations or refinements, that to say anything is
>
> (A. *a*) always to perform the act of uttering certain noises (a «phonetic» act), and the utterances is a phone;
>
> (A. *b*) always to perform the act of uttering certain vocables or words, i.e. noises of certain types belonging to *and as* belonging to a certain vocabulary, in a certain construction, i.e. conforming to and as conforming to a certain grammar, with a certain intonation, &c. This act we may call a

«phatic» act, and the utterance which it is the act of uttering a «pheme» (as distinct from the phememe of linguistic theory); and

(A. *c*) generally to perform the act of using that pheme or its constituents with a certain more or less definite «sense» and a more or less definite «reference» (which together are equivalent to «meaning»). This act we may call a «rhetic» act, and the utterance which it is the act of uttering a «rheme»[82].

This can be summarised as:

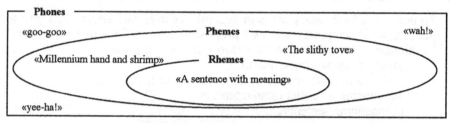

Figure 5: Phones, Phemes and Rhemes

There are obviously a myriad of noises that humans can vocalise; babies babble a wide range of syllables, and, responding to what they hear around them, begin to restrict themselves to only those in use in their language. These noises are all phones. Austin's phemes are distinguished among those noises by being well formed syllables or words belonging to the vocabulary of the language. Austin later clarified the distinction between phemes and rhemes:

> The pheme is a unit of *language*: its typical fault is to be nonsense – meaningless. But the rheme is a unit of *speech*; its typical fault is to be vague or void or obscure, &c.[83]

Obviously all rhemes are phemes, and all phemes are phones. We cannot utter a sentence with meaning unless we are also uttering vocables that are well formed according to the rules of a language and we cannot do that without making a sound. In the analysis of utterances the distinction between these parts of speech is an abstraction. Again it is the consideration of how communication can fail that enabled Austin to separate them.

---

[82] J.L. AUSTIN, *How to Do Things with Words*, 92.
[83] J.L. AUSTIN, *How to Do Things with Words*, 98.

Such terms and the distinctions have not caught on among other linguistic philosophers or students of language. It is the following distinctions, and neologisms, which achieved fame:

> The act of «saying something» in this full normal sense I call, i.e. dub, the performance of a locutionary act, and the study of utterances thus far and in these respects the study of locutions, or of the full units of speech[84].

However, when we say something we can also perform an act in saying it. The act achieved *in* the locution is the illocutionary act.

> To perform a locutionary act is in general, we may say, also and *eo ipso* to perform an illocutionary act, as I propose to call it. Thus in performing a locutionary act we shall also be performing such an act as:
> asking or answering a question,
> giving some information or an assurance or a warning,
> announcing a verdict or an intention,
> pronouncing sentence,
> making an appointment or an appeal or a criticism,
> making an identification or giving a description,
> and the numerous like[85].

We report locutions as direct speech in inverted commas. «He said to me "Shoot her!"»[86] is one of Austin's examples of a report of a locution. What he said involved a noise, something to be heard – a phone. The noise conformed to a certain vocabulary, namely the English language. It was identifiable as two words, «shoot» and «her». It has the structure of verb then object, thus it is a pheme. «Shoot» is an imperative meaning «fire a gun» and «her» referred to that woman – it makes sense and it has reference – it is a rhetic act. Something has been said in our normal understanding of speech. We have a locution: «Shoot her!» But what *is being done* in saying «Shoot her!» is the speaker imploring, advising, ordering or what? When we describe the event as «He ordered me to shoot her» (Note the absence of quotation marks around the two key words, the description no longer reports the direct speech but rather what it meant), we are identifying what was done. An order was given. What Austin called the illocution:

> We constantly do debate [...] in such terms as whether certain words (a certain locution) *had the force of* a question, or *ought to have been taken as*

---

[84] J.L. AUSTIN, *How to Do Things with Words*, 93.
[85] J.L. AUSTIN, *How to Do Things with Words*, 98.
[86] J.L. AUSTIN, *How to Do Things with Words*, 101.

an estimate and so on.

I explained the performance of an act in this new and second sense as the performance of an «illocutionary» act, i.e. performance of an act in saying something as opposed to performance of an act of saying something; I call the act performed an «illocution» and shall refer to the doctrine of the different types of function of language here in question as the doctrine of «illocutionary forces»[87].

Austin identified something other than meaning in utterances. He noted that they impact on their hearers in ways beyond logic. What we say has a force that is partly independent of sense and meaning. Two speakers can make the same utterance with different levels of force. The lecture is over when the lecturer declares it so, not when a student makes that remark as an observation.

6.5 *We Say Things to Influence People*

«John, I am out of flour» is a locution. Given uptake by a dutiful son, it will have the illocutionary effect of being an instruction. John will go to the shop. Consider the further possibility of a concealed motive behind this utterance. A girl has started working as a shop assistant in the local store and she strikes the mother as the sort her son ought to meet. We could imagine her admitting, «By saying that I was out of flour, I got John and Mary to meet up!»

There is yet a further sense in which to perform a locutionary act, and therein an illocutionary act, may also be to perform an act of another kind. Saying something will often, or even normally, produce certain consequential effects upon the feelings, thoughts, or actions of the audience, or of the speaker, or of other persons: and it may be done with the design, intention, or purpose of producing them[88];

This is the act that Austin called a «perlocution» what is done *by* the locution being said. *In* what was said above there was an instruction, but some matchmaking was achieved *by* what was said.

Thus we distinguished the locutionary act (and within it the phonetic, the phatic, and the rhetic acts) which has a *meaning*; the illocutionary act which

---

[87] J.L. AUSTIN, *How to Do Things with Words*, 99-100.
[88] J.L. AUSTIN, *How to Do Things with Words*, 101.

has a certain *force* in saying something; the perlocutionary act which is *the achieving of* certain *effects* by saying something[89].

Such effects that a perlocutionary act achieves can often be accomplished in an entirely non-verbal way.

> It is characteristic of perlocutionary acts that the response achieved, or the sequel, can be achieved additionally or entirely by non-locutionary means: thus intimidation may be achieved by waving a stick or pointing a gun. Even in the cases of convincing, persuading, getting to obey and getting to believe, we may achieve the response non-verbally; but if there is no illocutionary act, it is doubtful whether this language characteristic of perlocutionary objects should be used. Compare the use of «got him to» with that of «got him to obey». However, this alone is not enough to distinguish illocutionary acts, since we can for example warn or order or appoint or give or protest or apologize by non-verbal means and these are illocutionary acts. Thus we may cock a snook or hurl a tomato by way of protest[90].

Communication is, therefore, broader than merely utterances. Gestures such as cocking a snook[91] and hurling a tomato are illocutionary acts, partly because of their conventional nature. Austin's use of «additionally» is significant. The total speech situation may involve all sorts of gestures that enhance the illocutionary force. «I warn you to get off my property» is a much more forceful statement when the speaker is pointing a shotgun.

The Code Model had it that the result of successful communication was that the mental state of the addressee corresponded to that of the speaker – the assumption of semantic transparency in communication. Austin, with his attention to ordinary language, showed that utterances are often far from transparent. What is said is intended to be understood by the hearer but that is not necessarily the speaker's only purpose in making the utterance. Human converse is not simply the exchange of data – it involves fiction, exhortation, persuasion, argument, manipulation, bargaining and outright lying among many other behaviours. Statements have a purpose, motives lie behind speech and that motivation may not always be apparent to the hearer.

> The perlocutionary act always includes some consequence, as when we say «By doing x I was doing y» we do bring in a greater or less stretch of «con-

---

[89] J.L. AUSTIN, *How to Do Things with Words*, 121.
[90] J.L. AUSTIN, *How to Do Things with Words*, 119.
[91] A gesture of contempt made with one thumb on the nose and fingers spread out.

sequences» always, some of which may be «unintentional». Thus we can import an arbitrarily long stretch of what might also be called the «consequences» of our act into the nomenclature of the act itself is, or should be, a fundamental commonplace of the theory of our language about all «action» in general[92].

When we talk about an action, we often include those consequences until a second act by the agent or another person. In response to the question «What did you do?», the answers given can include «I moved my finger», «I pulled the trigger», «I fired the gun», «I shot the tree beside Fred», but when Fred shoots back that is a different action.

Many illocutionary acts invite a response or a follow on. An order invites the response of obedience. The responsibility for the consequences of the act depends largely on the relationship of the parties and the nature of the illocutionary act. The general who gives a legitimate order is held responsible for the consequences. The youth who asks his friend to join him in a crime might be said to be leading him astray but is not responsible for his friend agreeing to his request. Orders do not give the addressee any freedom; the response is «one-way»[93]. By contrast, «Asking whether you will» is «two-way». It requires more than uptake; it requires the second party to choose. The act that follows is normally spoken of as being the friend's action and responsibility, not that of the youth who invited him, unlike the situation where the order was given.

Austin treated language, not as semantically transparent, but as capable of Machiavellian complexity. His starting point was ordinary language, not an artificial model, and in day-to-day life we communicate to influence others, overtly and covertly. We consider a communication to *have worked* when it achieves the *effect* we wanted.

6.6 *What is Truth?*

In mathematics Gödel had shown that truth was of greater significance than provability. Now, with respect to ordinary language, Austin succeeded in showing that there are other types of conditions than truth for the happy outcome of communication. Austin contrasted the simple two-valued truth model of the logical positivists with the more subtle role of the word «true» in real life contexts.

---

[92] J.L. AUSTIN, *How to Do Things with Words*, 107.
[93] See J.L. AUSTIN, *How to Do Things with Words*, 117.

In real life, as opposed to the simple situations envisaged in logical theory, one cannot always answer in a simple manner whether it is true or false. Suppose that we confront «France is hexagonal» with the facts, in this case, I suppose with France, is it true or false? Well, if you like, up to a point; of course I can see what you mean by saying that it is true for certain intents and purposes. It is good enough for a top-ranking general, perhaps, but not for a geographer. «Naturally it is pretty rough», we should say, «and pretty good as a pretty rough statement». But then someone says: «But is it true or is it false? I don't mind whether it is rough or not; of course its rough, but it has to be true or false – it's a statement, isn't it?» How can one answer this question, whether it is true or false that France is hexagonal? It is just rough, and that is the right and final answer to the question of the relation of «France is hexagonal» to France. It is a rough description; it is not a true or a false one[94].

«France is hexagonal» looks exactly like the kind of proposition that the logical positivists had worked with successfully. Shapes were data from sense experience for them, and «This is square» like «This is red» was an elementary proposition. Austin's example was chosen for its close resemblance, but also for its striking difference. Is it true or false? The answer depends on context. Mathematically, the answer is no. France is not a perfect hexagon, but not even the logical positivists expected to encounter perfect mathematical shapes. For schoolchildren who learn that Italy

Figure 6: A Hexagon?

is shaped like a boot, if one of them were to write in a test that «France is hexagonal», it would be marked as correct. A cartographer who made the same assertion would be considered by professional colleagues to be dramatically oversimplifying.

The logical positivists had truth as a binary attribute of elementary propositions. It was either «on» or «off» and it connected the proposition to the real world. Truth for Austin was much more complex and relational. It relates not only to the proposition but also to the hearer, and the context of the utterance.

It is essential to realize that «true» and «false», like «free» and «unfree», do not stand for anything simple at all; but only for a general dimension of being a right and proper thing to say as opposed to a wrong thing, in these

---

[94] J.L. AUSTIN, *How to Do Things with Words*, 143.

circumstances, to this audience, for these purposes and with these intentions[95].

When, in ordinary language, we speak of something as «true» we are not simply connecting a proposition with sense experience. We do take the external world into account but what is true and proper to say depends on who is talking, whom they are talking to and the purpose of the utterance. Austin showed the logical positivist model to be only a pale shadow of our everyday truths.

> In general we may say this: with both statements (and, for example, description) and warnings, &c., the question can arise, granting that you had the right to warn and did warn, did state or did advise, whether you were right to state or warn or advise – not in the sense of whether it was opportune or expedient, but whether, on the facts and your knowledge of the facts and the purposes for which you were speaking, and so on, this was the proper thing to say.
> This doctrine is quite different from much that the pragmatists have said, to the effect that the true is what works, &c. The truth or falsity of a statement depends not merely on the meanings of word but on what act you were performing in what circumstances[96].

In addition to immediate sense experience of the external world we experience very directly an external, socially-constructed world. When a person communicates they are not usually the individual scientific observer, the paradigm for the logical positivists. The speaker and the addressee are persons within society. They have expectations of each other.

> It seems, rather, that believing in other persons, in authority and testimony, is an essential part of the act of communicating, an act which we all constantly perform. It is as much an irreducible part of our experience as, say, giving promises, or playing competitive games, or even sensing coloured patches[97].

People not only sense red squares, they also experience trust. Trust is ordinary and ubiquitous. No utterance is isolated from the flow of communication in society. The speaker and the addressee will not have been raised by wolves, nor are they likely to live alone deep in a forest. Knowing *because we have been told*, understanding what we see on the

---

[95] J.L. AUSTIN, *How to Do Things with Words*, 145.
[96] J.L. AUSTIN, *How to Do Things with Words*, 145.
[97] J.L. AUSTIN, «Other Minds», 83.

basis of that knowledge, is part of our experience. The world is seen from *within a human culture* by every human observer.

> Generally the effect [of a happy illocutionary act] amounts to bringing about the understanding of the meaning and of the force of the locution. So the performance of an illocutionary act involves securing the *uptake*[98].

If the mayor were to solemnly and with champagne name a ship and then, for whatever reason, no-one ever used the name but consistently referred to her by some prior appellation, then the naming act would have failed. When a teacher declares «I taught this topic but my class did not understand it», then the teacher has *covered* the topic but not *taught* the pupils. A cryptic warning may fail to warn because it is not understood. The illocutionary force of the utterance again depends on the context, and critically on the understanding and appreciation by the addressee. «Uptake» is another internal world phenomenon.

6.7 *Emotions and the Inner World*

The logical positivists distrusted emotions and preferred observation. In seeing the actions of another person they knew they could not *directly* perceive emotions, only physical manifestations. How were they to know that these were not a sham? Austin had a far more positive view of the inner world of emotions and how they are shown and understood:

> There is a peculiar and intimate relationship between the emotion and the natural way of venting it, with which, having been angry ourselves, we are acquainted. The ways in which anger is normally manifested are natural to anger just as there are tones naturally expressive of various emotions (indignation, &c.). There is not normally taken to be such a thing as «being angry» apart from any impulse, however vague, to vent the anger in the natural way[99].

Austin agreed that we do not directly perceive another's emotions. However, he considered that the witness to a display of emotion will also have experienced that feeling to some degree, have some idea of what it is like, and will know how it is naturally and conventionally expressed. Moreover, the witness does have a way of tapping in to what is going on within the person experiencing the emotion.

---

[98] J.L. AUSTIN, *How to Do Things with Words*, 147.
[99] J.L. AUSTIN, «Other Minds», 76-77.

There remains, however, one further special feature of the case, which dif-
ferentiates it radically from the goldfinch case. [Why one can confidently
assert «That is a goldfinch».] The goldfinch, the material object, is, as we
insisted above uninscribed and *mute*: but the man *speaks*. In the complex of
occurrences which induces us to say we know another man is angry, the
complex of symptoms, occasion, display, and the rest, a peculiar place is
occupied by the man's own statement as to what his feelings are. In the
usual case, we accept this statement without question, and we can then say
that we know (as it were «at second-hand») what his feelings are: though of
course «at second-hand» here could not be used to imply that anybody but
he could know «at first-hand», and hence perhaps it is not in fact used[100].

Thus Austin was content that a witness can usually know with certainty
what emotion they are seeing. The testimony of the person is going to
be accepted unless it is in contradiction to their behaviour. We know
what it is to be angry, how it manifests itself in us. When we experience a situation in which a man, red in the face and clenching his fists,
shouts «I am bloody furious», we *know* that man is angry.

We have entrée to the inner worlds of other persons precisely in
communication. By listening to the I-statements addressed to us we ap-
prehend, albeit fallibly, their emotions, thoughts and intentions. Moreover we form an understanding and appreciation of our own inner
world of consciousness through interaction, through relating our experiences to the accounts that others give of their own.

This acceptance of the accessibility and normality of emotion in
communication is very significant. In Austin's understanding, emotion,
as conveyed by gesture, tone, and the like, while not usually changing
the meaning of an utterance can strongly affect the illocutionary and
perlocutionary force associated with the locution.

6.8 *Descriptive Statements are Performative Utterances*

In *Philosophical Investigations* Wittgenstein repudiated the views he
himself had developed thirty years earlier in *Tractatus Logico-
Philosophicus*. Austin managed a similar feat within the scope of a single work: *How to Do Things with Words*.

He began by identifying his few examples of performative utterances
– marrying, christening, betting. He showed that grammatically they
are identical in form to descriptive statements (which he calls consta-

---

[100] J.L. AUSTIN, «Other Minds», 81-82.

tive utterances); yet they do not describe some other reality, nor can they be called true or false. Instead they *do* something. By being uttered when all the conditions for felicity are met, they *achieve* something in the world. In contrast constative utterances – statements characterised by having a truth value – such as «this is red» merely report on reality. Having established the existence of some clearly performative verbs Austin went hunting for more. As already noted, he found many and categorised them: verdictives, exercitives, commissives, behabitives and expositives[101]. The next task he set himself was to clearly distinguish performative from constative utterances so as to establish the two as separate classes.

His method of looking at grammar and usage failed to give any sure test for determining whether an utterance was performative or constative or neither. He therefore started right back at the beginning and built up the notion of the *force* of utterances as opposed to their sense and reference.

A warning, which is performative, has *illocutionary force*. «To warn» is to make an illocutionary act that is achieved in the uttering. The verb «warn» is not always explicit. The context of the speech act matters. If two people were in a car rapidly approaching a set of traffic lights and the passenger were to say «This is red» with the intent and tone of a warning, then it would indeed *carry the force* of a warning. The very example of a constative utterance, which in this case would have a truth value and does truly or falsely describe reality, is acting as a performative. The classes are not disjoint. Some utterances can belong to both. Moreover, in going through the dictionary and categorising each verb, Austin came across one that is especially critical and problematic.

> Surely «to state» is every bit as much to perform an illocutionary act as, say, «to warn» or «to pronounce». Of course it is not to perform an act in some specially physical way, other than in so far as it involves, when verbal, the making of movements of vocal organs; but then nor, as we have seen, is to warn, to protest, to promise or to name. «Stating» seems to meet all the criteria we had for distinguishing the illocutionary act. Consider such an unexceptional remark as the following: In saying that it was raining, I was not betting or arguing or warning: I was simply stating it as a fact[102].

---

[101] See J.L. AUSTIN, *How to Do Things with Words*, 151-152.
[102] J.L. AUSTIN, *How to Do Things with Words*, 134.

This had major significance for Austin's theory. He had set out to show there was a distinct class of utterances that unlike descriptive statements, *did something*, the performative utterances. Now his own method revealed ordinary language data that contradicted his hypothesis of their being separate. It proved impossible to keep the performatives distinct from the constatives because a constative does act as a performative. Moreover, all descriptive statements can be rephrased in the equivalent form «I state that ...», in which form they behave in the same ways as performative utterances where the performative is the verb «to state».

Instead of achieving his aim, Austin had found a result that is even more significant. All descriptive statements are performative utterances, but not all performative utterances are constative. The class of performatives, turns out to embrace all constatives. Instead of identifying a separate property, Austin had found one of greater generality. Descriptive truth, far from being elementary, was shown by Austin to be secondary to illocutionary force.

The final way Austin characterized the situation was:

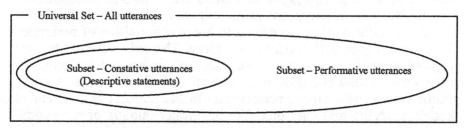

Figure 7: Final Constative-Performative Relationship

Moreover the doctrine of infelicities applies equally well to descriptive statements: «we find that statements *are* liable to every kind of infelicity to which performatives are liable»[103].

For a constative statement «This is red» to be a happily accomplished communication, all six rules of the Doctrine of Infelicities need to be fulfilled. The speakers need to make the utterance in a context where the addressee considers colour to be relevant. They need to be the type of person whose authority with respect to the identification is trusted. For example, they ought not be colour-blind. If it is a complete *non-sequitur* in the conversation, it is likely to be ignored – the given case

---

[103] J.L. AUSTIN, *How to Do Things with Words*, 136.

must be appropriate. If the description is not correct and complete – «This is bred» or «This is ...», then the statement will have failed. Future conduct can lead the statement to be not accepted – «This is red. No, it's blue»[104]. The simple statement that Russell and Whitehead treated as elementary, when scrutinised in the Austin style, proves to operate in a fashion similar to the performance of a ritual. It can fail in all sorts of ways other than truth.

Thus Austin was led to a conclusion quite different from what he had set out to show:

> We have here not really two poles [performative and constative utterances], but rather an historical development. Now in certain cases, perhaps with mathematical formulas in physics books as examples of constatives, or with the issuing of simple executive orders or the giving of simple names, say, as examples of performatives, we approximate in real life to finding such things. It was examples of this kind, like «I apologize», and «The cat is on the mat», said for no conceivable reason, extreme marginal cases, that gave rise to the idea of two distinct utterances[105].

Austin claimed that constative utterances are a modern phenomenon. Historically performatives are prior, ordinary discourse deals almost entirely in performatives, according to his new definition of performatives as utterances with illocutionary force. The only example he was prepared to concede of a constative which is perhaps not performative is the very rarefied one of a mathematical formula in a physics book. «Force equals mass times acceleration» in that context is a statement describing reality and only that. Yet his earlier quoting of the «unexceptional» remark «I was not betting or arguing or warning, I was simply stating it as a fact»[106] puts «stating» on a par with clear performatives. To state the formula is to do something, namely to state it as fact. To describe the world is also to perform an action.

> Furthermore, in general the locutionary act as much as the illocutionary is an abstraction only: every genuine speech act is both. (This is similar to the way in which the phatic act, the rhetic act, &c., are merely abstractions.) But, of course, typically we distinguish different abstracted «acts» by

---

[104] See J.L. AUSTIN, *How to Do Things with Words*, 122.
[105] J.L. AUSTIN, *How to Do Things with Words*, 146.
[106] J.L. AUSTIN, *How to Do Things with Words*, 134.

means of the possible slips between cup and lip, that is, in this case, the different types of nonsense which may be engendered in performing them[107].

What Austin has shown is that every genuine speech act is *both* a locution, which has meaning, and an illocution, which has force.

6.9 *An Austin-style Analysis*

One aspect of Austin's method for establishing distinctions was to try and invent a story in which the language conveying that distinction could plausibly be used[108]. To sum up Austin's contribution fittingly, consider the following extension of the example proposed earlier.

The story: A car, travelling at close to the speed limit in a suburban street is approaching an intersection where the traffic light is *green*. In the passenger seat is a driving instructor and his pupil is at the wheel. The instructor with a look of horror points at the traffic signal and in a fearful tone cries «This is red!» The student slams the brakes on and the car comes to a shuddering halt.

– The *locution*, what was said, namely «This is red!» was a descriptive statement that was *false*.
– The *illocution*, what was intended in saying «This is red!» was *a warning* to the pupil, and this was successfully achieved despite having been unnecessary.
– The *perlocutionary effect* on the addressee is getting him to stop the car – entirely as a consequence of the utterance. Otherwise the driver would have carried on through the intersection.

Factors enhancing the illocutionary force of the utterance were the gesture, the facial expression, the tone of voice and the relationship of authority between the instructor and the pupil. There was obviously uptake of the utterance on the part of the driver. He took it as a warning of such potency that it overrode the evidence of his own eyes.

7. The Uptake of Austin's Ideas

John Austin was an admired and influential lecturer at a prestigious English university. He was at his peak in the tumultuous post-war period when the universities were thronged with students. Undergraduates who were ex-servicemen brought a different perspective and energy to

---

[107] J.L. AUSTIN, *How to Do Things with Words*, 147.
[108] According to J.O. URMSON, «J.L. Austin», 234.

their philosophy. Austin was not perceived as a warm figure, but he was deeply respected, his humour was enjoyed, and his ideas were effectively and powerfully communicated. His theories were expressed in lectures long before they were published. His publications were not numerous, but his contacts with the student body were extensive and, particularly for those who joined in his research projects, intense.

Context affects uptake according to Austin's presentation of speech acts. It is not immaterial to the initial uptake of Austin's own ideas that he was a decorated intelligence officer who had played an important part in the allied victory, nor that he died suddenly of cancer at a comparatively young age. Most of the Austin material now available was published posthumously thanks to the initiative of his students. These publications, in particular *How To Do Things with Words*, ensure an enduring impact, but his first and greatest impact was on the students of Oxford University themselves.

Any set of ideas that is fruitful is capable of more than a single interpretation and application. It is therefore not surprising that Austin's ideas have been developed in diverse ways by different people working in a variety of fields. A lack of unanimity in interpretation is also to be expected. The following survey makes no claim to be comprehensive, but attempts to identify some «disciples» and key contributions to the reception and development of Austin's material, with a particular focus on theological applications.

7.1 *Philosophy – Speech Act Theory*

One of Austin's students, John Searle, took up his mantle. He has become the other name most frequently associated with «Speech Act Theory». Searle established this position with his 1969 work, *Speech Acts: An Essay in the Philosophy of Language*, which elaborated and extended Austin's ideas with some significant differences. One of these differences is on the distinction between the locutionary and illocutionary act. Searle did not follow Austin's self-professedly vague distinction between the act performed *in* saying something and that performed *by* saying something. He replaces it with the «utterance» and «propositional act». Searle provides more logical rigour than that offered by Austin, a contribution appreciated more by philosophers than by those engaged in literary analysis. An example of this rigour can be seen in his analysis of the illocutionary act of making a promise:

Given that Speaker S utters a sentence T in the presence of a hearer H, then, in the literal utterance of T, S sincerely and non-defectively promises that p to H if and only if the following conditions 1-9 apply.[109]

1	*Normal input and output conditions obtain.* [...] It should be noted that this condition excludes both impediments to communication such as deafness and also parasitic forms of communication such as telling jokes or acting a play.	
2	*S expresses the proposition that p in the utterance of T.*	Propositional content conditions
3	*In expressing that p, S predicated a future act A of S.*	
4	*H would prefer S doing A to his not doing A, and S believes H would prefer his doing A to his not doing A.*	Preparatory conditions
5	*It is not obvious to both S and H that S will do A in the normal course of events.*	
6	*S intends to do A.*	Sincerity condition
7	*S intends that the utterance of T will place him under an obligation to do A.*	Essential condition
8	*S intends (i-1) to produce in H the knowledge (K) that the utterance of T is to count as placing S under an obligation to do A. S intends to produce K by means of the recognition of i-1, and he intends i-1 to be recognized by virtue of (by means of) H's knowledge of the meaning of T.*	
9	*The semantical rules of the dialect spoken by S and H are such that T is correctly and sincerely uttered if and only if conditions 1-8 apply.*	

Searle continues working and contributing in this field. He defended Austin's ideas against criticisms by Jacques Derrida[110]. He is concerned

---

[109] See J. SEARLE, *Speech Acts*, 57-61.

[110] J. SEARLE, «Reiterating the Differences: A Reply to Derrida», *Glyph* 1 (1977), 198-208. In his «Signature Event Context» Derrida had attacked the notion of performative utterance, claiming Austin reflected philosophy's tendency to privilege speech over writing. For him the key feature of language is that it is *iterable* – the signs can be repeated in different contexts. Language is precisely that which can be *taken out of context*. Derrida demonstrated his point when, in his lengthy response to Searle, he

with the social reality that is a significant part of our world, and the role of performative utterances with respect to this. He identified two classes of fact:

> We need to distinguish between *brute facts* such as the fact that the sun is ninety-three million miles from the earth and *institutional* facts such as the fact that Clinton is president. [...] Institutional facts require special human institutions for their very existence. Language is one such institution; indeed it is a whole set of such institutions[111].

Moreover he claimed that it is precisely through performative utterances that institutional facts are established and maintained:

> One of the most fascinating features of institution facts is that a very large number, though by no means all of them, can be created by explicit performative utterances. Performatives are members of the class of speech acts I call «declarations». In declarations the state of affairs represented by the propositional content of the speech act is brought into existence by the successful performance of that very speech act. Institutional facts can be created with the performative utterance of such sentences as «The meeting is adjourned», «I give and bequeath my entire fortune to my nephew», «I appoint you chairman», «War is hereby declared», etc. These utterances create the very state of affairs that they represent; and in each case, the state of affairs is an institutional fact[112].

The phrase that Searle identified as paradigmatic for establishing an institutional fact is «*X* counts as *Y*» and its variants. For example «This note counts as legal tender». Such a performative utterance, when happy, creates a new social reality. Searle recounts the observation of many sociologists, that institutions are strengthened by use rather than worn out. Individual notes get worn by use, but the institutional reality of currency is strengthened by every transaction.

Perhaps the pithiest summary of Searle's contribution is that of Kevin Vanhoozer: «If Austin is the Luther of speech act philosophy, John Searle may be considered its Melancthon – its systematic theologian»[113].

---

quoted all of Searle's text, almost entirely out of context, in support of the other side of the argument.

[111] J. SEARLE, *The Construction of Social Reality*, 27.
[112] J. SEARLE, *The Construction of Social Reality*, 34.
[113] K.J. VANHOOZER, *Is There a Meaning in this Text?*, 209.

7.2 Linguistics – Pragmatics

There is a helpful tripartite division of the field of linguistics[114]: first *Semantics*, the study of meaning; second *Syntax*, the study of the formal relationships of the signs used to each other, the structures of language; third *Pragmatics*, the study of language in use. Pragmatics can claim to be the heir of a very long academic tradition stretching back to the classical study of rhetoric. Austin's work has much application to that category and, in practice, galvanised the field.

H. Paul Grice was another of Austin's students. His first publication, the seminal article «Meaning» shows Austin's influence in the clarity of the language and the willingness to present a process of thought rather than a set of conclusions. This article gives his very important definition:

> We may say that «*A* meant [in the non-natural sense] something by *x*» is roughly equivalent to «*A* uttered *x* with the intention of inducing a belief by means of the recognition of this intention»[115].

He distinguishes «natural meanings», like the symptoms which are, naturally associated with a disease, «Those spots meant measles», from non-natural, arbitrary, symbolic associations. For example: «Those three rings on the bell (of the bus) mean that the «bus is full». Most of our utterances are of the second type. Grice has it that the intention of the speaker and the recognition of that intention by the hearer is crucial to meaning. The meaning is not *in the words* – they are secondary to what the speaker is trying to get across[116].

Grice took on Austin's points about context and the fact that illocutions are conventional and set about elaborating the rules that are implicit in the conventions of communication. In 1967 he followed his professor by giving the William James Lectures at Harvard. He expounded a theory of conversational «implicature». By conversational implicatures he meant the inferences that the speaker intends the hearer

---

[114] This division was coined by the ideal-language philosopher, C.W. MORRIS, in *Foundations of the Theory of Signs* (1938).

[115] H.P. GRICE, «Meaning», 384.

[116] There is an ambiguity in the word «act». It can mean (a) a psycho-physical gesture on the part of an individual, or (b) the bringing about of a state of affairs (on the part of an agent). Intention is important for the first understanding, which is that of Grice and Searle, and this has become the accepted approach of Speech Act theory. It has been argued by Marina Sbisà («Communicating citizenship») that the latter view can be found in Austin.

to draw from an utterance. These enable the hearer to understand more from an utterance than is contained in its propositional content. A hearer reads in implications from context and from their encyclopaedic knowledge of the world and makes assumptions about the intention of the speaker.

Alan: «I have a headache».
Joan: «I have an aspirin»[117].

As *code*, Joan's utterance is merely an assertion, but conversational implicature holds that, given the previous utterance and the knowledge that aspirin is a medication to counter headaches, it is actually *intended* as an offer by Joan to provide Alan with that drug.

Within the lecture series Grice outlined the main types of implicature, characterized them, and proposed rules of communication which were specifications of a most general «co-operative principle». This principle, often abbreviated to CP, maintains that coherence and continuity in ordinary dialogue are made possible by the partners' adhering to the following implicit maxims:

1. *Quantity* – the contribution must be informative but not overly informative
2. *Quality* – the contribution must be truthful, based on evidence, and not knowingly false
3. *Relation* – contributions must be relevant
4. *Manner* – contributions must avoid obscurity, ambiguity, unnecessary prolixity and must be orderly[118].

These rules guide our conversation because they are rational, efficient ways to achieve our common ends. CP may be unfulfilled in various ways which Grice reduced to standard types: unintentional failures, and various knowing transgressions that he termed «violations»: opting out, clashes, and a deliberate «flouting» of a maxim in a way that actually serves the cooperative principle.

7.3 *The Social Sciences – Discourse Analysis*

In the early 1970s the work of Austin was discovered by practitioners of an emerging cross-discipline that styled itself as «Discourse Analysis». They found in Speech Act theory a method to account for the rela-

---

[117] Examples from S. Lanser, «(Feminist) Criticism in the Garden», 71.

[118] Maxims of the Cooperative Principle from H.C. WHITE, «Introduction to Speech Act Theory and Literary Criticism», 7.

tions between utterances as social interactions[119]. Practitioners of this discipline apply highly scientific methodologies to the analysis of inter-actions as diverse as charismatic oratory, the use of puns and jokes, courtroom speeches, and news interviews[120].

7.3.1 Anthropology – Ritual Criticism

In a 1988 issue of *Semeia*, dedicated to the topic of Speech Act the-ory and its applications, Ronald Grimes made a tentative beginning to «the task of ritual criticism»[121]. Austin had outlined the various infelici-ties that speech acts were prone to. Grimes notes that most of Austin's ideas are also applicable to ritual. He suggests that a full ritual criticism would have to account for more than speech; it would have to include non-verbal gestures and more. He offers various extensions to Austin's typology of infelicities such as «contagion» where the act leaps beyond proper boundaries, «opacity» where the act is unrecognisable or unin-telligible, and «misframe» where the genre of the act is misconstrued.

Grimes considers that «non-fulfilments» (which he calls «breaches») *necessarily* involve words, and he omits this category from his ritual infelicities. This conclusion is not obvious, since fulfilment will usually involve an action, for example paying up on the bet which was ritual-ised with a handshake. Grimes takes his supporting examples from the Bible, and the context of the article (in an issue of a magazine which styles itself as «an experimental journal devoted to the exploration of new and emergent areas and methods of biblical criticism») suggests he is hoping that ritual criticism will find applications to the scriptural text.

7.4 *Literature – Speech Act Theories of Text*

There existed in the mid-to-late twentieth century an Anglo-American style of literary criticism entitled «New Criticism», with European siblings identified with the phrase «the Death of the Author». The exponents of these styles of criticism considered that only the text

---

[119] See T. VAN DIJK, «Discourse Analysis as a New Cross-Discipline», 5.

[120] See J. M. ATKINSON, «Refusing Invited Applause: Preliminary Observations from a Case Study of Charismatic Oratory»; J. SHERZER, «Puns and Jokes»; P. DREW «Analyzing the Use of Language in Courtroom Interaction»; J. HERITAGE «Analyzing News Interviews: Aspects of the Production of Talk for an Overhearing Audience».

[121] R.L. GRIMES, «Infelicitous Performances and Ritual Criticism», 103-122.

itself mattered. The context, the social and psychological environment that produced it, was to be disregarded. Speech Act theory, as it had been developed by Searle and Grice, with its affirmation of the importance of context and the intention of the speaker, was picked up by those who considered this approach unbalanced.

There were philosophical difficulties inherent in this application. Austin had concentrated on spoken utterances. He had explicitly identified plays and poems as «non-serious» and «parasitic» on direct speech. In terms of speech act theory what status does literature have? An influential answer was given by literary critic Richard Ohmann who suggested that literary works only *pretend* to make illocutionary acts:

> *A literary work is a discourse abstracted or detached, from circumstances and conditions which make illocutionary acts possible; hence it is discourse without illocutionary force* [122].

For him, literature is mimetic, it imitates what happens in ordinary discourse. When we read James Joyce's hellfire sermon, we are not moved as the characters in the novel are. We can appreciate the effects, but we recognise that it is fiction; it is not reality. The text is an «act» only in the theatrical sense and the author is acting not *doing*. This seems to fit with Austin's line that: «If the poet says "Go and catch a falling star" or whatever it may be, he doesn't seriously issue an order»[123].

For those who have been deeply moved by novels, plays and poems, let alone those whose lives have been transformed by the words of scripture, this solution does not accord with their experience. The poet may not be seriously issuing an order, but he *is* doing something. Mary Louise Pratt offered an alternative approach which considers text not as the imitation of conversation, but as a subset of a particular class of conversation – the telling of tales. In ordinary discourse stories are told. The issues mentioned above with respect to literature therefore already exist within the context that Austin was addressing. What is happening in speech act terms when the speaker tells about what he did in his holidays?

According to Pratt the speaker is «verbally displaying a state of affairs»[124] which in some way is *remarkable*. The speaker finds them interesting, and worthy of reflection, and invites the hearer to join him in

---

[122] R. OHMANN, «Speech Acts and the Definition of Literature», 13 (emphasis his).
[123] J.L. AUSTIN, *How to Do Things with Words*, 228.
[124] M.L. PRATT, *Towards a Speech Act Theory of Literary Discourse*, 136.

this. Storytelling is thus different from a simple assertion or a representative speech act, it is a «display text» that invites the hearer to have an imaginative and affective involvement in it, and to respond to it.

The poet referred to by Austin, John Donne, averts to this recounting of the remarkable further into the same poem: «Thou, when thou return'st, wilt tell me / All strange wonders that befell thee». Far from lacking real illocutionary force, such accounts can carry considerable powers of influence and persuasion. There are levels of illocutionary activity involved when direct speech is reported, that of the character, and that of the narrator. For Pratt much conversation belongs to this class of «exclamatory assertion» as do «many if not all literary works». Both theories are influential and they are not mutually exclusive. For obvious reasons those who have applied speech act theory to scriptural texts have welcomed Pratt's analysis.

7.4.1 Interpreting Action – A Speech Act Theory of Deeds

Kevin Vanhoozer, in a work concerned with countering the «Death of the Author» approach of literary critic Stanley Fish, addresses the issue of actions that are meaningful. He points out four similarities between such an action and the Austin-Searle understanding of a speech act[125]:

«(1) *The "doing" of an action corresponds to the locution»*. Something being done is like something being said. Once said or done it is «fixed» in the past – a mark is made on the world.

«(2) *Actions have objects or "propositional contents"»*. In an action a subject operates on an object. If a door were to be opened, then the door is part of the propositional content of the action. It is the object acted upon. It is objective and therefore able to be shared with and identified by others. The action can be remembered in future and even commemorated by repeating it.

«(3) *Actions have a particular force»*. The agent takes up a certain stance with respect to the object of the action. One who opens a door «addresses» it differently from one who intends to shut it, paint it, or knock on it. According to Vanhoozer «What I do in taking up a particu-

---

[125] See K.J. VANHOOZER, *Is There a Meaning in this Text? The Bible, The Reader and the Morality of Literary Knowledge*, 221. The dialogue of opposition with Stanley Fish is signalled by Vanhoozer's choice of title in contrast to that of Fish's 1980 work: *Is there a Text in This Class?*.

lar stance toward the door corresponds to the action's illocutionary force»[126].

«(4) *Actions often have effects, both planned and unexpected*». The intention of the agent – to welcome a guest – may be fulfilled by opening the door. Knocking over the umbrella stand could be an unintended consequence. What is done *by* opening the door corresponds to the perlocutionary effect of an utterance.

A theory which was developed in the context of present tense first-person utterances in ordinary serious conversation is thus being applied not only to a much wider range of discourse situations, but also to text, ritual and meaningful action.

7.5 *Theology*

7.5.1 Religious Language – Self-Involvement

The very first application of Austin's ideas to another field of intellectual endeavour was in the area of religious language. Donald Evans, yet another of Austin's students, published his *The Logic of Self-Involvement: A Philosophical Study of Everyday Language with Special Reference to the Christian Use of Language about God as Creator* in 1963, shortly after Austin's own work was available to the general public. In it he attempts to show that the use of such language as «God is my creator» logically implies one making self-involving commitments. The force of the assertion requires the speaker to acknowledge their status and role and carries concomitant feelings and attitudes. Invoking biblical language necessarily involves taking up certain relationships with God and one's fellow creatures.

Further progress in what constitutes religious language is evidenced by the 1972 work of James Smith and James McClendon, who built on Searle's treatment of a promise and attempted to define logically a confessional speech act:

[Imagine] that when Luther at Worms said «Here I stand», he was misunderstood as reporting his location in the cathedral: «I'm over here, Sir, by the north transept. Were you looking for me?» But that would make more than one mistake: not only a mistake about the sense and reference of the speaker's words, but also a mistake about the kind of speech-act he was performing. Luther was not describing or reporting; he was confessing.

---

[126] K.J. VANHOOZER, *Is There a Meaning in this Text?*, 221

And confessing entails bearing witness; not only taking a stand, but showing it. Which is different, as we have said, from stating it[127].

There is a philosophical problem, known as Moore's Paradox[128], which involves identifying exactly what is wrong with the statement «It is raining, but I don't believe it». The sentence is grammatically well formed, the wrongness does not lie in the syntax. Speech Act theory shows that the origin of the paradox is at the pragmatic level. The utterance attempts two opposed acts. Assertions about brute facts imply a confession of belief in them.

7.5.2 The Parables as Performative Utterances

In 1970, in a closely reasoned philosophical article, Anthony Thiselton addressed the analysis of parables by Ernst Fuchs and suggested that Speech Act theory could throw light on their operation:

> They function *partly* as performatives. As we have seen, Fuchs believes that the parables constitute linguistic acts of calling (*berufen*), promising (*verheissen*), giving (*geben*), or demanding (*fordern*). He also believes that they effect an offer (*Angebot*) a proclamation (*verkündigen*), a pledge (*Zusage, Einsatz*), a naming (*nennen*), permission (*Erlaubnis*), admission (*Einlass*), claim (*Anspruch*), and especially verdict (*Urteil*). Each of these twelve terms for various uses of language belongs firmly to the category of illocutionary acts. Thus giving, proclaiming, claiming, and naming, explicitly feature in Austin's list of exercitives; promising and pledging appear in his list of commissives; and a whole range of words is listed as verdictives. If «permit» is taken as «grant», «demand» as «order», and so on, virtually all of Fuchs's terms are listed by Austin alone. Their function, or part-function, as performatives seems thus to be adequately confirmed. And the importance of a working distinction between performatives and assertions has been sufficiently demonstrated by Austin and Evans[129].

Thiselton has continued working and publishing in this and related fields. In a 1974 article, by applying Austin's ideas to blessings and curses, he debunked very effectively the notion that the ancient He-

---

[127] J. SMITH – J. MCCLENDON, «Religious Language after J.L. Austin», 62.

[128] George Edward Moore (1873-1958) used the phrase in a lecture at Cambridge, contrasting it with «It's raining, but he doesn't believe it» which is perfectly acceptable. According to university legend, Ludwig Wittgenstein, on hearing of the paradox, went to Moore in the middle of the night and got him to repeat the lecture.

[129] A.C. THISELTON, «The Parables as Language-event » 446.

brews thought of words as magical[130]. The continuing influence of Thiselton has gained new impetus with the recent highly successful entry into the field of his doctoral student Richard Briggs[131]. He has reviewed in a very thorough and insightful fashion the applications of Speech Act theory to Biblical interpretation.

7.5.3 Old Testament Prophecy as Speech Acts

The role of the Old Testament prophets as spokesmen of God has proved to be a fruitful area for the application of Speech Act theory. Walter Houston found Austin's distinction between illocutionary and perlocutionary effects helpful in accounting for the phenomenon of prophecies of future events which fail to occur, for example Jonah's preaching of the destruction of Nineveh:

> A prophetic utterance which produces the effect of repentance followed by remission of the punishment may not be the only «successful» kind of prophetic utterance, yet it has to be seen as successful in a perlocutionary sense even though the event announced does not occur. But in that case the word neither asserts a future state of affairs (assertive) nor commits its ultimate author, God, to future action (commissive). My suggestion that it declares a state of judgement is at least a possible alternative[132].

Also concerned with how prophecy operates, Nicholas Wolterstorff develops some of Searle's ideas and considers the variations in degree and mode of superintendence that might be involved in what he calls «double agency discourse». He considers examples like:
– A document is prepared for the president and he signs it.
– A speech is written for him and he delivers it.
– A letter is written by his secretary and signed on his behalf.
– A warning is issued in his name by an ambassador.
He applies the model of «deputized discourse» to the message of the prophets:

> If the ambassador was deputized to say what he did say in the name of his head of state, then the head of state speaks (discourses) by way of the utter-

---

[130] A.C. THISELTON, «The Supposed Power of Words », 283-99.

[131] R.S. BRIGGS, «The Uses of Speech-Act Theory» and *Words in Action*.

[132] W. HOUSTON, «What did the Prophets Think they were Doing? Speech Acts and Prophetic Discourse in the Old Testament», 184.

ings of the ambassador; locutionary acts of the ambassador count as illocutionary acts of the head of state[133].

This notion of «more than one voice» involved in a single utterance had previously been introduced in French writings on Speech Act theory with respect to irony and indirect speech. François Récanati calls it polyphony (*polyphonie*) and distinguishes between the speaker (*locuteur*) who makes the utterance and the announcer (*énonciateur*) who is responsible for the illocutionary act[134].

7.5.4 A Dialogue in John's Gospel – A Speech Act Reading

Speech Act theory has a natural application to text that records or imitates speech. For example, J. Eugene Botha applies it to the dialogue of the encounter between Jesus and the Samaritan woman as it is presented in John's gospel (John 4:1-42). The locutions in this text have to make sense as a conversation as well as advancing the purposes of the evangelist. Botha also points out that the author is seeking to actively engage the intellect and imagination of the reader. In John's gospel a key tactic to this end is his use of irony:

> The object of the highest expression is not to *represent* a fact of feeling to a passive participant … but to make him really *see* by stimulating his imagination. If you wish to produce this effect, you cannot do it by mere word, you must get the hearer's imagination to help. And thus it often comes about that while the lower stages of feeling can be expressed, the higher stages must be suggested. In the ascent the full truth will do; but the climax can only be reached by irony[135].

The scriptural authors are not writing for a passive audience. They expect their words to be read aloud to catechumens and believers. They write to encourage and strengthen faith. They are providing material for discussion and preaching. They expect a fair amount of «processing» of their text by the recipients. In the terminology of Grice, they deliberately «flout» the maxim of Manner[136]. The obscurity of a metaphor is not a violation of the cooperative principle because it ultimately serves

---

[133] N. WOLTERSTORFF, *Divine Discourse*, 45.

[134] F. RECANATI, *Les Énoncés Performatifs*, 220.

[135] J.E. BOTHA, *Jesus and the Samaritan Woman*, 170.

[136] The cooperative principle implies the maxim of Manner: «Contributions must avoid obscurity, ambiguity, unnecessary prolixity and must be orderly». H.C. WHITE, «Introduction to Speech Act Theory and Literary Criticism», 7.

the principle by engaging and involving the attention and insight of the hearer at a particularly high level. According to Botha the metaphoric content of scriptural texts does not reduce their illocutionary and perlocutionary impact, but rather enhances it:

> The communicatory effect of the metaphor is much greater than that of the usual assertive, because of its non-literalness and the fact that it is extremely economical – very few words can implicate as much information as many sentences can. As with the irony the effect of discovery and the satisfaction of grasping what is meant is also significant and makes for a very strong means of communication[137].

Speech Act theory shows just how much work the attentive listener or reader does in unpacking the content and deliberate implications of a communicative act. An effective communication motivates the recipients. If the content and form engage the recipients they are prepared to put more effort into processing the communication. When their processing reveals more and more to them about the world and about themselves, thereby giving them a moment of insight, then the communication has been highly effective indeed.

7.5.5 Liturgy – Performative Language

In a 1973 article Jean Ladrière summed up a central problem involved in the theology of liturgy:

> The basic problem is to discover how liturgical language works. Clearly this kind of language cannot be analysed in terms proper to information theory: it does not consist in the reporting of events, the description of objects, the formulation of theoretical hypotheses, the statement of experimental findings, or the handing on of data. It is characterized in that it is a certain form of operation; it puts something into practice: in short it possesses an «operativity». It is not merely a verbal commentary on an action external to itself; in and of itself, it is action[138].

Given this introduction, it is not surprising that he draws on Austin's distinction between constative statements and performative ones. He identifies a threefold performativity of liturgical language. The first performativity, «*existential induction*», is the operation of an expressive form which awakens in the person who uses it a certain affective

---

[137] J.E. BOTHA, *Jesus and the Samaritan Woman*, 174.
[138] J. LADRIÈRE, «The Performativity of Liturgical Language», 51.

disposition, this being a perlocutionary effect. Saying prayers of gratitude to God leads the person doing the praying to feel grateful. The second, «*institution*», is the effect of liturgical language with its heavy use of the «we» and «us» of collective speech thereby «instituting» «that operative reciprocity which constitutes the reality of a community»[139]. Joining with others in collective prayers leads to that group of people being understood, by themselves and others, as a collective. The third, and for him most fundamental, aspect is «*presentification*» whereby the language makes present for the participants the reality it speaks of. When the Lord's Prayer is introduced as the prayer that Jesus taught his disciples to pray, those who pray it are responding as disciples to that instruction. Ladrière explains sacramentality, and the sacrament of the eucharist in particular, in terms of the last category, acknowledging that «mere linguistic analysis does not suffice to reveal this kind of performativity»[140].

7.5.6 A Speech Act Approach to Sacramental Causality

In 1975 A.P. Martinich engaged in a dialogue with B.R. Brinkmann in *The Heythrop Journal*. Their topic was the issue of sacramental causality, which they presented as one of the most difficult in the tradition. According to Martinich, no single theory enjoyed majority support among theologians and the most popular suffered from the failure of having the sacramental action seeming to compel God to act. He quoted Rahner's criticism of the three traditional theories:

> In all these theories it is noteworthy that the fact that the sacraments are signs plays no part in explaining their causality. Their function as signs and their function as causes are juxtaposed without connection. The axiom everywhere quoted, *sacramenta significando efficiunt gratiam*, is not in fact taken seriously[141].

Attempting to take seriously the axiom that «sacraments cause grace by signifying» leads Martinich to a speech act theory of sacramental causality. He uses Searle's analysis of a promise as a model for developing a speech act analysis of the conditions for the successful performance

---

[139] J. LADRIÈRE, «The Performativity of Liturgical Language», 59.

[140] J. LADRIÈRE, «The Performativity of Liturgical Language», 61.

[141] K. RAHNER, «The Church and the Sacraments», 218, as quoted by Martinich, «Sacraments and Speech Acts», 414; (Sacraments cause grace by signifying – See St. Thomas Aquinas, *Super Sent.*, lib. 4 d. 23 q. 1 a. 2 qc. 2 s. c. 2).

of each of the sacraments. As he indicates, there is nothing new in his material about what is required for the performance of the sacraments; this has been well discussed in the tradition. The novelty is in the way this style of analysis presents the material, and he suggests various insights. Furthermore he develops correspondences between some of the key terms of sacramental theology and those in use in speech act theory. He takes pains to establish the role of conventions in the effects of the sacraments:

> In sacramental theology, *res et sacramentum* corresponds to the illocutionary effect and *res tantum* to perlocutionary effect of speech act theory. The successful performance of a sacramental speech act entails the reception of the *res et sacramentum*. In the abstract the *res et sacramentum* has been defined as a «character of the soul» or an *ornatus animae*. More concretely, the *res et sacramentum* or illocutionary effect of baptism and confirmation is members in the Church, of orders a rank in the church hierarchy. These descriptions make the conventional aspect of the *res et sacramentum* clear. [...] The *res tantum* or perlocutionary effect of a sacrament is its grace. Unlike an illocutionary effect, perlocutionary effects do not infallibly follow upon the successful performance of a sacrament and do not depend upon conventions for their reality[142].

In response to Martinich, Brinkmann suggests that he «may be trying to get too much mileage out of Austin's "performative utterance"»[143], and that any theory of sacraments must allow for their eschatological dimension. Thus if a sacrament is an illocutionary act, it is one without «even a thinkable term to the act»[144].

8. What Austin Offers to This Thesis

This thesis is concerned with how the sacraments of the Church work. Any full theory of sacramental efficacy will be concerned not only with the utterances and visible signs of the present celebration of the sacraments but also with:
– the history of the liturgy and rituals in which the sacraments find their context;
– the saying, deeds and person of Jesus Christ who institutes the sacraments;

---

[142] A.P. MARTINICH, «Sacraments and Speech Acts», 415.
[143] B.R. BRINKMANN, «"Sacramental Man" and Speech Acts Again», 418.
[144] B.R. BRINKMANN, «"Sacramental Man" and Speech Acts Again», 419.

- the sign-actions of the prophets who establish the typology that Christ and the Church invoke;
- the sacred texts that give access to salvation history and are proclaimed in the liturgy.

None of these were Austin's field of endeavour; he was concerned with linguistic philosophy and held the chair of Moral Philosophy. Speech acts were the area of Austin's most original and valued contributions. The relevance of his ideas becomes apparent by viewing prophetic actions and sacraments as communicative acts.

Austin shows that every speech act usually carries more than true or false information. In his doctrine of forces he has shown that potentially every speech act has locutionary, illocutionary and perlocutionary effects. A speech act is not merely a true or false report as the Descriptive Fallacy would have it. Speech acts are performative utterances and, significantly, when Austin reaches for clear examples of what it means to be a performative, two of the exemplars are christening and marrying – utterances central to the sacraments of Baptism and Matrimony.

Secondly, Austin draws attention to the context of the words involved in the act of communication, that is to «the total speech act in the total speech situation». He connects elements of this context to the utterance by way of his doctrine of forces. Not only can the context change the sense and reference of the words, it can also enhance or limit the illocutionary and perlocutionary force of the utterance. Austin also identifies conventional cases where the force is conveyed entirely by non-verbal means.

Austin is far from atomic in his approach to communication; he has a holistic view of what is involved. In the final chapter we will take up his considerations of the existing relationship between speaker and addressee, the notion of «uptake» and his style of analysis of the «total speech situation» trying to take account of the factors which enhance the force of a communicative act.

It is the breadth of the different applications of Austin's theory that show its potential to provide the connections that this thesis seeks. The theory has found application at many of the points relevant to this present enquiry. It has been applied to the teachings of the Old Testament prophets, to the parables and words of Jesus, to liturgy and to sacraments. A theory that can throw light on each of these areas independently clearly has potential to illuminate them when considered in connection with each other.

Figure 8: Jürgen Habermas, 1995

Chapter II

Jürgen Habermas and Communicative Action

1. Introduction

The previous chapter described how speech act theory was initiated by John Austin, developed by his students and successors, and applied in various disciplines. This chapter indicates how Austin's ideas came to be implanted in a different philosophical context and were there developed into the theory of communicative action. This theory, produced by Jürgen Habermas over 30 years with the help of assistants and teams of researchers, is closely argued by him in numerous publications, most especially in his two-volume work of that name.[1] By attending to its context and the central concepts of his theory, this chapter provides an introduction to the theory. Particular attention is given to the context and the central personality involved, because, as this theory states:

> If the investigations of the last decade in socio-, ethno-, and psycholinguistics converge in any one respect, it is on the often and variously demonstrated point that the collective background and context of speakers and hearers determine interpretations of their explicit utterances to an extraordinarily high degree[2].

---

[1] J. HABERMAS, *Theorie des kommunikativen Handelns*. I. *Handlungsrationalität und gesellschaftliche Rationalisierung*. II. *Zur Kritik der funktionalistischen Vernunft*, 1981; English trans., *The Theory of Communicative Action*. I. *Reason and the Rationalization of Society*. II. *Lifeworld and System: A Critique of Functionalist Reason*, 1984, 1987.

[2] J. HABERMAS, *The Theory of Communicative Action*, I, 335.

Thus an understanding of the theory of communicative action is facilitated by gaining an appreciation of the Habermas's academic and cultural context.

2. The Frankfurt School

The expression «the Frankfurt School» was a term coined in the 1960s to label a group of neo-Marxist philosophers associated with the Institute for Social Research in Frankfurt. During the student protests of 1968 this group acquired media fame and a «mythic status» as a key source of the ideas acclaimed by the student radicals. The chant of «Marx, Mao, Marcuse!» invoked a triad of Karl Marx, Chairman Mao Zedong, and Herbert Marcuse – the last being a philosopher of the Frankfurt School[3]. The relationship between the Frankfurt School philosophers and the students of 1968 was not always uncritical. One of the younger philosophers, Jürgen Habermas, met a hostile reception when he asked a student meeting that had been listening to the stirring oratory of Rudi Dutschke[4] if their challenging authority was not masochistic and whether Dutschke's ideology was perhaps «left-wing fascism»[5]. For the students, the Frankfurt School epitomised modern European Marxist thought, but they discovered within it a sensitivity to various forms of domination and a reluctance to accept anything without question. The history of the School and the biography of Habermas show that neither characterisation is without foundation.

2.1 *The Institute for Social Research*

On November 14, 1951, in Frankfurt am Main, the Institute for Social Research[6] reopened. It had been shut down by the Nazis in 1933

---

[3] Roberto Bartali, an Italian sociologist, refers to «il ma-ma-maismo, un'ideologia composita derivata dalla triade Marx-Mao-Marcuse ed elevata dai sessantottini a nuovo vangelo». See *Il «Sessantotto»* [Accessed 24 February 2005] on http://www. robertobartali.it/cap01.htm.

[4] Rudi Dutschke (1940-1979) was a sociology student of the Free University. He had been a conscientious objector to military service when he was an active member of the Protestant Church in East Germany. As a result, he had not been able to study in the East, and had fled to West Berlin just before the Berlin Wall went up. A charismatic public speaker with radical democratic ideas, Dutschke was presented by the media as «red Rudi» and as the epitome of the rebellious student leader.

[5] R. WIGGERSHAUS, *The Frankfurt School*, 619.

[6] *Institut für Sozialforschung*.

but continued operating in exile in America. Now, at the invitation of the acting chairman of Frankfurt University[7] and the Mayor of the City, it was being re-established in its place of origin. During his speech, Max Horkheimer quoted from his 1931 inaugural lecture as director of the Institute declaring that their goal was «to organise studies based on current philosophical issues, on which philosophers, sociologists, economists, historians, psychologists would unite in continual interdisciplinary cooperation»[8].

Rolf Wiggershaus has a list of five characteristics of what constitutes a «school» in the philosophic/artistic sense[9]. He claims these were present, at least during the 1930s, in the group that came to be known as «the Frankfurt School»:

1. An institutional framework – the Institute for Social Research
2. A charismatic leader with a new theoretical programme – Max Horkheimer
3. A manifesto – Horkheimer's 1931 lecture: *The Present State of Social Philosophy and the Tasks Facing an Institute of Social Research*[10].
4. A new paradigm – an aggressively cross-disciplinary approach they called «Critical Theory»[11] intended to both understand society and provide it with the tools for emancipatory change.
5. A journal and other outlets for publishing their work – the *Zeitschrift für Sozialforschung* (Journal of Social Research).

One of the people attracted into the academic environment of the re-established institute was a young newspaper journalist called Jürgen Habermas. He described the setting:

---

[7] The complexities and difficulties of the time are revealed in the fact that the Klingelhöfer who issued the invitation in 1946 was the same person who in 1938 had signed the decree in which the Ministry of Culture ordered the Institute's books to be dispersed. See R. WIGGERSHAUS, *The Frankfurt School*, 398.

[8] Institut für Sozialforschung an der Johann Wolfgang Goethe-Universität Frankfurt am Main, *Ein Bericht über die Feier seiner Wiedereröffnung*, 1952, 10.

[9] R. WIGGERSHAUS, *The Frankfurt School*, 2.

[10] M. HORKHEIMER, *Die gegenwärtige Lage der Sozialphilosophie und die Aufgaben eines Instituts für Sozialforschung*.

[11] In 1937 Horkheimer wrote an essay entitled «Traditional and Critical Theory». He characterized traditional theory as closed Cartesian systems of logical statements, and contrasted it with Marx's critique of political economy which remains connected to practical life and is governed by «an interest in rational conditions». See R. BUBNER, «Habermas's Concept of Critical Theory», 44-45.

Time had a dual-layered quality in the institute. During the fifties there was probably no other place in the whole Federal Republic, in which the intellectual twenties were so explicitly present. Certainly the old staff members of the institute, like Herbert Marcuse, Leo Löwenthal and Erich Fromm, also Franz Neumann and Otto Kirchheimer, had remained in America. However, also names like Benjamin and Scholem, Kracauer and Bloch, Brecht and Lukács, Alfred Sohn-Rethel and Norbert Elias, of course the names of Thomas and Erika Mann, Alban Berg and Arnold Schönberg or those of Kurt Eisler, Lotte Lenya and Fritz Lang circulated in completely natural fashion between Adorno, Gretel and Horkheimer[12].

The litany of names which Habermas recalls provides a snapshot of the major players of the first generation of the Frankfurt School and the authorities they acknowledged:
- **Herbert Marcuse** (1898-1979) was a Marxist philosopher and social theorist;
- **Leo Löwenthal** (1900-1993), interested in Judaism, socialism and psychoanalysis, was the editor of the Institute's journal, *Zeitschrift für Sozialforschung*;
- **Erich Fromm** (1900-1980) was a psychoanalyst and Freudian of the left, who attempted to combine Freud's theory of instinctual drives with Marx's class theory;
- **Franz Neumann** (1900-1954) and **Otto Kirchheimer** (1905-1965) were legal and state theorists;
- **Theodor Wiesengrund-Adorno** (1903-1969) was a philosopher with expertise in music criticism and musical aesthetics;
- **Margarete** («Gretel») **Adorno,** née Karplus (1902-1993), was a chemist and secretary to her husband Theodor; and
- **Max Horkheimer** (1895-1973), philosopher and sociologist, was the director of the Institute.

All were Jews, at least by the definition used by the Nazis. They were the «old staff members of the Institute»[13]

The names that were commonplace for the returned staff are from the pre-war academic and cultural environment of Frankfurt:
- **Walter Benjamin** (1892-1940) was a Marxist literary critic and philosopher;
- **Gershom Scholem** (1897-1982) founded the scholarly study of the Kabbalah;

---

[12] J. HABERMAS, «Dual-Layered Time», 52-3.
[13] J. HABERMAS, «Dual-Layered Time», 52.

- **Siegfried Kracauer** (1889-1966) was a journalist, sociologist, film historian and founder of the sociology of film;
- **Ernst Bloch** (1885-1977) was a Marxist philosopher;
- **Bertholt Brecht** (1898-1956) a Marxist playwright;
- **Georg Lukács** (1885-1971) was a Marxist philosopher, writer, and literary critic;
- **Alfred Sohn-Rethel** (1899-1990) was a Marxist philosopher;
- **Norbert Elias** (1897-1990) was a sociologist and founder of process sociology;
- **Thomas Mann** (1875-1955) was a novelist and literary critic;
- **Erika Mann** (1905-1969), his daughter, was a writer and actor;
- **Alban Berg** (1885-1935) and **Arnold Schönberg** (1874-1951) were composers.
- **Kurt Eisler** is presumably a reference to **Hanns Eisler** (1898-1962), composer of East Germany's national anthem, who collaborated with Brecht, Bloch and Adorno in works on the role of music in culture;
- **Lotte Lenya** (1898-1981) was a singer and actor; and
- **Fritz Lang** (1890-1976) was film director, famous for his grim futuristic film *Metropolis*.

The interests of Horkheimer and Adorno are reflected in this eclectic collection. Philosophy, sociology, psychology, law, film, theatre and music are well-represented, though, strangely given the cross-disciplinary thrust of the Institute[14], no historian or economist is mentioned.

Habermas recalled entering this setting feeling like «the clumsily uneducated boy from the province whose eyes were opened by the big city»[15].

3. A Biographical Sketch of Jürgen Habermas

Jürgen Habermas was born in Düsseldorf in 1929 and he grew up in Gummersbach where his father was director of the Chamber of Commerce. His grandfather was a minister and director of the local semi-

---

[14] Horkheimer had declared in his 1931 opening address that he hoped «to set up, along with my associates, at least on a very small scale, a regime of planned work on the juxtaposition of philosophical construct and empiricism in social theory» M. HORKHEIMER, *Die gegenwärtige Lage der Sozialphilosophie und die Aufgaben eines Instituts für Sozialforschung*, as quoted by R. Wiggershaus, *The Frankfurt School*, 38-9.

[15] J. HABERMAS, «Dual-Layered Time», 55.

nary, but Jürgen, through upbringing or personal choice, admits to no religious affiliation. At birth he had a cleft palate; corrective surgery left him with an asymmetric face and a slight lisp. With the others of his generation he entered the Hitler Youth. In a magazine interview, Habermas admitted:

> Philosophers live finally from their own intuitions, and those intuitions are not acquired by reading philosophic texts. They are acquired in certain particular individual experiences while growing up – rather negative experiences of violation, indignation and Kränkung[16].

One of these negative experiences was the revelation of the atrocities of the Second World War. When Habermas was 15 years of age the first documentaries about the concentration camps were shown. That, with the information coming from the Nuremberg Trials convinced him «that we had been living in a politically criminal system»[17].

At the universities of Göttingen and Bonn he studied philosophy, history, psychology and literature. He did his doctoral thesis on the German idealist Schelling[18]. His retrospective judgement of this period is harsh: «We had studied at the morally deteriorated universities of the Adenauer era that were marked with self-pity, suppression and insensitiveness»[19]. He contrasted that with his subsequent experience of the Institute of Social Research: «I had grown up in the dominant tradition, that had persisted during the Nazi-era and now I found myself in a milieu in which everything was alive that had been eliminated by the Nazis»[20].

In 1953 Habermas initiated a heated public debate by criticizing Heidegger, in a newspaper article, for publishing without comment or apology, his 1935 lectures (An Introduction to Metaphysics[21]) which included a discussion on the «inner truth and greatness» of the Nazi movement. Habermas perceived the culture of his childhood to have

---

[16] M. STEPHENS, «Jürgen Habermas: The Theologian of Talk», 21. Habermas speaks good English. His vocabulary failed him on one word, which translates as «an injury to one's feelings».

[17] M. STEPHENS, «Jürgen Habermas: The Theologian of Talk», 23.

[18] The title of his thesis was Das Absolute und die Geschichte: Von der Zweispältigkeit in Schellings Denken (The Absolute and History: The Duality in Schelling's Thought).

[19] J. HABERMAS, «Dual-Layered Time», 54-5.

[20] J. HABERMAS, «Dual-Layered Time», 55.

[21] M. HEIDEGGER, Einführung in die Metaphysik, Tübingen, 1953.

been dangerously sick and, so, was sensitive to any symptoms of relapse. As he said later:

> I knew that, despite everything, we should live on in the anxiety of regression, that we would have to carry on in that anxiety. Since then I have cast about, sometimes here, sometimes there, for traces of a reason that unites without effacing separation, that binds without denying difference, that points out the common and the shared among strangers, without denying the other of otherness[22].

The themes he identifies as central for his life are a trust in reason, in community and in intersubjective bonding – something that unites while permitting diversity.

In 1956 Habermas was employed by the Institute for Social Research as a researcher. He worked as assistant to Theodor Adorno for six years. In 1961, after Horkheimer had refused to approve as *Habilitationschrift* his monograph *The Structural Transformations of the Public Sphere*[23], he left to become a *Privatdozent* in Marburg. Through the intervention of Wolfgang Abendoth he habilitated there. On the initiative of Hans-Georg Gadamer and Karl Löwith, Habermas was appointed to a chair as extraordinary professor of philosophy at Heidelberg, even before completing his *Habilitation*.

In 1964 he returned to Frankfurt to take over the chair that Horkheimer held as professor of sociology and philosophy. His inaugural lecture was «Knowledge and Human Interests: A General Perspective»[24]. One of the statements in that lecture signalled what was to be a major theme of his life's work:

> What raises us out of nature is the only thing whose nature we can know: *language*. Through its structure, autonomy and responsibility are posited for us. Our first sentence expresses unequivocally the intention of universal and unconstrained consensus[25].

The classical Marxist takes «labour» as the basic form of human action. Early in his career Habermas had turned instead to communication and the use of language.

---

[22] J. HABERMAS, *The Past as Future*, 119-120.

[23] Subsequently published to considerable acclaim as *Strukturwandel der Öffentlichkeit*, Neuwied – Berlin 1962.

[24] Included in the book of the same name: *Erkenntnis und Interesse*, 1968.

[25] J. HABERMAS, *Knowledge and Human Interests*, 314.

He was on the staff of the university and lecturing in the Institute for Social Research throughout the turbulent period of the student protests. Then, for a 10 year period (1971-81), Habermas took on the director-ship of the *Max Planck Institute for the Research into the Conditions of Life in the Scientific-Technical World* in Starnberg (near Munich) where he established teams of researchers and philosophers working on various projects[26]. It is from within this environment that the works *Communication and the Evolution of Society* and the two volumes of *The Theory of Communicative Action* emerged. The works are directed and co-ordinated by Habermas and thoroughly imbued with his vision. They are the result of a co-operative process somewhat akin to Austin's proposal for how philosophy ought progress.

It is during this period that Habermas signalled a significant depar-ture from the methodology of the earlier Critical Theorists. One prob-lematic for them was the basis on which they made their criticisms. Hegelian and Marxist theories involve the notion of progress towards a better world. Against the hypothetical future the present can be cri-tiqued. Much of the Frankfurt School's critique of the reification of so-ciety assumed that what they criticized was self-evidently wrong. In his work, Habermas sought a theoretical foundation that could be used as a basis for culture critique and to point out the direction of emancipation for societies. He turned to deep theories of communication and tried to develop a «Universal Pragmatics», and in doing so he chose to «draw primarily on the theory of speech acts initiated by Austin»[27]. His incor-poration of English linguistic philosophy was a significant departure from the predominantly German and Marxist philosophical sources used by the Frankfurt School.

After a visiting professorship in Berkeley, Habermas returned to Frankfurt University in 1981 and took up again the professorship of

---

[26] Being identified as a Marxist has not always helped Habermas's academic ca-reer. He commented in an interview: «that other university, which is located next to the seat of the government of Bavaria, could not bring itself – even after repeated at-tempts – to take the routine decision of granting the position of honorary professor to the director of the neighboring Max Planck Institute». J. HABERMAS, *Autonomy and Solidarity*, 214.

[27] J. HABERMAS, *Communication and the Evolution of Society*, 7. This statement first appeared in 1976 within «Was heist Universalpragmatik» in *Sprachpragmatik und Philosophie*, edited by Karl-Otto Apel.

philosophy[28]. In 1986 he received a major five-year grant which he used to fund a research project on the philosophy of law and democratic theory. This collaborative working environment gave rise to *Between Facts and Norms*[29].

The transition made in 1994 to emeritus professor of philosophy ended neither Habermas's publishing nor his involvement with the public. He has a very high media profile in Germany despite refusing to appear on television. The newspapers seek his comments on the issues of the day. In the year of writing, 2004, 10 years after his «retirement» and in his 75th year, Habermas is a key figure in three academic events which have been publicized world-wide:
- 19 January – Habermas debated with Cardinal Ratzinger on the theme of «Duel of the Spirits: Towards a political and moral basis for a liberal state». The debate took place in Munich under the auspices of the *Katholische Akademie Bayern*.
- 4 March – He gave the keynote address to a symposium at the Austrian Academy of Sciences in Vienna entitled «Right / History / Religion: The Significance of Kant for current philosophy».
- 15 October – He is to give a public lecture on «The Kantian Project of Cosmopolitan Law» at Purdue University in Indianapolis.

Habermas, at the January debate, was introduced by the director of the Catholic Academy, Dr. Florian Schuller, as the «most influential German philosopher since Marx, Nietzsche and Heidegger; his role seems even to be that of a public conscience of the political culture of the country»[30].

4. Habermas's View of Philosophy

Horkheimer and the Critical Theorists were dismissive of «traditional theory», including philosophy since Descartes, which, in their view, was a closed system of logically linked statements that, while internally

---

[28] Germany was late in following the worldwide trend of giving Sociology independent academic status. The chair that Horkheimer and Habermas had held covered *both* philosophy and sociology, which was well-suited to the project of Critical Theory. While Habermas was absent from Frankfurt the chair was divided into two positions.

[29] J. HABERMAS, *Faktizität und Geltung*, Frankfurt 1992

[30] Reported in *Rheinischer Merkur*, January 22, 2004: «seit Marx, Nietzsche und Heidegger einflussreichste deutsche Philosoph, seine Rolle scheint sogar die eines öffentlichen Gewissens der politischen Kultur des Landes zu sein».

consistent, had little to do with practical life. Any theory which was not closely inter-related with praxis would itself be a source of exploitation. Their paradigm of critical thought was Marx's «critique of political economy». Habermas shares this viewpoint, and declares: «as long as philosophy remains caught in ontology, it is itself subject to an objectivism that disguises the connection of its knowledge with the human interest in autonomy and responsibility»[31]. To the requirement that critical thought be connected with practical interest, Habermas adds the criterion of reflexivity; a truly critical theory ought to be able to criticize itself. He perceives ontology as unaware of the interests it is serving. Similarly he critiques so-called objective empirical science in his work, *Knowledge and Human Interests*. Habermas identifies some «critical social sciences»[32] as having an *emancipatory interest*. The paradigm of this for him was psycho-analysis. In that discipline the clients, trapped by irrational psychoses, are enabled to find liberation through reflecting on the bases of their thinking and acting. For Habermas, philosophy is to serve this emancipatory interest.

The roles that Habermas assigns to philosophy are famously summed up in the title of one of his articles: «Philosophy as Stand-In and Interpreter»[33] He and Richard Rorty[34] in debate rejected the traditional roles taken by philosophy, which they referred to as «usher and judge». Rorty proposed that it also should give up being «guardian of rationality». Habermas strongly disagreed on that point. Habermas offered the role of stand-in (*Platzhalter*), where the seat philosophy keeps is that of «empirical theories with strong universalistic claims»[35]. He outlined the task of philosophy as interpreter as follows:

> Philosophy also occupies a position with two fronts [...] On the one hand, it directs its interest to the foundations of science, morality, and law and attaches theoretical claims to its statements. Characterized by universalistic problematics and strong theoretical strategies, it maintains an intimate relationship with the sciences. And yet philosophy is not simply an esoteric component of an expert culture. It maintains just as intimate a relationship with the totality of the lifeworld and with sound common sense, even if in a

---

[31] J. HABERMAS, *Knowledge and Human Interests*, 310.

[32] J. HABERMAS, *Knowledge and Human Interests*, 310.

[33] J. HABERMAS, «Philosophy as Stand-In and Interpreter», 296-315.

[34] Richard Rorty (1931-) of Stanford University is a leading American pragmatic philosopher.

[35] Quoted by D. RASMUSSEN, *Reading Habermas*, 21.

subversive way it relentlessly shakes up the certainties of everyday practice[36].

«Lifeworld» is the background set of convictions held by members of a culture and is a concept that will be explored further below. Philosophy is to act as bridge between this everyday aspect of the world and the findings of abstruse science. Science specializes, but philosophy, as Habermas understands it, must stay linked to the commonplace.

One aspect of the task of «interpreter of the lifeworld» is reminding society of important historical truths that many would rather forget. The term Habermas uses for this process «anamnestic reason» appropriated from Walter Benjamin. For Benjamin it was the «mystical force of retroactive reconciliation». Habermas describes it more prosaically: «Remembrance preserves from decay things which we regard as indispensable, and yet which are now in extreme danger»[37]. He proposes the example of keeping alive an accurate memory of the Holocaust. For the health and sanity of western society it is important that it not be forgotten or suppressed. Anamnestic reason concerns the interconnection between philosophy and contingent history emphasised by Habermas. He characterises ontological philosophy as concerned with timeless universals, whereas his pragmatic philosophy is situated in the midst of contingent reality and thoroughly tied to human history.

Habermas shares with Austin an opposition to the Positivist philosophical approach.

> Positivism, and in this context I would include Popper's philosophy under this heading, sees its task as being to establish the objective status of the sciences, to privilege them as the sole legitimate form of knowledge and the only way to achieve systematic cognitive progress. The theoretical-political impulse underlying the Vienna Circle was to draw a demarcation line between science and «metaphysics», in other words, all other kinds of knowledge which were thereby downgraded to mere forms of expression[38].

The physical sciences have enjoyed enormous success over the last 200 years. Habermas perceives a danger associated with this. The approach that has been fruitful can come to be thought of as the *only* good way forward. Branches of knowledge that do not fit that model are deval-

---

[36] J. HABERMAS, *The Philosophical Discourse of Modernity*, 208.
[37] J. HABERMAS, *Religion and Rationality*, 131-2.
[38] J. HABERMAS, *Autonomy and Solidarity*, 55.

ued. Habermas intends to champion a wider view of what constitutes knowledge.

5. Habermas's Method

Habermas's methodology is deliberately distinct from the transcendental and ontological tradition. Those approaches are deductive; building a structure that claims certainty on a foundation of axioms. Habermas, by contrast, does philosophy in much the same way he does sociology and in a fashion similar to those theorists of linguistics who adopt a reconstructive approach. He collects data about what does happen and seeks to construct a theory to explain this evidence. That theory is then tested against further data, and adapted in response to perceived shortcomings in order to provide greater generality and explanatory power. The theory is hypothetical and liable to be modified in response to new data or criticism.

Habermas is famous for how seriously he takes his critics and his willingness to argue constructively with them[39]. Later works explicitly cite objections to earlier formulations of his thought and address the issues they raise. Habermas believes that in free discourse the «better argument» has a chance to be heard. His personal style is consistent with his theories. Habermas is enormously eclectic in his quest for data to ground his theorising. He uses material developed by primary research of the Frankfurt Institute and the Max Planck Institute. He draws on the research results of Noam Chomsky[40] in linguistics, of John Austin and John Searle in speech-act theory, of Max Weber[41] in sociology, of George Herbert Mead[42] in pragmatic philosophy, of Talcott Par-

---

[39] A representative example is the volume by B. THOMPSON – D. HELD, ed., *Habermas: Critical Debates* which contains articles critiquing aspects of Habermas's thought and Habermas's lengthy «Reply to My Critics».

[40] Noam Chomsky (1928-), an American linguistic philosopher and author of *Syntactic Structures* (1957); see J. HABERMAS, *The Theory of Communicative Action, I*, 8-20.

[41] Max Weber (1864-1920), a German economist and sociologist, is one of the founders of modern sociology. He conceived of sociology as a comprehensive science of social action. He is the author of *The Protestant Ethic and the Spirit of Capitalism*, a seminal essay on the differences between religions and the relative wealth of their followers.

[42] George Herbert Mead (1863-1931), an American philosopher and founder of Pragmatism. His ideas were posthumously published by his students. See C.W. MORRIS, ed., *Mind, Self, and Society* (1934) .

sons[43] in systems theory, of Karl Popper on the philosophy of science, of Theodor Adorno and Walter Benjamin on theories of the arts. There is a reciprocal influence between Habermas and his friend the philosopher Karl-Otto Apel[44]. He is interested in Freud's ideas of psychoanalysis and Erich Fromm's attempts to apply those ideas to entire societies. He draws on both Kohlberg[45] and Piaget[46] for theories of development. He tries to take into account the vast sweep of history, while also responding to the *Zeitgeist* of this age. Moreover, his drawing together of all these threads is not mere compilation or anything resembling popularisation. Habermas is very selective in what he takes from each source and often reconstructs, or at least recasts, the material in question to fit in with his project.

6. Habermas's Results

6.1 *Three Worlds of Discourse*

In his exploration of sociology, Habermas discovered the writings of I.C. Jarvie[47] and, within them, an application of Karl Popper's theory of «three worlds». Influenced by Jarvie, Habermas traced these ideas to their source. Popper, who was concerned with the development of sci-

---

[43] Talcott Parsons (1902-1979) an American functionalist sociologist who attempted to integrate all the social sciences into a science of human action. In *The Social System* (1951), Parsons argued that the crucial feature of societies, as of biological organisms, is homeostasis (maintaining a stable state), and that their parts can be understood only in terms of the whole.

[44] Karl-Otto Apel (1922-), emeritus professor of philosophy at the University of Frankfurt am Main, with specialisations in ethics, philosophy of language and human sciences.

[45] Lawrence Kohlberg (1927-1987) a psychologist and professor at Harvard University. He started as a developmental psychologist in the early 1970s and became famous for his later work in moral education and moral reasoning. Kohlberg's theory of moral development emphasizes that moral reasoning develops in stages. His stages of moral development first appeared in the 1970 essay «Education for Justice: A Modern Statement of the Socratic View» which was reprinted in his work *Essays on Moral Development* (1981).

[46] Jean Piaget (1896-1980) a Swiss psychologist and structuralist philosopher, author of many works on human development including, *L'épistémologie génétique*, Paris 1970; English trans., *The Principles of Genetic Epistemology*, 1972.

[47] Ian Charles Jarvie (1937-), a philosopher and professor at York University, Canada. Jarvie was one of Popper's students, and has addressed the ideas and legacy of Popper in his own works. The work of Jarvie cited by Habermas is *Concepts and Society* (1972) which Jarvie describes as «a Popperian philosophy of the social».

entific thought, outlined the theory in a 1967 address to the Third International Congress for Logic, Methodology and Philosophy of Science:

> Without taking the words «world» or «universe» too seriously, we may distinguish the following three worlds or universes: first the world of physical objects or of physical states; secondly, the world of states of consciousness, or mental states, or perhaps of behavioural dispositions to act; and thirdly, the world of objective contents of thought, especially of scientific and poetic thought and of works of art[48].

Popper aimed to establish the independent, objective reality of bodies of scientific knowledge. Physical objects, such as rocks, have a reality entirely independent of the observer who may count them, build with them, or trip over them. The frustration experienced by a person who has tripped over a rock is a different class of reality, dependent on the observer and internal to him or her. When some person conceives of counting rocks, and communicates this notion, another sort of entity has come into existence. The natural numbers, once invented or (significantly) *discovered*, exhibit a kind of independence from the minds of those who conceived them. They provide solutions for some difficulties but contain in themselves further problems. The idea of the natural numbers implies that of the prime numbers, for example. Some of the further properties of primes have been discovered, yet they are still generating problems of interest to mathematicians and code-breakers. One person (a first world entity) may *know* a lot of mathematics (the consciousness of this is a mental state and thus belongs to the second world), but the system of mathematical *knowledge* (a third world entity) is now beyond the capacity of any individual human thinker.

---

[48] K.R. POPPER, *Objective Knowledge*, 106. Karl Raimund Popper (1902-1994) was born in Vienna but emigrated because of concern about the rise of the Nazis. He lectured in philosophy at Canterbury University, Christchurch, New Zealand, from 1937 to 1945, and then took up the position of Reader in Logic and Scientific method at the London School of Economics. Within three years he was made professor and lectured there until he retired from full-time teaching in 1969. His first major work *Logik der Forschung* (1935) was published in English as *The Logic of Scientific Discovery* only in 1959. He extended his theories of science to history and society, publishing *The Poverty of Historicism* (1957) and winning fame with his 1945 work: *The Open Society and Its Enemies*. As a trenchant critic of Communism, his theories have attracted considerable attention from Marxist philosophers, who, oddly, usually avoided mentioning his name. Habermas departs notably from this tradition in his explicit, *positive* citation of Popper.

Popper's Three Worlds[49]

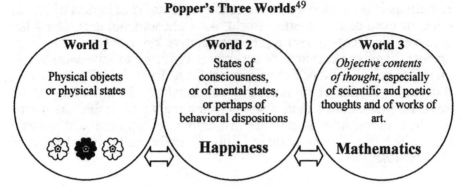

Figure 9: Popper's Three Worlds

Popper populated his third world with scientific theories, hypotheses and problems, reflecting his focus of interest: the philosophy of science. He did, however, allow in «poetic thought and works of art», thereby suggesting that there could be a reality and independence to standards of beauty and norms other than scientific truth. Significantly, for Habermas, Popper's first and third worlds interact by way of the second. Scientific theories may be stored in computer or printed in books (first world objects) and may impact on the design of first world objects (like computers) but they always make the transition from third to first world by way of the subjective experience of a thinking subject (the second world).

Popper's vision appealed to Habermas, but it would be deceptive to simply equate Habermas's three worlds with those of Popper. Habermas explains his different starting point as follows:

> The phenomenologist does not rely upon the guiding thread of goal-directed or problem-solving action. He does not, that is, simply begin with the ontological presupposition of an objective world; he makes this a problem by inquiring into the conditions under which the unity of an objective world is constituted for the members of a community. The world gains objectivity only through *counting* as one and the same world *for* a community of speaking and acting subjects[50].

---

[49] A similar diagram to this is provided by Popper and Eccles, *The Self and Its Brain*, 359.

[50] J. HABERMAS, *The Theory of Communicative Action*, I, 12.

Habermas is not interested in the ontological status of bodies of knowledge, or even of the external world. As a phenomenologist, using language as his access to reality, the interpretive key is *what sort of utterances* a linguistic community accepts as referring to «the world». His question, reminiscent of Searle's institutional facts, is: «What *counts as* the world *for* this communicative community?» In providing an answer, he first makes a distinction between the world in the foreground, the focus of our interest, and the vast amount of unquestioned information which we simply assume. This latter he calls the «lifeworld» (*Lebenswelt*).

6.1.1 Lifeworld

Edmund Husserl is the name most associated with the term «lifeworld» which for him constituted the natural world in which we live:

> Science [...] presupposes as its point of departure, both historically and for each new student, the intuitive surrounding world of life, pregiven as existing all in common[51].

For Husserl, before we start theorizing about the world, there is a reality which we all experience and accept. This was a major theme in his philosophy which he developed throughout his academic career.

The term «lifeworld» was enthusiastically picked up in sociology, and used in varying senses; some were clearly derived from Husserl, others less so. Habermas, despite being familiar with Husserl, gives a different sense to the term than he did. Where the lifeworld was the «ground» for Husserl, for Habermas it is the «background». Husserl had it as «the object of straight-forward experience»[52] and as «a realm of original self-evidences». It is a more mysterious kingdom for Habermas:

> Searle encounters this layer of worldview knowledge functioning in everyday life as the background with which a hearer has to be familiar if he is to be able to understand the literal meaning of speech acts and to act communicatively. He thereby directs our gaze to a continent that remains hidden so long as the theoretician analyzes speech acts only from the perspective of the speaker who relates his utterances to something in the objective, social, and subjective worlds. It is only with the turn back to the context-forming horizon of the lifeworld, from within which participants in communication

---

[51] E. HUSSERL, *The Essential Husserl*, 363.
[52] E. HUSSERL, *The Essential Husserl*, 366.

come to an understanding with one another about something, that our field of vision changes in such a way that we can see the points of connection for social theory within the theory of communicative action[53].

Thus, for Habermas, the lifeworld is «a layer of worldview knowledge» – knowledge *of* the world, rather than the natural world which we experience. It is a set of assumptions rather than a concrete context of life: «Subjects acting communicatively always come to an understanding in the horizon of a lifeworld. Their lifeworld is formed from more or less diffuse, always unproblematic, background convictions»[54]. While Husserl has *everyone* intuiting it, Habermas has the members of a particular communicative community being «sociated» into it through learning the language and imbibing the culture[55]. According to Habermas, members of different communities can inhabit *different* lifeworld*s*. For Husserl the lifeworld was always singular. As Habermas has it, the lifeworld is not an unchanging given for all people of every generation, rather, for any given community, their lifeworld develops in history:

> The lifeworld also stores the interpretive work of preceding generations. It is the conservative counter-weight to the risk of disagreement that arises with every actual process of reaching understanding; for communicative actors can achieve an understanding only by way of taking yes/no positions on criticizable validity claims[56].

The lifeworld is given to each generation. When, in public discourse, the members of a communicative community interpret the world they incrementally sustain and add to the lifeworld. The lifeworld received by the next generation will be subtly different.

Habermas distinguishes in modern societies between *lifeworld* and *system*. The lifeworld sustains and is sustained by communicative action. It is concerned with the symbolic reproduction of society. It is the storehouse of culture and the relationships that constitute society. It also contains «the patterns of motivation and the stock of competencies for speech and action»[57] which Habermas calls «structures of personality». However, the material reproduction of society is split off from the

---

[53] J. HABERMAS, *The Theory of Communicative Action*, I, 337.
[54] J. HABERMAS, *The Theory of Communicative Action*, I, 70.
[55] See J. HABERMAS, *The Theory of Communicative Action*, I, 82.
[56] J. HABERMAS, *The Theory of Communicative Action*, I, 70.
[57] H. BAXTER, «System and life-world », 47.

lifeworld and handed over to institutions that are not controlled by communicative action. This is «system» – those administrative areas controlled by the «steering mechanisms» of money and power.

The characteristics Habermas ascribes to the lifeworld, he acknowledges as unusual:

> The fundamental background knowledge that must tacitly supplement our knowledge of the acceptability conditions of linguistically standardized expressions if hearers are to be able to understand their literal meanings, has remarkable features; it is an implicit knowledge that cannot be represented in a finite number of propositions; it is *holistically structured* knowledge, the basic elements of which intrinsically define one another; and it is a knowledge which *does not stand at our disposition*, inasmuch as we cannot make it conscious and place it in doubt as we please[58].

It is our shared experience of the lifeworld that makes communication possible. To conduct a conversation, even about the weather, requires the participants to make large assumptions about what is appropriate, relevant, and interesting, and about what knowledge and attitudes the hearer can be expected to have. In bringing up a topic of conversation a part of that unproblematic background is brought forward. Lifeworld becomes world. Each participant has their own grasp on that world – their own mental map of the way reality is. In the dialogue they reveal their understanding and check it against that revealed by the other. Using reason, experience, and authority they modify their maps in accord with what the dialogue reveals. Their maps are partial and fallible. Partners in true dialogue are open to having their views changed. As Habermas has it:

> If full agreement [...] were a normal state of linguistic communication, it would not be necessary to analyze the process of understanding from the dynamic perspective of bringing about an agreement. The typical states are in the gray areas in between: on the one hand, incomprehension and misunderstanding, intentional and involuntary untruthfulness, concealed and open discord; and, on the other hand, pre-existing and achieved consensus. Coming to an understanding is the process of bringing about an agreement on the presupposed basis of validity claims that can be mutually recognized. In every day life we start from a background consensus pertaining to those interpretations taken for granted among participants. As soon as this consensus is shaken, and the presupposition that certain validity claims are satisfied (or could be vindicated) is suspended, the task of mutual interpretation

---

[58] J. HABERMAS, *The Theory of Communicative Action*, I, 336.

is to achieve a new definition of the situation which all participants can share[59].

The lifeworld is a pre-existing consensus but each dialogue participant has only a limited grasp of it, just as no individual mathematician now knows all mathematical knowledge. Humans are socialized into their lifeworld in their upbringing, and their understanding is maintained and updated in every conversation. Habermas lists the deliberate and unintentional types of misunderstanding that can feature in a dialogue. A normal conversation is a process of moving towards mutual comprehension. Habermas allows for the role of ignorance and malice. He has a far from idealistic view about the meeting of minds involved in daily converse:

> For both parties the interpretive task consists in incorporating the other's interpretation of the situation into one's own in such a way that in the revised version «his» external world and «my» external world can be relativized in relation to «the» world, and the divergent situation definitions can be brought to coincide sufficiently. [...] Stability and absence of ambiguity are rather the exception in the communicative practice of everyday life. A more realistic picture is that drawn by ethnomethodologists – of a diffuse, fragile, continuously revised and only momentarily successful communication in which participants rely on problematic and unclarified presuppositions and feel their way from one occasional commonality to the next[60].

It is only the common lifeworld that holds everything together. Institutions, customs and culture give a common, unquestioned horizon that interprets experiences and enables dialogue. Nobody understands the whole. Everyone has partial maps of the world, which they are constantly checking against the maps of those whom they are in dialogue with. [See figure 10 overleaf.] Each participant in dialogue has a large amount of background knowledge, assumptions about the way the world is and about what can and cannot be said. From all that background of shared assumptions, those in conversation with each other thematize and differentiate the particular topic under discussion. In Habermas's terms, they explicitly attend to a part of the lifeworld, whereupon it ceases to be lifeworld and becomes «world». The language used further demarcates this into three worlds of reference: the objective, the subjective, and the social.

---

[59] J. HABERMAS, *Communication and the Evolution of Society*, 3.
[60] J. HABERMAS, *The Theory of Communicative Action*, I, 100.

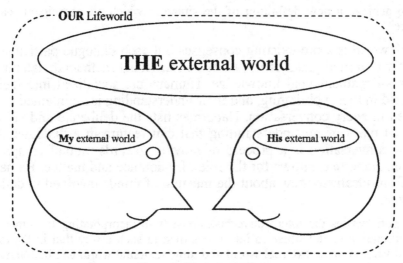

Figure 10: Maps of the World

6.1.2 The Objective World

Popper's first world consisted of objects that have physical existence and he contrasted this to his third world of systems of knowledge. Habermas notes:

> Popper's theory of the third world explains how cultural semantic contents and symbolic objects can be understood as something in the world, and can at the same time be distinguished as higher-level objects from (observable) physical and (experienciable) mental episodes[61].

The importance for Habermas of Popper's theory is that he has shown how «semantic contents of symbolic formations»[62] are treated as *things* in the world. Everyone has access to the natural numbers. Simple statements about them (e.g., $11 + 17 = 28$) can be checked for truth by anyone acquainted with arithmetic. Numbers are abstractions, they do not have a physical existence, but they are public and accessible to all.

> These «unembodied world 3 objects» are an important indicator of the independence of the world of objective mind. Symbolic formations are, it is true, generated by the productive human mind; but though they are them-

---

[61] J. HABERMAS, *The Theory of Communicative Action*, I, 83.
[62] J. HABERMAS, *The Theory of Communicative Action*, I, 77.

selves products, they confront subjective mind with the objectivity of a problematic, uncomprehended complex of meaning that can be opened up only through intellectual labor. The *products* of the human mind immediately turn against it as *problems*[63].

Statements about these «unembodied objects» are akin to Searle's «institutional facts», they refer to realities of the human world that depend on humans for existence.

Habermas, using a phenomenological rather than ontological approach sees the objective world as the totality of entities about which true statements can be made[64]. It is the world of «existing states of affairs»[65]. While he does not explicitly advert to this, the implication is that all the objects from Popper's third world are within Habermas's objective world. Statements about institutional facts are true statements; the entities they refer to are the «unembodied world 3 objects» of Popper's theory. Mathematics and many less scientific symbolic systems belong in Habermas's objective world. «Your sign is Taurus» is a statement that can be made truly. The person addressed and the astrological predicate belong together in the objective world.

A particular communicative community may accept as true, statements that members of another community contest. For Habermas «facts» are statements that are universally accepted in the communicative community and they have objective status, even if this «fact» may elsewhere or subsequently not be accepted. Lifeworlds have existed where it was taken for granted that the earth was flat. Habermas's objective world is that which our collective map of reality refers to and, like all maps, that collective understanding is selective, anthropocentric, and can err. However, Habermas does seem to concede a kind of ontological reality as the basis of the objective world. As he says:

Cognitive dealings with perceptible and manipulable objects, and expressions of subjective experiences are in contact with external or internal nature through stimulation of our senses or through our needs and desires. They are in touch with a reality that not only transcends language but is also free of symbolic structures[66].

---

[63] J. HABERMAS, *The Theory of Communicative Action*, I, 77, (emphasis his). The phrase «embedded world 3 objects» is from K. POPPER – J. ECCLES, *The Self and Its Brain*, 41.
[64] See J. HABERMAS, *The Theory of Communicative Action*, I, 52.
[65] J. HABERMAS, *The Theory of Communicative Action*, I, 88.
[66] J. HABERMAS, *The Theory of Communicative Action*, II, 61.

External nature has a special pre-symbolic existence. There is an unde-niable realness to what can be seen and handled, and it is human to ac-cept that others see and handle the same objects, and assume that they, too, experience them in the same way. Yet the world experienced by humans is overlaid with symbols and symbolic formations. To speak of external nature is to interpret it symbolically. True statements are made about external nature and about the symbolic formations. External real-ity and symbolic formations constitute the «objective world» – an indi-vidual's reactions to that world belong, however, to a different frame of reference.

6.1.3 The Subjective World

Popper's second world is associated with a clear and simple type of utterance – first person expressive assertions. When a person declares, «I feel happy!» their statement is likely to be accepted by the hearers, since it refers to the world which they, alone, have privileged access to – their internal state. Similar statements in the third person can get a very different reception. «He feels happy» tends to invite the riposte, «How do you know?» We have direct access to our own internal states, not to those of others. When the statement is made in the third person it is a proposition about an objectified person.

In Habermas's model this second world is assimilated, virtually as is, from Popper. The difference is, that, rather than claim an ontological reality for it, Habermas describes it in phenomenological terms. Where Popper has «states of consciousness» Habermas identifies this world as the correlate of the totality of all «expressible subjective experi-ences»[67]. «Subjective experiences» and «states of consciousness» ap-pear equivalent, but the addition of «correlate» and «expressible» makes a difference. Popper asserts that mental states exist. Habermas, more indirectly, asserts that there is a category of expressions used by communicative subjects in speaking of such experiences. He affirms the existence of this category of statements and labels what they refer to as the «Subjective World». Habermas makes no assertion about whether the mental states exist, what concerns him is that language re-ferring to them does exist. His phenomena are the statements about in-ternal experiences rather than the experiences.

---

[67] See J. HABERMAS, *The Theory of Communicative Action*, I, 70.

The objective world is overlaid with symbols so that subjects are conditioned by their lifeworld even in their experiencing of objective reality. Similarly, they are conditioned by their language, culture and upbringing in how they interpret and express their subjective experiences. There is a pre-symbolic reality to emotions, but for them to be expressed, in any way, is for them to be somehow symbolized and thereby interpreted. Society affirms some emotions and discourages others; some expressions win sympathy, others are spurned. The speaker may have privileged access to his internal states but the expression of them is something public and relational. Habermas is not concerned with atomic individuals observing an objective world; he is developing a critical theory of societies. Using language as his starting point, he sees individuals as inescapably relational, as strongly linked into a social world.

6.1.4 The Social World

Habermas posits the existence of a third world dramatically different from that proposed by Popper. Popper's was a world of the intellect; Habermas's is one of the will. Popper was concerned with scientific theories. Habermas is seeking an all-embracing conception that explains why humans interact as they do, and how societies do and should function. Popper does not account for the motive power of values and norms, which are a major concern for Habermas:

> In this respect Popper's model of the third world is particularly implausible, for the action-orienting power of cultural values is at least as important for interactions as that of theories. [...] this approach would make it necessary to expand Popper's version of the third world in such a way that the normative reality of society would own its independence vis-à-vis subjective mind not only – and not primarily – to the autonomy of truth claims, but to the binding character of values and norms. That raises the question of how the components of cultural tradition that are relevant to social integration can be understood as systems of knowledge and connected with validity claims analogous to truth[68].

Factual statements directed to the objective world claim to be true, yet there are values other than truth. What moves us to act may be good, or beautiful, rather than true. These action-motivations are expressed in what Habermas calls «ought-statements» or commands that are ac-

---

[68] J. HABERMAS, *The Theory of Communicative Action*, I, 81.

cepted as justified by the addressees[69]. Just as he defines the objective world in terms of the factual statements that can be made about it, so he defines the social world as «the totality of all interpersonal relations that are recognized by members as legitimate»[70] and that are expressible by justified ought-statements.

Teachers and pupils are entities in the objective world, but one component of our cultural tradition is the correct teacher-pupil relationship. This relationship belongs to Habermas's social world. All pupils know that they ought to respect their teacher. Teachers are aware of what is appropriate behaviour for them and their students within the academic context. A young pupil whose parent is their teacher at school often has difficulty switching between the behaviours that are normal within the family and those that are right in the classroom. The child and their parent are the same persons in both contexts; it is the relationship and the corresponding expectations that are different. Such relationships are neither true nor false, Habermas calls them «legitimate» and the actions motivated by legitimate relationships he calls «right» (richtig).

These relationships and the behaviours they mandate are the fabric that holds society together. Children, through experience, play, story, and instruction, are taught the different relationships and how they should behave within each. These relationships cannot be touched, but they can certainly be experienced. They are an external institutional reality and constitute a significant part of our lifeworld. Facts about them are assigned by Habermas to the objective world, but the relationships themselves – the object of all right imperatives – constitute a world of reference in themselves.

6.1.5 Lifeworld and Worlds

When people act communicatively they do not refer to the lifeworld, which is assumed, but to the worlds of reference: their own subjective experience through expressive I-statements, the objective world through factual statements, or the social world through imperatives or ought-statements. These references can be explicit or implied in the dialogue. By distinguishing these aspects of communication Habermas identifies how:

---

[69] See J. HABERMAS, The Theory of Communicative Action, I, 88.
[70] J. HABERMAS, The Theory of Communicative Action, I, 52.

the concepts of the three worlds serve here as the commonly supposed system of coordinates in which the situation contexts can be ordered in such a way that agreement will be reached about what the participants may treat as a fact, or as a valid norm, or as a subjective experience[71].

Habermas's Three Worlds

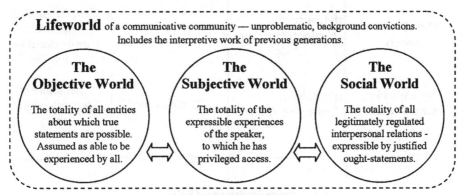

Figure 11: Habermas's Three Worlds

The three worlds are a central part of Habermas's theories, providing a foundation for his theory of communicative action, the validity claims implicit in speech, and an explanation for Austin's «force and meaning». He claims that the human personality is formed in relation to this frame of reference[72], that it is reflected in the first, second and third person pronouns used in all languages[73], and that development in societies is directly related to the rationalising of the lifeworld[74]. He claims that the three worlds are the underlying structure of how all humans understand the world and act upon it.

Each of these three domains of reality operates differently in language. The attitude taken up by the speaker in each case is different, what is being done in speaking differs, and there is a different «validity claim» made in terms of each world. Habermas summarises[75]:

---

[71] J. HABERMAS, *The Theory of Communicative Action*, I, 70.

[72] See J. HABERMAS, «Moral Development and Ego Identity», 69-94.

[73] See J. HABERMAS, *Communication and the Evolution of Society*, 106-107.

[74] See J. HABERMAS, «Modernization as Societal Rationalization» in *The Theory of Communicative Action*, I, 216-242.

[75] J. HABERMAS, *Communication and the Evolution of Society*, 68.

Domains of Reality	Modes of Communication: Basic Attitudes	Validity Claims	General Functions of Speech
«The» World of External Nature	Cognitive: Objectivating Attitude	Truth	Representation of Facts
«Our» World of Society	Interactive: Conformative Attitude	Rightness	Establishment of Legitimate Inter-personal Relationships
«My» World of Internal Nature	Expressive: Expressive Attitude	Truthfulness	Disclosure of Speaker's subjectivity
Language	----------------	Comprehensibility	----------------

Figure 12: Domains of Reality

Notice that Habermas further distinguishes *the linguistic medium itself* as a special region of reality. He describes it as having a peculiar half-transcendence, presumably because it belongs both to «my» world and to «our» world.

Habermas does not consider these domains to be mutually exclusive, rather they are a reflection of a communicative attitude. One can speak of a flag as an object in the external world or as a symbol in our inter-subjective reality that evokes patriotism. When language is talked *about* then language is both the medium of discourse and the object of discourse.

The lifeworld is the locus of any communicative interaction. Sharing the same language and culture, members of a social group confidently and unreflectively assume they share all that the lifeworld holds.

> The lifeworld is, so to speak, the transcendental site where speaker and hearer meet, where they can reciprocally raise claims that their utterances fit the world (objective, social, subjective), and where they can criticize and confirm those validity claims, settle their disagreements, and arrive at agreements[76].

---

[76] J. HABERMAS, *The Theory of Communicative Action*, II, 126.

When one actor introduces a theme, parts of the lifeworld are brought into the foreground. The objective and the social worlds are taken as shared, each has sole access to their own subjective world. Habermas provides this diagram of the interactions between the worlds[77]:

World-Relations of Communicative Acts (CA)

The double arrows indicate the world-relations that actors (A) establish with their utterances (CA).

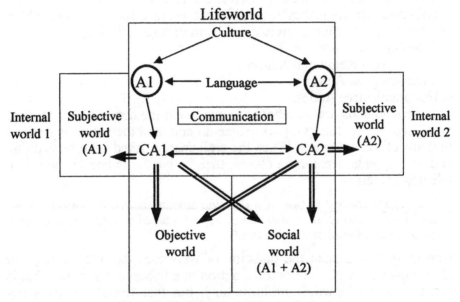

Figure 13: World-Relations of Communicative Acts

Communication «takes place» in the lifeworld, with both parties embedded in the same culture and schooled in the same language. Each communicative action, at least implicitly, is in relation to all three worlds. The communicative actor reveals his own subjectivity, presents facts and adverts to norms. For the communicative action to be successful agreement in communication about the theme needs to be established so the plans of action can be formulated and consented to.

---

[77] Diagram from J. HABERMAS, *The Theory of Communicative Action*, II, 127

6.2 *Concepts of Action*

The basis of Habermas's revision of critical theory is *communicative action*. «Action» is a term in common use which proves difficult to define in philosophical terms. Is breathing an action? Is *not* going to school? Where does the action of the agent begin and end: «pressing the dispenser of the spray can», «writing graffiti on the wall», «making a protest», «contributing to the depletion of the ozone layer» are action-descriptors that could all be applied to the same event.

Habermas distinguishes four different «concepts» of action. These models are used, often interchangeably, in different disciplines:
1. Teleological Action
2. Normatively Regulated Action
3. Dramaturgical Action
4. Communicative Action

1) *Teleological Action* where the one doing the action either is, or is presumed to be, attempting to realize an end, and the action is defined in terms of that intention. When the craftsman is asked what he is doing and he responds, «making a chair», then he has described his action in teleological terms.

> The central concept is that of a *decision* among alternative courses of action, with a view to the realization of an end, guided by maxims, and based on an interpretation of the situation[78].

Habermas leaves open the question of who does the interpreting. An anthropologist might interpret the action of a tribesman in a way that is accepted as valid within anthropology, but that would not have occurred to the man doing the action. This view of action had a pre-eminent place in philosophy and theology, particularly in the traditions influenced by Aristotle.

2) *Normatively Regulated Action* is a conception of action that has come from Law and Sociology. Unlike teleological action which is defined by the interpretation of a single individual, it is the normative values of a particular social group which establish what constitute the limits and the understanding of the action. Members of the group in particular circumstances are *entitled* to expect a certain behaviour. A driver who extends her arm from the car window may have the inten-

---

[78] J. HABERMAS, *The Theory of Communicative Action*, I, 85.

tion of drying her nail polish, but her action will be taken by other motorists, *and the courts*, as constituting a turn signal.

> All members of a group for whom a given norm has validity may expect of one another that in certain situations they will carry out (or abstain from) the actions commanded (or proscribed). The central concept of *complying with a norm* means fulfilling a generalized expectation of behavior[79].

As Habermas makes clear, this explanation of action applies only to those who accept the norms and to situations in which those norms apply. The model is powerful in explaining characteristics of different cultures, and the variations that can occur within different contexts of the same community. Habermas also emphasizes that this view can account for non-actions; for people refraining from doing certain things.

3) *Dramaturgical Action* is a perception of action which has come from psychology and phenomenology. Using the analogy of the theatre it considers interactions between individuals in terms of stage actors and their public. Partners in dialogue alternate as public to each other's self-presentation. Involvement in an interaction necessarily involves the revelation, at least apparent, of some aspect of the actor's inner life; a disclosure of subjectivity.

> Thus the central concept of *presentation of self* does not signify spontaneous expressive behaviour but styling the expression of one's own experience with a view to the audience[80].

Habermas does not present dramaturgical action as a mask that the real person hides behind. Instead it is a mask that is donned to express, sincerely or otherwise, the inner self. The role that is taken up, the conventional language used, enable the speaker to make a self-presentation, to give to a public something of his subjective world. The couple who exchange vows, with high solemnity, in a marriage ceremony are engaging in dramaturgical action before an audience of the congregation, but most especially of each other. They use the staged event and the ritual, to both express and reinforce their subjective experience of love for, and commitment to, each other.

4) *Communicative Action* is a model that has emerged from economics and game theory. It is further developed and championed by

---

[79] J. HABERMAS, *The Theory of Communicative Action*, I, 85.
[80] J. HABERMAS, *The Theory of Communicative Action*, I, 86.

Habermas and is a central concept in his philosophy, as the title of his two-volume major work testifies. He defines it as follows:

> The concept of *communicative action* refers to the interaction of at least two subjects capable of speech and action who establish interpersonal relations (whether by verbal or extra-verbal means). The actors seek to reach an understanding about the action situation and their plans of action in order to coordinate their actions by way of agreement. The central concept of *interpretation* refers in the first instance to negotiating definitions of the situation which admit of consensus[81].

The notion includes both verbal and non-verbal communication. It is communication oriented towards action and the co-ordination of action. It is what enables people to work together and achieve common ends. It is the basis of human society and civilisation. As Habermas puts it:

> [I am not] saying that people ought to act communicatively, but that they *must* ... When parents educate their children, when living generations appropriate the knowledge handed down by their predecessors, when individuals cooperate, i.e. get on with one another without a costly use of force, they must act communicatively. There are elementary social functions which can only be satisfied by means of communicative action[82].

So communicative action is not some rarefied ideal behaviour but the normal everyday communication whereby people live and work together in harmony.

Consider the example of a wife asking her husband to pick up a loaf of bread at the supermarket: she assumes the existence of bread and the supermarket in the external world and she expresses her wish to have more bread in the house, thereby revealing something of her internal world. She knows that it is a legitimate request to make of one's spouse in the culture they share – «our» world. She is aware that he usually drives past the supermarket, and that he can do the task. She is attempting to co-ordinate their actions for the smooth functioning of their household. If her husband agrees and complies, then his actions during the day will be different from what they would have been if she had not spoken. The spouse might clarify the task to make sure he understands exactly what he is being asked to do. «White bread or wholemeal? One loaf or two?» He could explain that today he is taking the bus, and the task will be more difficult than she anticipates. It is even possible that

---

[81] J. HABERMAS, «Four Sociological Conceptions of Action», 136.
[82] J. HABERMAS, *The Past as Future*, 11.

he query her assessment of the need: «I think we have a lot of bread in the freezer». Together, in this simple everyday dialogue, they reach consensus about the state of the household bread supply and about what more is required. They express their wishes and plans. They exchange constative statements about external world factors until they achieve a sufficient shared understanding to agree on appropriate co-ordinated actions.

Habermas indicated above that it is through communicative action that «living generations appropriate the knowledge handed down by their predecessors»[83]. Communicative action is made possible by the lifeworld, but at the same time it maintains and reproduces the lifeworld:

> In coming to an understanding with one another about their situation, participants in interaction stand in a cultural tradition that they at once use and renew; in coordinating their actions by way of intersubjectively recognizing criticizable validity claims, they are at once relying on membership in social groups and strengthening those same groups; through participating in interactions with competently acting reference persons, the growing child internalizes the value orientations of his social group and acquires generalized capacities for action[84].

The actors apply the insights of tradition to the present situation and thus make the present part of that tradition. In acting together they recognize and take up legitimate roles in their social group and thereby strengthen its inter-subjective reality. Finally, their achieving of the action through their interaction impacts on their subjective worlds via their self-understandings of their capabilities. Another episode is added to the history of the community, members of the community exercise their belonging, and their personal stories are enhanced. All this can happen when understanding is achieved and communicative action happily accomplished, which raises the issue of what is needed for this happy outcome to be reached.

6.3 *Towards Universal Conditions of Possible Understanding*

In his characteristically terse style of writing, Habermas indicates his aim in developing the theories that he calls «Universal Pragmatics»: «The task of universal pragmatics is to identify and reconstruct univer-

---

[83] J. HABERMAS, *The Past as Future*, 11.
[84] J. HABERMAS, *The Theory of Communicative Action*, II, 137.

sal conditions of possible understanding [*Verständigung*]»[85]. It is to be universal in the sense of «species-wide». He intends it to be descriptive of the communication processes of the entire human race, independent of language and culture. He does not explicitly state the corollary but it seems reasonable that he would intend it to be applicable to all times. A set of theories that describes human communication in all cultures of our present age ought to be capable of describing the communication that occurred in the cultures of the past.

Habermas uses the term «Pragmatics» to distinguish his theories from linguistic and semiotic theories[86]. Linguistic theories, based on the logical analysis of language originated by Rudolf Carnap[87], focus on the structures of a particular language. Semiotics, developed by Charles Morris[88], is influenced by the model of information transmission (the encoding and decoding of signals between a sender and a receiver) and as the name suggests it puts the emphasis on the signs and symbols used in this transmission. In Universal Pragmatics Habermas does assume the existence of some language, but it can be *any* language shared by the speaker and hearer. He does not concern himself with a particular symbology but instead focuses on the *conditions* required for those symbols to achieve their end. It is also a pragmatic theory in the sense that Habermas rejects both simplistic idealism and simplistic materialism. Simplistic idealism claims that the mind makes up the world, simplistic materialism makes the reverse claim. Habermas takes a pragmatic realist approach, an interactive model whereby the mind and the world jointly make up the mind and world.

The end of human communication is understanding. The etymology of the German word Habermas uses is enlightening. The root of *Verständigung* is *Verstand*, meaning mind or intellect. *Verständigen* is to make oneself understood, to communicate. The suffix *-ung* indicates

---

[85] J. HABERMAS, *Communication and the Evolution of Society*, 1.

[86] See J. HABERMAS, *Communication and the Evolution of Society*, 5-8, where Habermas performs a preliminary delimitation of the object domain of Universal Pragmatics.

[87] Rudolf Carnap (1891-1970), a German-American philosopher, was a leading member of the Vienna Circle and a proponent of logical positivism. He outlined «formal semantics» in his *Meaning and Necessity: A Study in Semantics and Modal Logic*, Chicago 1947, 1956[2].

[88] Charles Morris (1901-1979), an American philosopher coined the term «semiotic» to describe the general theory of signs which he formulated in his, *Foundations of the Theory of Signs*, Chicago 1938.

a process filling something or reaching completion. *Verständigung* could also be translated as «agreement». We communicate to achieve commonality, to share a viewpoint. Information is exchanged not for its own sake but so that the hearer *can* understand what the speaker *does* understand. This understanding is what motivates the speaker to speak. In his use of «possible» in the phrase «universal conditions of possible understanding»[89] Habermas alludes to the fact that much human communication is unsuccessful. What determines success or failure, at a level of abstraction sufficient to make it universally applicable, is the aim of Habermas's investigation.

6.3.1 A General Theory of Speech Acts

Reconstructive language analysis attempts to make explicit the rules that a competent speaker of the language uses in order to utter well-formed sentences. Habermas assumes that competence and tries to go a step beyond it. A sentence can be grammatical yet fail to communicate. Competence in the language is necessary but not sufficient for communication that achieves shared understanding. In Universal Pragmatics Habermas is attempting to lay the foundations for something even more ambitious:

> A general theory of speech actions would thus describe exactly that fundamental system of rules that adult subjects master to the extent that they can fulfil the conditions for a happy employment of sentences in utterances, no matter to which particular language the sentences may belong and in which accidental contexts the utterances may be embedded[90].

Habermas assumes that the ability to communicate is a learned skill. He expects to be able to discover rules governing this behaviour. He takes note of theorists of human development, like Jean Piaget, to identify what it is that juveniles are not able to do. Those who have mastered the rules of communication are able to operate on many levels of play and seriousness. They can use wit and irony, tell stories, lie, and convey sober history. In his 1979 work, *Communication and the Evolution of Society*, Habermas parallels the evolution of human society as a whole with the development of the individual. His theories of communication competency are central for his analysis of the problem-solving ability of all human societies.

---

[89] J. HABERMAS, *Communication and the Evolution of Society*, 1.
[90] J. HABERMAS, *Communication and the Evolution of Society*, 26.

Hans-Georg Gadamer[91], one of the founders of the discipline of hermeneutics, had a conviction that by seeking truth in communication harmony would be achieved. According to him, communication in itself drives progress and leads to peaceful co-existence. Habermas studied under Gadamer. As a German who had experienced the Second World War and the impact of propaganda on the nations concerned, Habermas strongly disagreed with his teacher. He was very aware that communication could be systematically distorted. In seeking a theory to account for the *happy* employment of sentences in utterances he was always aware of the possibilities of distorted communication. His is a *critical* theory, he had a deep distrust of institutions, authorities and power structures.

6.3.2 Categorising Speech Acts

As part of his task of reconstructing universal conditions of possible understanding, Habermas separated speech acts into different types. He followed Searle with modifications, producing the diagram (figure 14) on the facing page. An *instrumental speech action* is one that communicates decision, dictum, command. For example: «Take a letter, Miss Jones». *Social action* by contrast is to do with the *lifeworld*, in areas where socialisation and cultural reproduction are at issue. Instrumental speech action tends to treat people as objects in the external world, social speech action treats them as subjects, as participants in the inter-subjective world. What Habermas here calls *symbolic actions* are self-expressions, one-way communications not using language. He gives as examples a concert, a dance – modes of communication that involve non-propositional systems of symbolic expression[92]. *Strategic actions* are oriented to the actor's success. In speech this involves the speaker making an utterance of which the purpose is other than it purports to be. The often-absent student asks the professor a question, not to clarify the point, but to draw attention to his presence. «It is this model of action that lies behind decision-theoretic and game-theoretic approaches in economics, sociology, and social psychology»[93].

---

[91] Hans-Georg Gadamer (1900-2002), a German hermeneutic theorist and a major influence on Habermas. His most famous work is *Wahrheit und Methode*, 1960.

[92] See J. HABERMAS, *Communication and the Evolution of Society*, 41.

[93] J. HABERMAS, *The Theory of Communicative Action*, I, 85.

DERIVATION OF THE ANALYTICAL UNITS OF THE THEORY OF SPEECH ACTS[94]

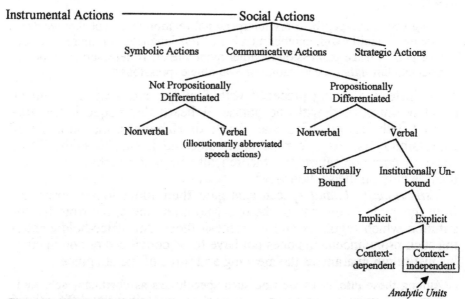

Figure 14: Analysis of Actions

Habermas focuses on *communicative action* – communication oriented at reaching understanding. A *propositionally differentiated* action is one that contains a reference to some real or imaginary object and a predicate expression for whatever the speaker wants to attribute to it or deny to it. A traffic officer pointing to a car and waving his hand can tell the driver of the car to move it. The car is indicated and the attribute associated with it. In contrast, if the traffic officer were to throw up his hands in horror he would communicate shock, but in an undifferentiated way. A shout of «Fire!» is an abbreviated speech action which is understood to mean «Some part of this building is on fire and you should evacuate». The verbal utterance is not propositionally differentiated but it is understood as if it were.

Habermas chooses to ignore *non-verbalised* actions and bodily expressions, and contexts that produce shifts in meaning. To justify doing

---

[94] Diagram from J. HABERMAS, *Communication and the Evolution of Society*, 40.

so, he invokes a weakened form of Searle's «principle of expressibility»[95]:

> In a given language, for every interpersonal relation that a speaker wants to take up explicitly with another member of this language community, a suitable performance expression is either available or, if necessary, can be introduced through a specification of available expressions[96].

Thus, instead of being preceded with a nudge and a wink, a remark could be introduced with the phrase «I heard this risqué joke». Expressed with less precision than Searle or Habermas, the principle of expressibility is: «If it can be communicated it can be said». Thus, since all communication can theoretically be made verbal, Habermas focuses only on the spoken word.

Institutionally bound speech acts gain their illocutionary force not from the evident sincerity of the one who utters them, but from the institution which regulates and «enforces» them. An office-holder making such pronouncements does not have to be convinced or convincing, his institution guarantees the meaning and force of the utterance.

> Among these utterances we find such speech acts as «betting», «christening», «appointing», and so on. Despite their propositionally differentiated content, they are bound to a single institution (or to a narrowly circumscribed set of institutions); they can therefore be seen as the equivalent of actions that fulfil presupposed norms, either non-verbally or in an illocutionarily abbreviated way. The *institutional bond* of these speech acts can be seen in (among other things) the fact that the permissible propositional contents are narrowly limited by the normative meaning of betting, christening, appointing, marrying, and so on. One bets for stakes, christens with names, appoints to official positions, marries a partner, and so on[97].

The examples offered by Habermas throw light on how an institution can be vitally concerned with the correct interpretation of an utterance. In New Zealand the Totalisator Agency Board controls all betting on horse races. It allows telephone bets to be placed by account holders. The precise interpretation of a telephone utterance can make a difference of thousands of dollars. When a judge utters the sentence on a

---

[95] Searle's Principle of Expressibility is: «For every meaning x, it is the case that, if there is a speaker S in a language community P who means x, then it is possible that there is an expression in the language spoken by P which is an exact expression of x». Quoted in J. HABERMAS, *Communication and the Evolution of Society*, 39.

[96] J. HABERMAS, *Communication and the Evolution of Society*, 40.

[97] J. HABERMAS, *Communication and the Evolution of Society*, 38.

convicted felon the justice system works extremely hard to ensure that the precise significance of his words is clear. The *force* of his words comes not from him but from the institution backing him.

Habermas chose to focus his attention on *institutionally unbound utterances*. Following his version of the principle of expressibility he further narrowed this to *explicit* and *context-independent*. He asserts that what is implicit can be made explicit and if the context modifies an utterance a more complex utterance could express this in a context-independent form[98].

6.3.3 Categorising Interactions

When Habermas addressed the categorisation of actions again, some years later, in his first volume of *The Theory of Communicative Action*, he approached it as a «limit case» of a speech act. Recognising that most human interactions contain a mix of instruction, comment, assertions of a role, and self expression, he constructs theoretical «pure» types of interaction, shown in the table on the next page (Figure 15). He continues to distinguish communicative action from strategic action, but now divides communicative action into three types – «conversation», «normatively regulated action» and «dramaturgical action».

A *perlocution* is Austin's term for an utterance intended to affect behaviour. A mother who says to her son «You look so much handsomer with your hair short» could be engaging in strategic action to get him to have a haircut. She might achieve the same end with an imperative «Go and get your hair cut!» Her utterances relate to the external world and she is likely to choose the remark she finds to be more effective. Neither remark looks for any other response other than compliance. Refusing an imperative involves rejecting the authority of the one who uttered it. Such remarks can be embedded in a conversation but are not characteristic of it.

A conversation, as Habermas understands it, has a very different dynamic[99]. A conversation is not purposive activity. It is not a mechanism for co-ordinating individual actions. It involves the discussion of themes. One of the most important special cases of conversation is argumentation. The characteristic speech act of conversation is a *consta-*

---

[98] See J. HABERMAS, *Communication and the Evolution of Society*, 38-9, where he delimits the pragmatic units of analysis.

[99] See J. HABERMAS, *The Theory of Communicative Action*, I, 327.

tive where the «speaker refers to something in the objective world and in such a way as they would like to represent a state of affairs»[100]. If one speaker asserts, «The weather has been mild this month», he or she is making a claim about the reality of the external world. One who responds, «I have found it to be quite cold», would be contesting the *truth* claim raised by the first speaker.

Pure Types of Linguistically Mediated Interaction[101]

Types of action / Formal Pragmatic Features	Strategic Action	Conversation	Normatively Regulated Action	Dramaturgical Action
Characteristic Speech Acts	Perlocutions Imperatives	Constatives	Regulatives	Expressives
Functions of Speech	Influencing one's opposite number	Representation of states of affairs	Establishment of interpersonal relations	Self-representation
Action Orientations	Oriented to success	Oriented to reaching understanding	Oriented to reaching understanding	Oriented to reaching understanding
Basic Attitudes	Objectivating	Objectivating	Norm-conformative	Expressive
Validity Claims	(Effectiveness)	Truth	Rightness	Truthfulness
World Relations	Objective world	Objective world	Social world	Subjective world

Figure 15: Pure Types of Interaction

A *regulative speech act*, by contrast, is to do with the social world. It involves a reference to something in the intersubjective reality of speaker and hearer whereby the speaker attempts to establish as legitimate an interpersonal relation. «Professor, I am a student in your class. May I make an appointment to see you?» Implicitly in the title used, and explicitly in the statement, the speaker claims a relationship with the hearer and on that basis requests a meeting. The class, which exists

---

[100] J. HABERMAS, *The Theory of Communicative Action*, I, 325.

[101] Based on the table in J. HABERMAS, *The Theory of Communicative Action*, I, 329.

in the objective world as a group of persons who gather, has a social reality – a network of relationships and corresponding norms.

In *dramaturgical* action a speaker uses expressive utterances to reveal to a public something of his or her internal world. «I intend to reform my behaviour this year». Since only the speaker has direct privileged access to their internal world the only way such a statement can be negated is by doubting the *sincerity* of the speaker's self-representation[102].

6.3.4 Non-verbal Communicative Actions

Habermas gives little attention to non-verbal communication. His focus is on explicit communication using words. However, in explaining this choice he provides a carefully chosen range of examples:

> Explicit speech actions always have a propositional component in which a state of affairs is expressed. Non-linguistic actions normally lack this component; thus they cannot assume representational functions. Signaling to a taxi so that I can begin working in my office at eight in the morning, reacting to the news of miserable marks with the desperate look of a father, joining a demonstration march, expressing non-acceptance of an invitation by not showing up, shaking a candidate's hand after he has passed the test, and so on and so forth, I observe or violate conventions. Naturally these normative expectations have a propositional content; but the propositional content must already be known to the participants if the expressed behavior is to be understandable[103].

Signalling a taxi, by raising one's hand while standing on the side of the street and looking towards the vehicle, involves a gesture that is well-established and understood in global urban culture. It is a request for a particular service. The context establishes the different content of this gesture from the request of a student to leave a classroom and others which have similarities. Cultures include standardised gestures with understood content. Habermas does acknowledge the existence of «grammaticalized sign language, for example, the standardized language of the deaf and dumb»[104], but he treats this as functionally equivalent to verbal language.

---

[102] See J. HABERMAS, «Four Sociological Conceptions of Action», 135.

[103] J. HABERMAS, *Communication and the Evolution of Society*, 37.

[104] J. HABERMAS, *Communication and the Evolution of Society*, 38.

The father's desperate look is an expression of an emotion – disappointment. The form that this takes may be culturally conditioned. A Japanese father might express his disappointment in a different facial gesture from that chosen by an Italian. An emotion can be expressed in a propositionally differentiated verbal statement, «I am disappointed in your performance»; yet the verbal statement without the facial expression lacks impact. The non-verbal seems to connote more than the propositional statement expresses, and, when used in conjunction with a verbal expression, it increases its *illocutionary force*.

Joining a demonstration is expressing something with one's *presence*. Not showing up when invited is communication by one's *absence*. Context is important in the understanding. The former example is interesting because simply standing with a group is all that is required to communicate. The latter is the philosophically fascinating gesture that one can make by *not* doing something.

It is true that speech, also, requires prior knowledge on the part of the hearer. Language is a set of symbols and associated meanings established in the culture. For Habermas the important feature that distinguishes language from non-verbal systems of communication is the complexity of speech and the corresponding degrees of freedom that it gives the actor with respect to a recognised normative background[105]. It is possible to communicate with greater subtlety and precision in spoken words than it is by gestures alone.

6.4 *The Double Structure of Speech*

Austin had distinguished meaning and force, and called for a «doctrine of forces» to explain how utterances varied in impact and effect[106]. Searle gave examples of utterances of different illocutionary force with identical propositional content[107]. Habermas picked up this thread of argument, applying it to explicit illocutionary utterances:

Any number of examples of the *speech-act-invariance of propositional content* can be provided – for instance, for the propositional content «Peter's smoking a pipe» the following:

---

[105] See J. HABERMAS, *Communication and the Evolution of Society*, 38.

[106] As a representative example, see J.L. AUSTIN, *How to Do Things with Words*, 99-100.

[107] J. SEARLE, *Speech Acts*, 22; Searle's examples are implicit illocutionary utterances: «1. Sam smokes habitually. 2. Does Sam smoke habitually? 3. Sam, smoke habitually! 4. Would that Sam smoked habitually».

«I assert that Peter smokes a pipe».
«I beg of you (Peter) that you smoke a pipe».
«I ask you (Peter), do you smoke a pipe?»
«I warn you (Peter), smoke a pipe»[108].

The propositional content with respect to Peter and his pipe smoking is the same throughout, but each of the four is a quite different speech act: an assertion, a supplication, a request for information, a warning. In this explicit form of the illocution, there are the words which signal the type of speech act and these words also *have a meaning*. Habermas infers that there are always two communicative levels operating in the communication of intentions:

(1)   the level of intersubjectivity on which speaker and hearer, through illocutionary acts, establish the relations that permit them to come to an understanding with one another, and

(2)   the level of propositional content which is communicated[109].

The relations are established through the meaning of the illocutionary verbs, explicit or implicit.

The utterance, «I warn you (Peter), smoke a pipe» had, for Austin, the illocutionary force of a warning. Habermas points out that while «smoke a pipe» has a meaning, so does «I warn you». He therefore interprets Austin's «force and meaning» as two categories of meaning. «Force then stands for the meaning of expressions that are originally used in connection with illocutionary acts»[110]. By identifying force as a type of meaning, Habermas looks as if he is collapsing Austin's distinction between force and meaning, but he recasts it as a distinction between meanings that relate to different worlds of reference. Illocutionary force is based on social world meaning, while propositional content – Austin's «meaning» – is directed to the objective world. Force concerns the establishment of interpersonal relations, while meaning relates to the representation of facts. Locutionary meaning is backed by the objective world, illocutionary force by the social world.

Austin in his conditions for felicity (refined by Searle in his definition of what constituted a promise) has a «sincerity condition»[111]. Habermas incorporated this into his «three worlds» reference frame.

---

[108] J. HABERMAS, *Communication and the Evolution of Society*, 41.
[109] J. HABERMAS, *Communication and the Evolution of Society*, 42.
[110] J. HABERMAS, *Communication and the Evolution of Society*, 49.
[111] See J. SEARLE, *Speech Acts*, 57-61.

The sincerity of an utterance is its correspondence with the *subjective* world of the speaker. Just as relationships have to be *right*, and propositions *true*, so does the speaker have to be *truthful*. What Habermas has done is to take Austin's insights on illocutionary force and put them into an elaborate and rigorous philosophical framework. The force of an utterance is *not* something magical. It does rely on the utterance being understood so it is dependent on the meaning of the utterance. Force is also affected by the context; the circumstances and especially the relationship between speaker and hearer.

Habermas has made it clear that Austin's «force» is a *social* phenomenon. Marrying, christening, betting, promising, and warning are embedded in a social matrix. Inasmuch as the hearer is socialized into that web-work of relationships, mores and customs, the force of the utterance will impact on them.

What Austin identified as two types of utterance – performative and constative – Habermas extends to two different worlds of reference: social and objective. Performative verbs are understood from within the social world of reference and it is that understanding which gives them their social force. Constative propositions are interpreted against the background of the objective world and are checked against our encyclopaedic knowledge of that realm.

Austin went on to show that constative and performative utterances were not distinct classes, but rather that the former was a subset of the latter. His explanation for this was in terms of locutionary and illocutionary force. Habermas dubs this the «two levels of meaning» of every utterance. There is the objective world meaning – the propositions that are judged for truth – and the social world meaning – which is assessed for normative rightness. Every utterance has an utterer (or text an author) and the hearer always takes up some social role in attending to the words (if only that of mocker). Any illocutionary verb, even the implicit «to state», is interpreted for its rightness in terms of the social world.

The interplay of utterance and worlds can be pictured as on the next page. When a doctor tells Peter, «I warn you, smoke a pipe» this utterance is heard and interpreted by Peter. From his knowledge of the objective world he is aware of a family of objects that are called «pipes»: hosepipes, drainpipes, copper pipes, exhaust pipes, and the like. In addition, he knows various meanings of the verb «to smoke».

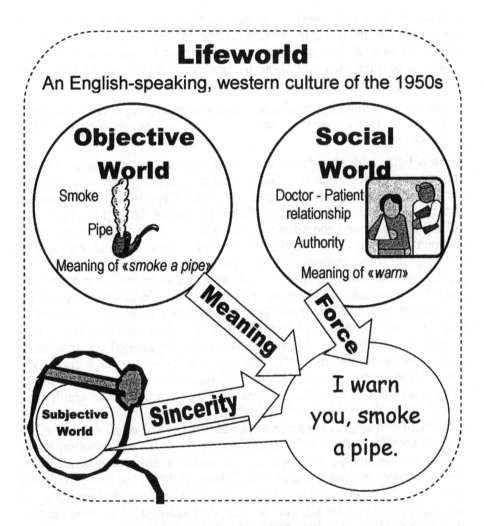

Figure 16: «I warn you, smoke a pipe»

From their combination in the sentence and contextual clues he takes it that what is being referred to is his smoking a tobacco pipe instead of some alternative – cigarette smoking or, less plausibly, not smoking at all. At the same time as understanding these objective realities, Peter is processing the social issues. As Habermas has it: «To be understood in a given situation, every utterance must, at least implicitly, establish and bring to expression a certain relation between the speaker and his counterpart»[112]. The verb used is «warn», the one doing the warning is his doctor, an authority figure whose advice in the field of health he respects. Is this advice about his personal image – he will look more manly smoking a pipe – or about his health? The force of the utterances is precisely the result of this social analysis.

> Thus the illocutionary force of an acceptable speech act consists in the fact that it can move a speaker to rely on the speech-act typical commitments of the speaker[113].

Even if Peter understands the doctor's statement and recognizes his authority, the warning can still fail if Peter doubts its *sincerity*. Is the doctor joking, or lying, or is he deadly serious? Even though Peter cannot directly access the subjective world of the doctor, he will read the tone of the utterance and the situation, and *may choose* to rely on the commitment to seriousness implicit in the statement. For the warning to have its full force, both parties involved must will it.

Most of the time we do not back up our statements. A response of complete cynicism would make communication impossible. Normally statements are taken on trust. This is why lies can work, as can influence and domination. Yet built into the structure of all ordinary discourse is the assumption that assertions can be backed up, that argument can be made, that what we say conforms to the world. This assumption is shown when consensus breaks down and we deal with a hard topic. The kinds of argument that we produce when challenged reveal the assumptions underlying our conversation. They show the priority of consensual agreement for the functioning of all discourse.

In Habermas's theory the performative-constative distinction made by Austin has been developed into an understanding of how all utterances in every language are implicitly backed up by the three worlds of reference. Since he declares this to be the universal underpinning of language he needs to account for the vast amount of communication that does not live up to his ideal.

6.5 *Systematically Distorted Communication*

Habermas is alert to the deliberate manipulation of communication in a society. The Critical Theorists were keen to critique both capitalist and communist societies. He notes that, in some societies, the «logic

---

[112] J. HABERMAS, *Communication and the Evolution of Society*, 34.
[113] J. HABERMAS, *Communication and the Evolution of Society*, 62.

accords with the grammar of systematically distorted communication and with the fateful causality of dissociated symbols and suppressed motives»[114].

Distortion can be the result of deliberate, *conscious* manipulation as in the case of wartime propaganda. According to Habermas it can also be *unconscious*, both on the individual and social level. A society can be systematically distorting communication about some issue and be unaware that it is doing so. Habermas offers a psychoanalytical explanation for this behaviour and connects it to his framework as follows:

> In situations of concealed strategic action, at least one of the parties behaves with an orientation to success, but leaves the others to believe that all the presuppositions of communicative action are satisfied. This is the case of manipulation [...] On the other hand, the kind of unconscious repression of conflicts that the psychoanalyst explains in terms of defense mechanisms leads to disturbances of communication on both the intrapsychic and interpersonal levels. In such cases at least one of the parties is deceiving himself about the fact that he is acting with an attitude oriented to success and is only keeping up the appearance of communicative action. The place of systematically distorted communication can be seen [in the diagram below][115].

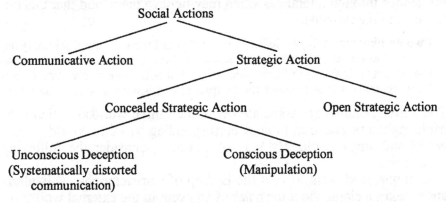

Figure 17: Locating systematically distorted communication

An example of unconscious deception at the individual level of communication would be the «stage mother» phenomenon: a parent who thinks that she is working for her child's best interests but is actually coercing the child to perform so as to make the parent feel successful. Such a mother is deceiving herself as well as her child as to her mo-

---

[114] J. HABERMAS, «Technology and Science as "Ideology"», 56-7.
[115] J. HABERMAS, *The Theory of Communicative Action*, I, 332-3.

tives. An example at the level of communication within a society is the apartheid regime that operated last century in South Africa. Even sectors of Christianity were subverted into supporting the suppression of the «children of Ham».

When deception, conscious or otherwise, is absent and

(a) all relevant voices are heard,
(b) the best all available arguments, given the present state of our knowledge, are accepted, and
(c) only the non-coercive coercion of the better argument determines the affirmations and negations of the participants[116],

then dialogue tends to what Habermas characterizes as the «ideal speech situation». This is the underlying reality of human communication that can be distorted but never completely obliterated.

6.6 Validity Claims

The neo-Kantian[117] concept of validity (*Geltung*) plays a key role in how Habermas understands communication. He notes that people are influenced through utterances when they believe them, and that this belief is not unreasonable:

> I would like, therefore, to defend the following thesis: In the final analysis, the speaker can illocutionarily influence the hearer and vice versa, because speech-act typical commitments are connected with cognitively testable validity claims – that is, because the reciprocal bonds have a rational basis[118].

The validity claims are associated with the «three worlds» – claims to truth, rightness and truthfulness corresponding to «the» world, «our» world and «my» world. By way of example, consider the following speech acts:

Example 1: «I went to visit the Bishop of Christchurch». This utterance makes a claim about the *truth* of an event in the external world.

---

[116] J. HABERMAS, *Autonomy and Solidarity*, 260.

[117] German neo-Kantianism was divided into: the «Marburg School» of H. Cohen (1842-1918) and P. Natorp (1854-1924), concerned mainly with the theory of knowledge and the philosophy of science, and the «Heidelberg School» of W. Windelbrand (1848-1915) and H. Rickert (1863-1936). Max Weber belonged to the latter school. His views are examined by Habermas in *On the Logic of Social Sciences*. For a critique of neo-Kantian influences on sociology, Habermas included, see G. ROSE, *Hegel Contra Sociology*, London 1981.

[118] J. HABERMAS, *The Theory of Communicative Action*, I, 63.

Example 2: «On being appointed to a diocese a religious priest ought to present himself to the bishop». This is an expression of what is *right*. It pronounces a norm of behaviour in a particular culture.

Example 3: «I enjoyed my visit to the Bishop of Christchurch». In addition to the external world reference to the visit, this statement contains a reference to an internal state – enjoyment. It is conceivable that it was *true* that the person visited the bishop but not *truthful* about having enjoyed it.

These statements can influence another person because they *make sense* and are *believable*. Statements which are not nonsense connect to reality – to one or more of the domains of reality that Habermas describes. It is their connection with reality that gives them impact. That link with the real can also be tested and that is what Habermas calls «redeeming the validity claim».

6.6.1 Redemption of Validity Claims

Each communicative speech act involves a claim to comprehensibility, linked to a particular language, and three validity claims linked with each of the three domains of reality. The freedom of the hearer to refuse to accept these claims requires there to be a mechanism in communication for dealing with doubt and denial:

> In the cognitive use of language, the speaker proffers Constative speech acts which contain the offer to recur if necessary to the *experiential source* from which the speaker draws the *certainty* that his statement is true. If this immediate grounding does not dispel an ad hoc doubt, the persistingly problematic truth claim can become the subject of a theoretical discourse[119].

To continue the examples offered in the section on validity above, if the hearer doubted the statement about having visited the bishop, then the normal constative speech act strategy is to provide more details of the experience. «I went to see him on Tuesday, at his house in Barbadoes Street. We talked about my studies at the Gregorian». The speaker touches back on his memories of the experience and offers supporting evidence. This is far from being a proof but involves a repeated claim to the truth of the external world event.

---

[119] J. HABERMAS, *Communication and the Evolution of Society*, 63.

In the interactive use of language, the speaker proffers a speech-act-immanent *obligation to provide justification [Rechtfertigungsverpflich-tung]*. Of course, regulative speech acts contain only the offer to indicate, if necessary, the *normative context* that gives the speaker the *conviction* that his utterance is right. Again, if this immediate justification does not dispel an ad hoc doubt, we can pass over to the level of discourse, in this case of practical discourse. In such a discourse, however, the subject of discursive examination is not the rightness claim directly connected with the speech act, but the validity claim of the underlying norm[120].

A hearer who queried the obligation to visit the bishop would gain a response along the lines of: «It is probably in canon law, but even if it is not it is the usual practice in the Christchurch Diocese and our bishop is a stickler for it». The normative context and the force of the norm is expressed, plus the depth of the conviction of the speaker.

The last of the validity claims, truthfulness, has the most important requirements for redemption and the only ones that are future oriented:

Finally, in the expressive use of language the speaker also enters into a speech-act-immanent obligation, namely the *obligation to prove trustworthy [Bewährungsverpflichtung]*, to show in the consequences of his action that he has expressed just that intention which actually guides his behavior. In case the immediate *assurance* expressing what is *evident* to the speaker himself cannot dispel ad hoc doubts, the truthfulness of the utterance can only be checked against the consistency of his subsequent behavior[121].

If the speaker asserted that he had enjoyed his visit to the bishop and the hearer doubted his sincerity, then there is nothing that can be said at that time to make it any more convincing. Only the speaker has access to his internal world. If his assertion about that world is doubted, then the way he acts *after* that event can be checked for consistency with what he said. If he is subsequently seen chatting happily with that bishop, it will seem that he is honest. If he shows evidence of dreading another encounter with the bishop, it will be thought he was insincere.

Utterances do not usually stand on their own. The hearer interprets what is said against the history of his relationship with the speaker. He assesses the speaker's maturity. He judges if the context is such that the speaker would benefit from telling a lie. He is likely to be aware of the speaker's reputation. Each utterance both expresses the ongoing relationship and is checked against it. When it seems consistent with the

---

[120] J. HABERMAS, *Communication and the Evolution of Society*, 63 (emphases his).
[121] J. HABERMAS, *Communication and the Evolution of Society*, 64 (emphases his).

existing relationship, it strengthens it. Society is built from these relationships.

6.6.2 Freedom to Refuse

The process of reaching agreement in a communicative speech act is not automatic, nor inevitable. The hearer can reject the offered content or the implied relationship. However, a refusal based on understanding is distinct from simply random rejection:

> The binding effect of illocutionary forces comes about, ironically, through the fact that participants can say «no» to speech-act offers. The critical character of this saying «no» distinguishes taking a position in this way from a reaction based solely on caprice. A hearer can be «bound» by speech-act offers because he is not permitted arbitrarily to refuse them but only to say «no» to them, that is, to reject them for reasons. [122]

The reasons for rejecting the speech act offer would not always be expressed. Habermas gives an illuminating example of what he means:

> Let us assume that a seminar participant understands the following request addressed to him by the professor:
> «Please bring me a glass of water» [123]

The hearer can deny the request in terms of the external world (a *truth* issue):

> «No. The next water tap is so far away that I couldn't get back before the end of the session».

Or he can contest the appropriateness of the utterance (a *rightness* issue):

> «No. You can't treat me like one of your employees».

Or he can doubt the motives of the Professor (a *truthfulness* issue):

> «No. You really only want to put me in a bad light in front of the other seminar participants».

Habermas claims that what he illustrates in this example holds true for *all* speech acts oriented to reaching understanding[124]. Speech acts can always be rejected under one or other of the three aspects – truth, right-

---

[122] J. HABERMAS, «Four Sociological Conceptions of Action», 172.

[123] J. HABERMAS, *The Theory of Communicative Action*, I, 306.

[124] See J. HABERMAS, *The Theory of Communicative Action*, I, 307.

ness and truthfulness. The hearer can say that the speaker is wrong about «the» world, about what is normatively acceptable in «our» world or the hearer can express doubt as to the sincerity of the speaker, about how truthfully they are presenting «their» world.

The ability to refuse has long been recognised as a particularly important human attribute. Habermas identifies two streams of philosophical thought to do with the issue:

> From Herder through Nietzsche to Heidegger and Gehlen, being able to say «no» has been repeatedly stressed as an anthropological monopoly of ours. The thesis put forward by Popper and Adorno in different versions, to the effect that reliable knowledge can only be gained through negation of statements, is based on the same insight[125].

This capacity to freely deny is of profound significance for human nature and the growth of organised knowledge, especially natural science, is the result of the critical attitude that this freedom permits.

6.7 *Success in a Speech Act*

A speech act succeeds if it achieves its goal. Habermas describes that goal as follows:

> The goal of coming to an understanding *[Verständigung]* is to bring about an agreement *[Einverständnis]* that terminates in the intersubjective mutuality of reciprocal understanding, shared knowledge, mutual trust, and accord with one another. Agreement is based on recognition of the corresponding validity claims of comprehensibility, truth, truthfulness, and rightness[126].

Notice how the three worlds structure and the three validity claims underlie this definition. Knowledge relates to the external world, trust to a normatively right relationship, and accord flows from the internal worlds of the speaker and hearer. Every speech act, at least implicitly, engages all three domains of reality.

---

[125] J. HABERMAS, «The Three Roots of Communicative Action», 174. J.G. Herder (1744-1803) an advocate of cultural pluralism. F. Nietzsche (1844-1900). M. Heidegger (1889-1976) – perhaps especially *On the way to Language* 1959. A. Gehlen (1904-1976). K. Popper (1902-1994). T. Adorno (1903-1969).For Popper versus Adorno see T.W. Adorno, ed., *Der Positivismusstreit in der deutschen Soziologie*, München 1969 (the Positivist Debate in German Sociology).

[126] J. HABERMAS, *Communication and the Evolution of Society*, 3.

For a speech act to bring about the interpersonal relation that the speaker intends, it needs to be comprehensible and acceptable. Moreover, since the hearer is free to refuse, it must be accepted to be successful. Habermas has two rules for acceptability: the *preparatory rule* and the *sincerity rule*[127]. These rules are taken from Searle's analysis of what constitutes a promise[128]. If these conditions are fulfilled and the hearer freely accepts the validity claims, then the communication has achieved its desired outcomes.

Knowing that the hearer is free to refuse and being desirous of communicating successfully, speakers often think out their line of argument before speaking. This element of rehearsal, reflecting on what one is about to say, opens up a new area of application of communication theory – the psyche.

6.8 *Reflectivity – Arguing with Yourself*

Universal Pragmatics started as a model for communication between persons. George Mead's[129] «social constitution of the self» considers communication with others as essential for self-awareness. Habermas applies communication theory to this inner dialogue:

> The model of inner dialogue, which Mead used rather too unspecifically, turns out in fact to be helpful. In anticipating from alter a negative answer to his own speech act, and raising against himself an objection that alter might raise, ego understands what it means to make a criticizable validity-claim. As soon, then, as ego masters the orientation to validity-claims, he can repeat the internalization of discursive relations once more. Now alter already encounters him with the expectation that ego is not assuming the communicative role of the first person only in a naive manner, but will expand it, if necessary, to the role of a proponent in argumentation. If ego makes this attitude of alter his own, that is to say, if he views himself through the eyes of an arguing opponent and considers how he will answer to his critique, he gains a reflective relation to himself[130].

Accepting that the partner in dialogue has the freedom to refuse, we can imaginatively rehearse dialogues. We take the part of the other in dia-

---

[127] See J. HABERMAS, *Communication and the Evolution of Society*, 65.

[128] J. SEARLE, *Speech Acts*, 63.

[129] George Herbert Mead (1863-1931) American pragmatist philosopher and sociologist. His most important writings are in the collection G. MEAD, *Mind, Self and Society*, Chicago 1934.

[130] J. HABERMAS, «The Three Roots of Communicative Action», 172.

logue with ourselves. We can test our own ideas, checking that *we* can redeem validity claims which *we* make. We can discover the limits of our knowledge or experience. The ability to argue becomes a vital tool for developing this skill of self-critique.

This internal dialogue enables critical thought about our own ideas and those presented to us. In recognising the freedom of others to refuse, we too learn to refuse assertions or instructions that do not correspond with our view of the true and the good. This connection could lead to profound implications of Universal Pragmatics on how we understand our own internal mental processes. The leap from external world to internal world illustrates the power and fruitfulness of this communication model.

6.9 *Discourse Ethics*

In line with his division of validity claims, Habermas considers moral «truths» not to be of the same order of validity as objective «truths»[131]. «Murder is wrong» is a different type of assertion from «Iron is magnetic». The former is a statement of normative rightness, the latter of objective truth. The first addresses the inter-subjective social reality, the second ontological external reality. Habermas considered the parallel between assertoric statements used in constative speech acts and normative statements used in regulative speech acts. The contrasts are as follows:

Statement	Speech Act	relates to	if it is	then it
assertoric	constative	facts	true	exists
normative	regulative	legitimately ordered interpersonal relations (norms)	right	ought be observed

Figure 18: Parallel between assertoric and normative statements

Habermas admits that the parallel is not exact. «A moral norm lays claim to meaning and validity regardless of whether it is promulgated or made use of in a specific way»[132]. So the normative proposition somehow exists independently of the utterance, which, according to Habermas, is not the same with the assertoric proposition. The claim to

---

[131] See J. HABERMAS, «Discourse Ethics», 180.
[132] J. HABERMAS, «Discourse Ethics», 181.

truth exists only in the speech act. The claim to rightness exists in relation to the norm and only secondarily in utterances expressing it.

Habermas seeks universal norms while accepting that some norms
vary from one culture to another. He distinguishes the recognition of
the social existence of a norm from its worthiness to be recognized[133].
Statements of norms, of what is right and proper in a society, are partially dependent on that society and on the language. The language
shapes the society and the society the language. For example, in Italian
there is a formal mode of the language for addressing people with
whom one is not well acquainted or whom one wants to treat respect-
fully. The norms for when it is right to use this mode, and when it is
not, depend both on the grammar of the language and the social distinctions made within the culture.

Throughout his discussion on ethics Habermas bases his approach on
his communication theory. Rather than a system of morality that works
«top down» from a set of absolute norms of behaviour, he starts from
utterances about what is right in ordinary conversation. Since we cannot discuss morality without employing statements about rightness, his
is a theory of these utterances rather than about morality in itself. It is
called discourse ethics because Habermas approaches ethics in and
through discourse. He makes this clear when he identifies the basis of
his ethics:

> In fact, I am defending an outrageously strong claim in the present context
> of philosophical discussion: namely that there is a universal core of moral
> intuition in all times and in all societies. I don't say that this intuition is
> spelt out the same way in all societies at all times. What I do say is that
> these intuitions have the same origin. In the last analysis, they stem from
> the conditions of symmetry and reciprocal recognition which are unavoid-
> able presuppositions of communicative action[134].

Starting from simple statements of what ought to be done in a particular
situation, Habermas looks for what enables some normative statements
to win arguments. A normative statement which is more compelling is
more general in its application. Norms are not some distant ideal for
Habermas, they are found within communications that lead to understanding. The weight of those normative expressions in discussion is

---

[133] See J. HABERMAS, «Discourse Ethics», 182.

[134] «Life-forms, Morality and the Task of the Philosopher» in J. HABERMAS,
Autonomy and Solidarity, 201.

his criterion for determining the general applicability of that norm. He acknowledges a debt to Stephen Toulmin[135] in this approach.

Like Kant[136], Habermas sought a principle of universalization and arrived at one which is more community-oriented and more pragmatic:

> **U**   *All* affected can accept the consequences and the side effects its *general* observance can be anticipated to have for the satisfaction of *everyone's* interests (and these consequences are preferred to those of known alternative possibilities for regulation)[137].

U is a rule of argumentation for the justification of a choice of a norm within a community. Habermas notes that normative validity-claims are used in ordinary life to *co-ordinate* action, and therefore he sought a principle based on the community rather than an atomic individual. He acknowledges that in the same situation different people can have different concerns and be taking care of different interests. His pragmatic approach morality is about the norms of communities. He considered how communities discuss and agree on norms for behaviour within their domain and generalised what underlies that process into U. Habermas carefully avoids classing norms with ontological truths. Having noted the asymmetry in the comparison[138] he keeps the normative apart from the assertoric.

Habermas also offers a reformulation of Kant's imperative in the light of discourse theory. He calls D a «principle of discourse ethics» and uses it to test norms for validity:

> **D**   Only those norms can claim to be valid that meet (or could meet) with the approval of all affected in their capacity *as participants in a practical discourse*[139].

Having based his approach to morality on his communication theory, Habermas also takes this criterion from there. Since norms can only be discussed by being expressed, and since U requires the satisfaction of everyone's interests, the only practical way this could be known would

---

[135] Stephen Toulmin (1922-) British philosopher, author of *The Uses of Argument*, Cambridge 1958.

[136] Immanuel Kant (1724–1804). The formulation of Kant's categorical imperative that Habermas has addressed is a principle of universalization which states: «I should always act in such a way that I am able at the same time to will that the maxim of my action be a universal law of nature».

[137] J. HABERMAS, «Discourse Ethics», 185.

[138] See J. HABERMAS, «Discourse Ethics», 181.

[139] J. HABERMAS, «Discourse Ethics», 185.

be for them to be talked out. Habermas is conscious that «our world» –
the inter-subjective reality – is constantly created and maintained in
human communication, and this is the domain where he locates norms.
Thus they must be connected to discourse and to the community that
shares in this discourse. Since the community can change over time, the
norms would be constantly open to revision. The validation is for a particular time and place, not for all times and all places.

6.10 *The Evolution of Societies and the Role of Religion*

Reconstructing Piaget and Kohlberg into a several-stage theory of the
evolution of societies, Habermas provided a sociological theory of human history. Societies must always deal with problems of survival, justice and legitimacy. There has been an overall increase in the size and
complexity of societies across history: from kinship groups, tribes,
through city states, kingdoms, empires, to the various forms of the
modern nation states. For Habermas the key to interpreting these
changes was the development in the problem-solving skills of society.
This process he calls «the Rationalization of Society».

Habermas views religion as a transitional stage in this evolution. One
of his most concise accounts of this is the table on the next page[140]. The
vertical axis shows stages of rationalization, the key skill involved being the ability to differentiate between the different validity claims.
Primitive societies with a mythical worldview do not distinguish between the laws of nature and the customs of their societies; all of life is
under the capricious control of the gods. The numbered boxes indicate
the direction of progress of societies. «The areas (1-2) and (3-4) stand
for the understanding in archaic societies, the areas (5-6) and (7-8) for
that in civilizations, the areas (9-10) and (11-12) for that of early modern societies»[141]. It is a progress from the undifferentiated to the differentiated and from the sacred to the profane. Note how the profane is
always a step more rational than the sacred.

---

[140] J. HABERMAS, *The Theory of Communicative Action*, II, 192, Figure 28; «Au-
ratic» in 9 is a term used by Walter Benjamin to describe original artworks that have
an «aura» of uniqueness, in contrast to mechanical reproductions. For an explanation
of this concept and an application of it to the situation of Jan Van Eyck's altarpiece (a
full-size reproduction sits above the altar, while the original is on display in another
room behind bullet-proof glass) see F. BAUERSCHMIDT «The Lamb of God in the Age
of Mechanical Reproduction», *Communio* 30 (2003) 581-98.

[141] J. HABERMAS, *The Theory of Communicative Action*, II, 191.

Domains of action / Differentiation of validity spheres	Sacred		Profane	
	Cultic Practice	Worldviews that steer practice	Communication	Purposive activity
Confusion of relations of validity and effect-iveness: performative-instrumental attitude	1. Rite (institutionalization of social solidarity)	2. Myth	—	—
Differentiation between relations of validity and effectiveness: orientation to success vs. to mutual understanding	5. Sacrament/prayer (institutionalization of paths to salvation and knowledge)	6 Religious and metaphysical worldviews	3. Communicative action bound to particular contexts and with a holistic orientation to validity	4. Purposive activity as a task-oriented element of roles (utilization of technical innovations)
Differentiation of specific validity claims at the level of action: objectivating vs. norm-conformative vs. expressive attitudes	9. Contemplative presentation of auratic art (institutionalization of the enjoyment of art)	10. Religious ethics of conviction, rational natural law, civil religion	7. Normatively regulated communicative action with an argumentative handling of truth claims	8. Purposive activity organized through legitimate power (utilization of specialized practical-professional knowledge)
Differentiation of specific validity claims at the level of discourse: communicative action vs. discourse	—	—	11. Normatively unbound communicative action with institutionalized criticism	12. Purposive activity as ethically neutral purposive-rational action (utilization of scientific technologies and strategies)

Figure 19: Progressive Rationalization of Society

Sacraments, religion and metaphysical worldviews were features of the great civilizations before the modern period. The worship of archaic societies had involved the magical rituals that were believed to compel a deity to affect the external world. By contrast the cultic practice of religions involves sacraments and prayer which are an institutionalized, non-magical way for the believer to communicate with the deity and to change *internally* as a result[142]. These practices are replaced in the early

---

[142] See J. HABERMAS, *The Theory of Communicative Action*, II, 418.

modern period by art appreciation and «civil religion» characterized by oaths in courtrooms and a rational understanding of natural law. When we arrive fully in the modern period:

> The two areas on the left in the bottom row of [the figure above] have been left empty because, with the development of modern societies, the sacred domain has largely disintegrated, or at least has lost its structure-forming significance. At the level of completely differentiated validity spheres, art sheds its cultic background, just as morality and law detach themselves from their religions and metaphysical background. With this secularization of bourgeois culture, the cultural value spheres separate off sharply from one another and develop according to the standards of the inner logics specific to the different validity claims[143].

Religion was good and useful, but now has had its day. According to Habermas the world religions were dominated by the «problem of suffering» (which he identifies with the need to explain the unequal distribution of society's resources[144]) and did so by dichotomous world views that contrasted this world with the world to come, or the world of appearances with the world of essences. Suffering was thereby given a religious explanation and anodyne. This is in continuity with the traditional Marxist view of religion, though Habermas does point out that it is not merely «for the masses»:

> The world religions pervaded both popular and high cultures, they owed their overwhelming efficacy to the fact that with the same set of assertions and promises they could satisfy the need for justification at very different levels of moral consciousness simultaneously[145].

Habermas is not merely restating Marx's dictum that «Religion is the opiate of the masses», he has organically connected these assertions to his theory of communicative action. According to him religious worldviews subtly limit communication. They attract intellectuals but «immunize» them against dissonant experiences:

> The immunization could succeed when an institutional separation between the sacred and the profane realms of action ensured that traditional foundations were not taken up in the wrong place; within the domain of the sacred, communication remained *systematically restricted* ...[146]

---

[143] J. HABERMAS, *The Theory of Communicative Action*, II, 196.
[144] See J. HABERMAS, *The Theory of Communicative Action*, II, 188-9.
[145] J. HABERMAS, *The Theory of Communicative Action*, II, 189.
[146] J. HABERMAS, *The Theory of Communicative Action*, II, 189 (emphasis his).

In a realm where some truths are sacred and institutionally defended unfettered discourse cannot take place. Meanwhile, the profane world is free to advance more rapidly on the path of rationalization. Habermas attributes the secularization of the modern world to the fact that «the modern form of understanding is too transparent to provide a niche for this structural violence by means of inconspicuous restrictions on communication»[147]. Within his framework, this is a good and emancipatory process. In a later work, Habermas acknowledged that what he gave above was a «one-sided functionalist description of religion» and that «the world religions do *not* function *exclusively* as a legitimation of governmental authority»[148]. He asserts that:

> As long as religious language bears with itself inspiring, indeed, unrelinquishable semantic contents which elude (for the moment?) the expressive power of a philosophical language and still await translation into a discourse that gives reasons for its positions, philosophy, even in its postmetaphysical form, will neither be able to replace nor to repress religion[149].

He thus acknowledges that he may have signalled the demise of religion prematurely and that religious language has a valuable inspirational role; it continues to offer individual existential comfort in societies in which it no longer has a structural role. He seems to expect philosophical discourse to take over these beneficial roles at some future date.

7. Conclusion

Habermas, with teams of researchers, worked on the theory of communicative action for over 30 years[150]. He extended the application of communication theory into the political philosophy and he is often invoked in the political sphere with direct application to the legal structures of modern states[151]. His thinking on the «public sphere» as the place of unconstrained discourse about public policy and the affairs of the state is influential among the media and in the governments of par-

---

[147] J. HABERMAS, *The Theory of Communicative Action*, II, 196

[148] J. HABERMAS, *Religion and Rationality*, 79 (emphases his).

[149] J. HABERMAS, *Nachmetaphysisches Denken*, 60.

[150] J. Habermas: «my research program has remained the same since about 1970» quoted by S. WHITE, *The Cambridge Companion to Habermas*, 7.

[151] For example Colin Farrelly in *An Introduction to Contemporary Political Theory*, London 2004, centres his treatment of the question «How substantive are the principles of democracy?» on the proceduralist theories and discourse ethics of Habermas.

ticipatory democracies. In the field of sociology, the applications of this theory to the functioning and evolution of societies are hailed as having considerable explanatory power. This chapter focused on central aspects of the theory of communicative action and upon Universal Pragmatics. Discourse is the basis of Habermas's theory. Commencing from Austin's insight that sentences are actions as well as descriptions, Habermas examined what it is that all language does. According to him, in and through language we both experience and construct the objective world. Through interaction we encounter and maintain the legitimate relationships that constitute our communities. The very structures of personality are the result of the processes whereby language and culture are learnt. In discourse humans discover how to relate to each other and the world and establish their identities. Habermas's is not a theory of atomic individuals; he deals with people always-already embedded in a symbolic system and the web of relationships which is language and culture. Habermas believes in reason and the power of the better argument. His theory is ultimately a rational one in which people, know truth, relate rightly, and express themselves sincerely. Denials, distortions, lies and manipulation are secondary and parasitical. There is much in the philosophy of Habermas that is compatible with Catholic theology. The generality of the theory and its foundation in communication suggest it could helpfully be applied to sacramental theology. The Marxist roots of the theory and its negative assessment of religion, signal there may be dangers to an uncritical adoption of his ideas.

Austin declared: «What we need besides the old doctrine about meanings is a new doctrine about all the possible forces of utterances»[152]. Habermas has responded to this challenge with his conception of the lifeworld and the three worlds of discourse. In his theory of the redeemable validity claims in communicative action he provides a rational basis for the illocutionary force of performatives utterances. Performatives work because of their link to the objective world of truth, the social world of legitimate relationships, and the inner world of the speaker. Truth, rightness, and sincerity enable those communicative actions which are the normal business of human society.

---

[152] J.L. AUSTIN, «Performative Utterances», 238.

Figure 20: Louise-Marie Chauvet, 2004

CHAPTER III

Louis-Marie Chauvet: Symbolic Efficacy

1. Introduction

The preceding chapters outlined speech act theory as originally pro-posed by John Austin and then as applied by a range of authors, in par-ticular its contribution to and development within Jürgen Habermas's theory of communicative action. This chapter addresses the work of another user of speech act theory, Louis-Marie Chauvet, who applies it to sacramental theology. His theory of symbolic efficacy is quite inde-pendent of Habermas, but in this chapter his ideas will be presented against the background of those of Habermas for the purposes of cri-tique, to make connections, and to suggest potential developments.

2. Louis-Marie Chauvet

In 1987 a lecturer from the Institut Catholique in Paris published a volume entitled *Symbole et Sacrement: Une relecture sacramentelle de l'existence chrétienne*. The author was Louis-Marie Chauvet, a priest of the diocese of Luçon. He taught sacramental theology at the Institut from 1974. This, his first major work, was recognised as a significant contribution to the field of sacramental theology and as a challenge to the classic theory of how sacraments work.

The name of L.-M. Chauvet is making an increasing impact in sacramental theology [...] the project aims at elaborating a «fundamental theology of sacramentality»; its scope is situated at the heart of modernity; this will imply a radical questioning of classical sacramental theology[1].

The size and complexity of the work must have been a factor in the eight-year delay before it appeared in English[2]. The impact of Chauvet's thought was enhanced by his simpler and updated treatment of the same topic in his 1997 work: *Les Sacrements: Parole de Dieu au risque du corps*. Within four years this had appeared in English as *The Sacraments: The Word of God at the mercy of the body*. This work at only 200 pages (in comparison to the 555 pages of its predecessor), without the dense academic footnoting and including more pastoral applications, has had greater popular appeal[3]. As one reviewer put it: «Chauvet is one of the very best sacramental theologians writing today. Students will find this book more accessible than some of his early work»[4].

Entirely faithful to the title of his major work, Chauvet provides a re-interpretation of Christian existence by a re-reading of the sacramental structure of that existence in a symbolic rather than ontological register. He presents the sacraments as mediations of grace within a symbolic order. He styles the classical scholastic theology as «onto-theology» and critiques it in terms of its presuppositions and negative consequences. While confronting a metaphysical issue he does not restrict himself to philosophy but draws on diverse fields – anthropology, linguistics, psychoanalysis, exegesis, ethics, liturgical history, christology, and ecclesiology – to further his argument. Chauvet draws explicitly on the work of J.L. Austin[5], but his main philosophical influence is Martin

---

[1] Camil Ménard reviewing *Symbole et sacrement* in *Studies in Religion / Sciences Religieuses* 1988, 376: «Le nom de L.-M. Chauvet s'impose de plus en plus en théologie sacramentaire [...] le projet vise à élaborer une «théologie fondamentale de la sacramentalité» (p. 8) dont la problématique se situe au coeur de la modernité, ce qui impliquera une remise en question radicale de la théologie sacramentaire classique».

[2] L-M. CHAUVET, *Symbole et Sacrement: Une relecture sacramentelle de l'existence chrétienne*, Paris 1987; English trans., *Symbol and Sacrament: A Sacramental Reinterpretation of Christian Existence*, tr. Patrick Madigan – Madeleine Beaumont, Collegeville MN 1995.

[3] In private correspondence (e-mail to M Duffy 9/9/2004), Fr Cyril Gorman of the Liturgical Press indicated that *The Sacraments* is selling at approximately twice the rate of *Symbol and Sacrament*.

[4] John Baldovin reviewing *The Sacraments* in *Theological Studies* 63 (2002) 419.

[5] Chauvet worked from the French translation of Austin's *How to do Things with Words* and reads him within a French school that includes the sociologist Pierre Bourdieu (1930-2002), author of *Ce que parler veut dire*, Paris 1982, and the linguist

Heidegger. Jürgen Habermas is cited only once – as the main inspirer of the «critical theory of ideologies»[6] which has criticized hermeneutics.

The scope of *Symbole et Sacrement* is considerable. It critiques the established instrumental theory of the efficacy of sacraments and attempts to recast all of sacramental theology on a new philosophical basis.

2.1 *Some of Chauvet's Theological Presuppositions*

In introducing his sacramental themes, Chauvet rejects scholasticism while accepting insights from Thomas Aquinas. By way of example, he locates the foundations of his sacramental theology as follows:

> Any theology worthy of its name must find some way to achieve a coherence between its *Christology* and its *sacramental theology*. We have indicated this when speaking of the *Commentary on the Sentences*: the intellectual scheme in the two domains is that of disposing causality. In the *Summa* it is, in both cases, a matter of instrumental efficient causality. While in the *Sentences* Thomas takes care not to attribute to the human nature of Christ a divine efficacy for our salvation, in the *Summa* the Aristotelian-Averroistic theory of communication between subordinated agents allows him to do full justice to the saying of St. John Damascene: «in Christ human nature was like the instrument of the divinity»[7].

Chauvet notes that this phrase of John Damascene is used by Aquinas some forty times and operates as an axiom of his christology. Chauvet, despite his rejection of instrumental efficient causality, affirms the Thomistic-patristic insight and accepts it as the basis for this coherent link between christology and sacramental theology:

> Further, «the principal efficient cause of grace is God, for whom the humanity of Christ is a *conjoined* instrument (like the hand), while the sacrament supplies an instrument that remains *distinct* (like the stick moved by the hand). It is thus necessary for the salvific power to pass from the divinity of Christ through his humanity and finally through the sacraments» (*ST*

Émile Benveniste (1902-1976) author of *Problèmes de linguistique générale*, Paris 1966.

[6] L-M. CHAUVET, *Symbol and Sacrament*, 67.

[7] L-M. CHAUVET, *Symbol and Sacrament*, 19-20 (emphases his). The John Damascene phrase «humana natura in Christo erat velut organum divinitatis» comes from *De Fide Orthodoxa* III, 15.

III q. 62, a. 5). One could not better express how closely sacramental theology is modeled on Christology[8].

Thomas Aquinas is clear that the Jesus of the ministry was no puppet manipulated by God. Jesus freely chooses to do the will of the Father and his human will joins with his divine will in the task of salvation. Humanity is thus saved «from the inside», from within humanity[9]. There is a double agency involved here:

> The humanity of Christ is an instrument of the divinity. But it is not an inert instrument, such as would merely be moved without in any way moving itself. It is a living instrument, with a spiritual soul, which itself acts even when it is being acted upon[10].

Patrick Gray characterizes double agency as «an attempt to understand that God makes the world make itself»[11]. In this case it is through the agencies of the divine and human wills of Christ that God makes the world *save* itself. In his humanity, Christ accepted to suffer and die. For Aquinas, the suffering and death of Christ is the source of the efficacy of the sacraments:

> From this it is manifest that in a special way the sacraments of the Church derive their power from the Passion of Christ, and that it is through the reception of the sacraments that the power flowing from this becomes, in a certain way, conjoined to us[12].

On the basis of his reading of Aquinas, Chauvet asserts:

---

[8] L-M. CHAUVET, *Symbol and Sacrament*, 20 (emphases his). *ST* III q. 62, a. 5: «Principalis autem causa efficiens gratiae est ipse Deus, ad quem comparator humanitas Christi sicut instrumentum conjunctum, sacramentum autem sicut instrumentum separatum. Et ideo oportet quod virtus salutifera derivetur a divinitate Christi per ejus humanitatem in ipsa sacramenta».

[9] See G. O'COLLINS, *Christology*, 155. He cites Irenaeus, «If a human being had not overcome the enemy of humanity, the enemy would not have been rightly overcome. On the other side, if it had not been God to give us salvation, we would not have received it permanently». *Adversus haereses*, 3.18.7.

[10] *ST* III, q. 7, a. 1, ad. 3: «Ad tertium dicendum quod humanitas Christi est instrumentum divinitatis, non quidem sicut instrumentum inanimatum, quod nullo modo agit sed solum agitur, sed tamquam instrumentum animatum anima rationali, quod ita agit quod etiam agitur».

[11] P. GRAY, «Making Us Ourselves», 126.

[12] *ST* II q. 62, a. 5: «Unde manifestum est quod sacramenta Ecclesiae specialiter habent virtutem ex passione Christi, cujus virtus quodammodo nobis copulatur per susceptionem sacramentorum».

The sacraments remain the *sacraments of the Incarnate Word*, from whom «they derive their efficacy» and to whom they «are conformed by the fact that they join the «word» to the sensible object, just as, in the mystery of the Incarnation, the Word of God is united to human flesh». (*ST*, III, q.60, Prologue to the «Treatise on the Sacraments» and a.6) The sacraments are thus appreciated as *prolongations of the sanctified humanity of Christ*[13].

While following Aquinas in seeing a connection between the sacraments and the humanity of Christ, Chauvet cites him while omitting all reference to the Passion. The suffering and death of Jesus which is such a major Thomistic theme with respect to the efficacy of the sacraments is less central for Chauvet. He interprets the Pasch of Christ in the broadest possible terms as he indicated in the diagram explanation below:

We can visualize what we understand by paschal mystery, taken in its full extension, by the following diagram:

Paschal Mystery of Christ

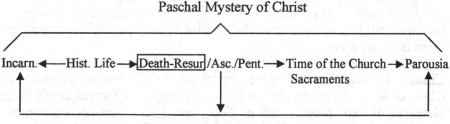

Incarn.◄——Hist. Life——►Death-Resur/Asc./Pent.——►Time of the Church——►Parousia
                                          Sacraments

Figure 21: Paschal Mystery of Christ

According to the diagram above, the sacraments appear not as the somehow static prolongations of the incarnation as such but as the major expression, in our own history, of the embodiment (historical/eschatological) of the risen One in the world through the Spirit, embodiment whose «fundamental sacrament» is the church visibly born at Pentecost. The sacraments are thus situated in the dynamism of a secular history reread as holy history[14].

Chauvet clearly wishes to affirm the importance of the death and resurrection of the Lord, but additionally to read it in a context that stretches from the incarnation to the *parousia*. Jesus Christ mediates the presence

---

[13] L-M. CHAUVET, *Symbol and Sacrament*, 20-21 (emphases his). *ST* III q.60: «Ab ipso Verbo incarnate efficaciam habent». *ST* III q.60 a.6: «cui sacramentum quodammodo conformatur in hoc quod rei sensibili verbum adhibetur, sicut in mysterio incarnationis carni sensibili est Verbum Dei unitum».

[14] L-M. CHAUVET, *The Sacraments*, 160.

of the hidden God for humanity. He does this throughout his life, and the Church, under his Lordship, continues this mandate after Pentecost.

2.2 *The Structure of Christian Identity*

Christian existence, according to Chauvet, is characterized by *mediation*. Christians have to renounce the direct, «gnostic» line to Jesus Christ, or to God[15]. God can only be truly known as revealed in and by the Christ – Jesus is the original sacrament who mediates God to humanity and humanity to God. Moreover, Jesus is risen, his body is not here, and for humanity to encounter him today the privileged locus to do so is in the symbolic mediation of the fundamental sacrament of the Church[16].

Accepting mediation involves *«agreeing to loss»*. Trusting Christ implies an acceptance of the hiddenness of God and the limitations of human knowing. God can only be known in Christ when it is realized that God cannot be known directly in himself. Yet, paradoxically, once the direct route is abandoned more is found in the mediation than might be expected. In encountering Christ, God is encountered. In mediation there is a *«presence in absence»*.

The encounter with Christ through the necessary mediation of the Church involves three elements which are in a dynamic interplay, as Chauvet shows in the model on the facing page[17]. Chauvet labels these elements of the Christian life as *Scripture, Sacrament* and *Ethics*, but he is not using the words in their usual senses. Scripture is the most deceptive of the three titles:

«Scripture» encompasses everything that concerns the understanding of the faith, starting with those glosses in the margins of the Bible which we call theology[18].

This is the dimension of knowledge in the Christian life. Standing alone it is insufficient, but it is an essential part of the tripod supporting Christian existence. Without knowing Christ and his teaching it is not possible to respond to them or to live them out.

---

[15] See L-M. CHAUVET, *Symbol and Sacrament*, 172.

[16] See L-M. CHAUVET, *Symbol and Sacrament*, 177.

[17] Illustration taken from L-M. CHAUVET, *Symbol and Sacrament*, 172. See also the simpler version in *The Sacraments*, 28.

[18] L-M. CHAUVET, *Symbol and Sacrament*, 178

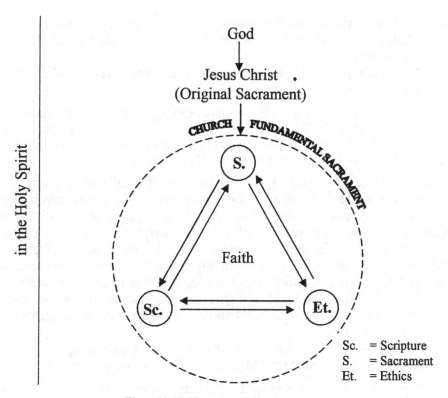

Figure 22: The Structure of Christian Identity

The second dimension involves «living symbolically what one is attempting to understand theologically» and hence:

> Under the term «sacrament» we place everything that has to do with the celebration of the Triune God in the *liturgy*. First, of course, the two paradigmatic sacraments of baptism and the Eucharist; but also the other five; and further still, even celebrations which are not strictly sacramental, whether in a small group or large, whether in a gothic cathedral or in an ordinary room. Prayer is partially included in ritual action, but only partially because the line between prayer and ritual is always a moving one[19].

Thus the term «sacrament» in the model equates with Christian *ritual*. It covers the seven sacraments, liturgy and «para-liturgy». What characterizes this dimension is the formal, group activity whereby what is known in the scripture/intellectual dimension is publicly acknowl-

---

[19] L-M. CHAUVET, *Symbol and Sacrament*, 179 (emphasis his).

edged. Private rituals are not among Chauvet's examples; he may intend therefore that ritual is an action of the Church only when at least two are gathered.

Chauvet admits that his third element in the model has «a rather large extension».

> Simply put, the element «ethics» includes every kind of *action* Christians perform in the world insofar as this is a testimony given to the gospel of the Crucified-Risen One and this conduct [...] concerns not only interpersonal «moral *praxis*» but also collective «social *praxis*»[20].

Ethics therefore covers all that Christians, individually or collectively, *do* because of their faith, with the exception of the ritual action that comes under «sacrament». Chauvet's model therefore divides the Christian life into an intellectual element (scripture), a ritual element (sacrament), and a pragmatic element (ethics). The Church reflects on what she believes, the Church worships, and the Church acts in the world. This has a resonance with the triad referred to by the Fathers of the Second Vatican Council: «In this way the church, in its *teaching*, *life* and *worship*, perpetuates and hands on to every generation all that it is and all that it believes»[21].

Chauvet goes on to claim that the structure underlying the sacraments closely corresponds with this structure of Christian identity:

> If every sacramental celebration thus implements the same process of gift / reception / return-gift, a process concretely corresponding to the figure Scriptures / Sacrament / Ethics, this cannot be by pure chance. In fact such a process can be understood as the very process of Christian identity. In other words, *every sacrament shows us how to see and live what transforms our human existence into a properly Christian existence*[22].

In Chauvet's vision sacraments are not merely «helps» to the Christian life, they are both exemplars and constitutive elements. In his consideration of Christian identity – of what it is that characterizes a truly Christian existence – Chauvet has come across a recurring patterning which he identifies as symbolic exchange. The triangle of a gift given, the gift received, and a return-gift made is for him not only the leitmotif of the seven sacraments and the liturgy of the Church, it is the funda-

---

[20] L-M. CHAUVET, *Symbol and Sacrament*, 179 (emphases his).
[21] *DV* 8 (emphasis added).
[22] L-M. CHAUVET, *The Sacraments*, 145 (emphasis his).

mental pattern whereby people become believers. This is the basis of his sacramental re-reading of Christian life.

3. The Structure of *Symbol and Sacrament*

Chauvet's work is organized like a doctoral thesis with an elaborate and detailed table of contents; his numbering system is nested five deep. Such is the wealth of detail that the overall structure is not immediately apparent. The diagram on the next page gives the top two levels of his headings revealing the logic that underlies the work. Chauvet begins by pointing to a new philosophical direction – «From the Metaphysical to the Symbolic». To justify this movement he critiques the former and outlines some of the advantages of the latter. He spends considerable effort establishing the principle of mediation which is fundamental to his understanding of symbolic efficacy. Since Chauvet's scope is not simply to explain the sacraments but to provide a new interpretation of the entirety of Christian existence, in Part 2 he goes on to outline the triad of Scripture–Sacrament–Ethics which provides the structure of this existence. He shows with examples how these interrelate to produce disciples and an ecclesiology. Parts 3 and 4 of the work are more explicitly sacramental. In the third part Chauvet explains how, through acts of ritual symbolization, the sacraments link the body of the disciple with the body of the Church and the cosmos. He addresses questions of the institution of the sacraments, the freedom and limitations of the Church with respect to the sacraments. He looks at how the sacraments make the Church and make Christians, and how they operate by revealing, and reveal in their operation. Finally, he considers the connections between sacramental theology and the Trinity, especially as this is revealed in the (broadly understood) Pasch of Christ. He treats of God as hidden, and pays particular attention to the role of the Holy Spirit. He presents his understanding of sacramental grace, and locates sacraments within the eschatological tension of salvation history.

Chauvet treats of topics from the philosophical, through social justice, to particular details of liturgical practice. He draws from multiple sources across several disciplines. This chapter addresses only his critique of metaphysics, understanding of language, use of Austin's linguistic philosophy, and theory of the symbolic efficacy of sacraments.

Part	Title		Chapter Title	Pages
1	From the Metaphysical to the Symbolic	1	Critique of the Onto-theological Presuppositions of Classical Sacramental Theology	39
		2	Overcoming Onto-Theology	38
		3	Mediation	26
		4	Symbol and Body	49
2	The Sacraments in the Symbolic Network of the Faith of the Church	5	Description of the Structure of Christian Identity	31
		6	The Relation between Scripture and Sacrament	69
		7	The Relation between Sacrament and Ethics	38
		8	How the Structure Functions: The Process of Symbolic Exchange	55
3	The Symbolizing Act of Christian Identity	9	The Sacraments: Acts of Ritual Symbolization	56
		10	The Sacraments as Instituted	32
		11	The Sacraments as Instituting	40
4	Sacramental Theology & Trinitarian Theology	12	The Sacraments of the New Pasch	41
		13	The Sacraments: Symbolic Figures of God's Effacement	58

Figure 23: Structure of *Symbol and Sacrament*

4. Chauvet's critique of Metaphysics

4.1 *Being* vs. *Becoming*

Chauvet identifies classical philosophical thought as focused on ends, finished products; on Being rather than Becoming. He analyses the *Philebus*, a late dialogue of Plato[23]. In that dialogue Socrates distinguishes *genesis* (becoming) and *ousia* (being). To answer the questions «Which one of the two is in a condition of *genesis*, the lover or the beloved? Which one is in a condition of *ousia*?», the interlocutors use the analogy of building a ship. As Chauvet has it:

> Thus, in the final analysis, it is this *technological* argument of shipbuilding that allows Socrates to carry off the decision and to set in place as a general law that all process is for the sake of *existence*[24].

Onto-theology gives priority to being. Chauvet argues that in this scheme of thought it is impossible to grasp the reality of relationships between human subjects, since these are necessarily always in process. «The human may never be adequately understood according to the technical mode of causality»[25]. According to him, traditional western philosophy finds a permanent state of incompleteness to be literally unthinkable.

Relationships between persons are not directly causal. Take the example of a man (the lover) who is in love with a woman (the beloved). The lover does not *cause* the beloved to love him in return, because she is another fully free subject. The beloved, as a free subject who knows and feels themselves to be loved, *chooses* to return love for love. Thus it is the beloved, not the lover, who is the cause of the affectionate response that establishes the reciprocal loving relationship. Ships are built, but a person cannot *make* another love him or her. Humans have the capacity to reject both love and grace.

Chauvet suggests that the tentative and necessarily incomplete character of human interpersonal relationships was why Aquinas avoided employing those relationships as an analogy for the relationship of God to the human being with respect to grace and the sacraments. An all-powerful God should not have to rely on the response of a human being to achieve what God wants. Aquinas developed his theory of sacramen-

---

[23] See L-M. CHAUVET, *Symbol and Sacrament*, 22.
[24] L-M. CHAUVET, *Symbol and Sacrament*, 23 (emphases his).
[25] L-M. CHAUVET, *Symbol and Sacrament*, 24.

tal efficacy between his *Commentary on the Sentences* and the *Summa*. In the former he described them as causal remedies for sin; in the latter, as sacred signs that sanctify human beings, thereby introducing the importance of signification. However, he adds that sacraments *effect* what they signify – they are instrumental causes of grace. Chauvet locates Aquinas's problem in:

> harmonizing two categories as completely foreign to one another as are «sign» and «cause», and doing so in such a way that the type of sign under examination would have these unique traits: it would *indicate what it is causing* and it would *have no other way of causing except by the mode of signification*[26].

From the *Sentences* to the *Summa*, Aquinas shifts his ground «*from disposing causality to instrumental causality*»[27]. However, for Chauvet he does not go far enough. Aquinas recognizes the importance of the sign but, locked into the technical-ontological mode, cannot take the step into the «symbolic order». This step is the major theme of *Symbol and Sacrament*. A question asked by Chauvet reveals his agenda:

> But may one simply decree, by a simple announcement, the replacement of an onto-theological logic of the Same, where the sacraments are controlled by their instrumental and causal system, with a symbolic representation of the Other, where they are appreciated as language acts making possible the unending transformation of subjects into believing subjects[28]?

A simple decree is not enough to achieve it, but this substitution is precisely Chauvet's aim. Instrumental causality is to be replaced by «symbolic representation of the Other» – which is going to involve the concept of *mediation*, and sacraments being appreciated as «language acts» that make possible the *unending* transformation (precisely the kind of permanent process which onto-theology has difficulty grasping) «of subjects into believing subjects».

Consistently in *Symbol and Sacrament* Chauvet goes against the mainstream of tradition; he prefers Becoming to Being, the subject to the object, the body to the abstract, and the contextualized historical to the eternal.

---

[26] L-M. CHAUVET, *Symbol and Sacrament*, 16 (emphases his).
[27] L-M. CHAUVET, *Symbol and Sacrament*, 16 (emphasis his).
[28] L-M. CHAUVET, *Symbol and Sacrament*, 45.

4.2 *Onto-Theology underrates language*

Thomas Aquinas summed up Aristotle's teaching on language: «The Philosopher says that words are signs for thoughts and thoughts are likenesses of things ...»[29] This suggests a hierarchy of word, thought and thing. Augustine declared:

> Given signs are those which living beings give to each other, in order to show, to the best of their ability, the emotions of their minds, or anything that they have felt or learnt. There is no reason for us to signify something (that is, to give a sign) except to express and transmit to another's mind what is in the mind of the person who gives the sign[30].

Thomas echoes this view: «Speaking to another is nothing else than manifesting the concept of the mind to that person»[31]. These explanations of human communication resemble the code model discussed above[32]. They assume a priority of thought above that of language. The person *has* the thoughts, the impressions, the states of soul, *then* signifies them with the arbitrary symbols of language, transmits them to another who interprets the significations and is thereby aware of the thoughts that are in the mind of the speaker. Thoughts are logically and chronologically before words. Chauvet, however, does not accept that things and thoughts are prior to language:

> Language *creates*, creates «things». This idea is absurd from the viewpoint of traditional metaphysics, which sees language only as an attribute that humans possess and as «an instrument for bestowing a name on something that is already there, already represented» or as a simple «means for displaying what presents itself by itself». This is precisely the view of language we must give up[33].

---

[29] *ST*, 1 q. 13, a. 1: «Dicendum quod secundum Philosophum, I Perihermeneias, voces sunt signa intellectum, et intellectus sunt rerum similitudines», Thomas is referring to Aristotle's *De Interpretatione* I, I, 16 a3.

[30] AUGUSTINE, *On Christian Teaching* II, II, 3: «Data vero signa sunt, quae sibi quaeque viventia invicem dant ad demonstrandos, quantum possunt, motus animi sui, vel sensa, aut intellecta quaelibet. Nec ulla causa est nobis significandi, id est signi dandi, nisi ad depromendum et trajiciendum in alterius animum id quod animo gerit is qui signum dat». *PL* 34, 37.

[31] *ST*, I, q. 107, a. 1: «Nihil aliud est loqui ad alterum quam conceptum mentis alteri manifestare».

[32] See Ch. I 6.1 above.

[33] L-M. CHAUVET, *Symbol and Sacrament*, 89 (emphasis his).

Chauvet is not denying the existence of the objective world, but rather asserting that human beings never know the world *as objective* alone. «Reality is never present to us except in a mediated way, which is to say, *constructed* out of the symbolic network of the culture which fashions us»[34]. People always know the world *as it is for them* – the world for humans is the one *subjectively* experienced. As Robert Bellah comments: «reality is seen to reside not just in the object but in the subject and particularly in the relation between subject and object»[35]. Humans do not perceive brute facts that stamp an impression on their intellect – they see «rocks» and «trees», «buildings» and «bus-stops». Humans cannot see without labelling, without interpreting. A blank stare is not human seeing. To see involves recognition – connecting what is before the person to their prior collection of culturally defined categories.

> It is similar to contact lenses which cannot be seen by the wearers since they adhere to their eyes but through which all their vision of the real is filtered. Therefore, the real as such is by definition *unreachable*. What we perceive of it is what is constructed by our culture and desire, what is filtered through our linguistic lens. But our perception has become so accustomed to this lens and this lens adheres so tightly to our perception that, almost as a reflex, we take the cultural for the natural and our desires for the real[36].

The key cultural construct that filters and focuses our view of the world is language. Words do not merely label, they transform – an entity out there in the real is brought into the presence of the human subject by being signified. It ceases to be real-as-such in *becoming* real-to-the-person-knowing-it.

> This is the distinctive *activity*, the primordial human activity; in this *poiesis* – and let us remember, all language is of its essence «poietic», all language is a «forgotten poem» – language kills entities as simple facts spread out before our eyes in order to resurrect them as signifiers of humans and for humans. It is in language that the «world» becomes for us a world that

---

[34] L-M. CHAUVET, *Symbol and Sacrament*, 84 (emphasis his).
[35] R. BELLAH, «Christianity and Symbolic Realism», 93. Bellah, a sociologist from the University of California, made this assertion as part of his keynote address to the Society for the Scientific Study of Religion and the American Academy of Religion on 25 October 1969.
[36] L-M. CHAUVET, *Symbol and Sacrament*, 86 (emphasis his).

speaks; it speaks in both senses of the word «speak», transitive and intransitive: it speaks us and it speaks to us[37].

The work that language does for the human subject is to create the world. What is out there is darkness and chaos – it is only the creative human word that enables human beings to speak the world into existence every time they look upon it.

Following Heidegger, Chauvet views the human person as always cocooned in and defined by language:

> That is why, continues Heidegger, «we speak when awake, we speak in our dreams. We speak continually, even when we are uttering no word and are only listening or reading; we speak even when, no longer really listening or reading, we immerse ourselves in work or give up and simply decide to do nothing». This clearly shows that humans and language are inseparable[38].

Humans cannot think thoughts without words and other symbols. Things are not used without being named, labelled and interpreted. The human world is not one of brute facts but of culturally classified and created facts.

4.2.1 Does Chauvet misrepresent Augustine and Aquinas?

Chauvet's view of language is clearly different from that of classical metaphysics. However, in establishing this difference he overstates it by attributing to Augustine and Aquinas an unlikely position. He characterizes their classical view in these terms:

> The human being is an entity that has, among other *attributes*, speech. Humans have language, instead of being originally possessed and constituted by it [...] They use language as necessary *tool for the translation* of their mental representations to themselves (thought) or to others (voice)[39].

In support of this position Chauvet makes an assertion about Augustine's view of language:

> According to Augustine, language is a consequence of original sin which has so dried up the inner source of direct knowledge of God that our first parents could no longer communicate with each other except through the skill (quite imperfect) of language. (*De. Gen. contra Manich.*, II, 31) This

---

[37] L.-M. CHAUVET, *Symbol and Sacrament*, 89 (emphasis his).

[38] L.-M. CHAUVET, *Symbol and Sacrament*, 57, citing M. HEIDEGGER, *Acheminement vers la parole*, 207 (*Unterwegs zur Sprache*, Tübingen 1959).

[39] L.-M. CHAUVET, *Symbol and Sacrament*, 33 (emphases his).

is a significant statement because it implies that God could have created humans beyond any real need for language... Without going that far, Augustine comes close to saying the same thing in another text, quoted and commented upon by Thomas to this effect, that «before [the fall], God perhaps spoke with Adam and Eve in the same way he communicates with the angels, that is by directly illuminating their intellects with God's permanent truth». (Augustine, *Super Gen. ad Litt.*, XI. *ST*, I, q. 94, a. 1. Cf. *De Veritate*, q. 18, a. 1-2)[40]

Ten years later in *Les Sacrements*, Chauvet repeats this point, in a less nuanced form:

Another theory is to see in language, as Augustine, then Thomas Aquinas did, a consequence of original sin, which presupposes that human beings had been created without language. (*ST* 1, q. 94, a. 1.)[41]

In the passage from the *Summa* referred to above, Aquinas cites the same text from Augustine as Chauvet. Thomas is concerned with how in original beatitude Adam knew God, whether in his Essence or not. He takes the negative opinion, and writes:

Hence Augustine says (*Gen. ad lit.* XI, 33) that, «perhaps God used to speak to the first man as He speaks to the angels; by shedding on his mind a ray of the unchangeable truth, yet without bestowing on him the experience of which the angels are capable in the participation of the Divine Essence». Therefore, through these intelligible effects of God, man knew God then more clearly than we know Him now[42].

Aquinas, in quoting Augustine, includes a word that Chauvet omits, namely «perhaps» – Augustine was advancing his notion as a speculation. Elsewhere in his writing he has entertained an alternative possibility:

But what manner of speech it was that God then uttered to the outward ears of men, especially in speaking to the first man, it is both difficult to discover, and we have not undertaken to say in this discourse. But if words alone and sounds were wrought, by which to bring about some sensible

---

[40] L-M. CHAUVET, *Symbol and Sacrament*, 33-34.
[41] L-M. CHAUVET, *The Sacraments*, 5.
[42] *ST* 1, q. 94, a. 1: «Unde dicit Augustinus quod *fortassis Deus primis hominibus antea loquebatur sicut cum angelis loquitur, ipsa incommutabili veritate illustrans mentes eorum; etsi non tanta participatione divinae essentiae quantam capiunt angeli.* Sic igitur per hujusmodi intelligibiles effectus Dei Deum clarius cognoscebat quam modo cognoscamus».

presence of God to those first men, I do not know why I should not there understand the person of God the Father[43].

Of more concern is Chauvet's logical leap from God's speech to human language. Surely how God communicates with Adam does not determine how Adam and Eve communicated. Yet Chauvet asserts «[after the fall] our first parents could no longer communicate with each other except through the skill (quite imperfect) of language», thereby implying that in the original beatitude (and therefore in God's fundamental plan for humanity) they conversed together via some kind of ray of illumination.

The Yahwist creation story has both Adam and Eve speaking before the fruit of the tree is consumed. The man gives names to all cattle, all birds of the sky, and all the wild beasts (Gen 2:20). When Augustine comments on this text, his version of it includes the line «according to what Adam called them, this is their name to this day»[44]. Elsewhere Augustine argues that Hebrew was the original language of humankind, surviving the Flood with Noah's family and taking its name from Heber his descendant[45]. Augustine would therefore consider the Hebrew names of the animals to be the names given them by Adam. It is remarkable that Chauvet does not advert to this clear example of pre-fall speech given that elsewhere he declares:

> [Language's] primary function lies elsewhere, in its unique capacity to place things at a distance by naming them, and thus representing them, thereby giving them speech. The result we have insistently said, is that the raw elements of the universe become a world of meaning in which human beings can dwell as subjects[46].

Another example of Adamic dialogue is when Yahweh brings the woman before the man who then says: «This one at last is bone of my bones and flesh of my flesh. She shall be called Woman, for she was taken from Man» (Gen 2:20). This involves a play on the sound of the

---

[43] AUGUSTINE, *De Trinitatis* II, 10: «Cujusmodi autem loquela tunc Deus exterioribus hominum auribus insonaret, maxime ad primum hominem loquens, et invenire difficile est, et non hoc isto sermone suscepimus. Verumtamen si solae voces et sonitus fiebant, quibus quaedam sensibilis praesentia Dei primis illis hominibus praeberetur, cur ibi personam Dei Patris non intelligam nescio». *PL* 42, 856-857.

[44] AUGUSTINE, *De Genesi contra Manichaeos* II, 1: «et secundum quod vocavit ea Adam, hoc est nomen eorum usque in hodiernum diem» *PL* 34,195.

[45] AUGUSTINE, *De Civitate Dei*, XVI, 11.

[46] L-M. CHAUVET, *The Sacraments*, 77.

Hebrew words *'iššā* (woman) and *'īš* (man). Augustine is well aware of this, ingeniously comparing it to the similarity between *virago* (a war-like or heroic woman) and *vir* (man)[47]. Furthermore, direct speech by Eve is part of the Genesis account in her dialogue with the serpent (Gen 3:1-5). All of this is *before* the Fall.

Given the above, on what basis does Chauvet conclude that «according to Augustine, language is a consequence of original sin»? The citation he gives in support is *De. Gen. contra Manich.*, II, 31. In that exact passage there is nothing relevant to the issue, but in the passage that immediately follows there is this text:

> For they made for themselves aprons from the leaves of the fig tree, but God made for them garments of skin. That is, having abandoned the face of truth, they sought the pleasure of lying, and *God changed their bodies into this mortal flesh in which deceitful hearts are hidden. For we should not believe that thoughts could be hidden in those heavenly bodies,* as they lie hidden in these bodies. Rather as some states of soul are apparent on the countenance, and especially in the eyes, so I think that in the clarity and simplicity of those heavenly bodies absolutely no states of the soul are hidden[48].

Augustine contrasts the «heavenly bodies» of before the Fall with «this mortal flesh». The latter enables human beings *to lie*. The heavenly bodies were far more expressive and revealing of the «states of the soul». Chauvet takes this as implying a direct soul-to-soul communication of truth that is replaced, in this mortal flesh, by the imperfect mediation of language. However, Augustine supports his argument by observing how some states of soul, of ordinary mortals, are apparent on the countenance. Anger would be one such. When lividly angry it is impossible to claim plausibly not to be upset. A hypothetical perfectly revealing body-language would not remove the need for spoken language, rather it would make *sincerity* totally evident. Augustine is not suggesting that there was no *spoken language* in Eden, he is claiming

---

[47] AUGUSTINE, *De Genesi contra Manichaeos* II, 18.

[48] AUGUSTINE, *De Genesi contra Manichaeos*, II, 32: «Ipsi enim sibi fecerunt praecinctoria de foliis fici, et Deus illis fecit tunicas pelliceas: id est, ipsi appetiverunt mentiendi libidinem relicta facie veritatis, et Deus corpora eorum in istam mortalitatem carnis mutavit, ubi latent corda mendacia. Neque enim in illis corporibus coelestibus sic latere posse cogitationes credendum est, quemadmodum in his corporibus latent: sed sicut nonnulli motus animorum apparent in vultu, et maxime in oculis, sic in illa perspicuitate ac simplicitate coelestium corporum omnes omnino motus animi latere non arbitror» *PL* 34, 21-213 (emphasis added).

there was no *falsehood* – Adam and Eve could not deceive each other. There was language in the Garden, and like everything else it is corrupted in the Fall. The distortion that language undergoes is that it now can convey lies as well as truth. A view of language which takes lying as an essential part of it – for example that of Derrida – might argue that Augustine allows for such language to come into existence only with the Fall. However, for Augustine himself, truth is what is fundamental to language.

Given the evidence of the Genesis story and Augustine's reading of it, noting that the direct illumination by God is a hypothesis and does not necessarily imply anything about human communication, to assert that Augustine and Aquinas presuppose «that human beings had been created without language»[49] is quite far-fetched. In seeking to distinguish his viewpoint from classical metaphysics, Chauvet has pushed Augustine and Aquinas into a position they are unlikely to have recognized as their own.

5. The Symbolic Order which Mediates Reality

Chauvet describes the world which human beings experience as the «symbolic order» and contrasts this with brute reality:

> This *symbolic order* designates the system of connections between the different elements and levels of a culture (economic, social, political, ideological – ethics, philosophy, religion ...), a system forming a coherent whole that allows the social group and individuals to orient themselves in space, find their place in time, and in general situate themselves in the world in a significant way[50].

What the translator has rendered as «connections» is «*rapports*» in the original[51]. It may be translated as «relations» which makes the similarity between Chauvet's symbolic order and Habermas's social world clearer[52]. Chauvet is referring to something close to Habermas's idea of «the totality of all interpersonal relations that are recognized by members as legitimate»[53].

---

[49] L-M. CHAUVET, *The Sacraments*, 5.
[50] L-M. CHAUVET, *Symbol and Sacrament*, 84-85 (emphasis his).
[51] L-M. CHAUVET, *Symbole et Sacrement*, 89.
[52] See Ch. II 6.1.4 above.
[53] J. HABERMAS, *The Theory of Communicative Action*, I, 52.

Chauvet distinguishes *sensation* and *perception* by giving the example of being hit on the head by a stone[54]. Humans and animals would experience an identical *sensation* of pain, but their *perception* of it is different. «What is perceived by the humans is not only physical reality that affects the senses but the «semiological layer» in which this event is embedded by the culture»[55]. The pain is sensed, but as soon as the stone is *named* it is perceived as an assault or an accident – it is given a *sign*ification, it is connected to a personal and cultural framework of meaning.

According to Chauvet it is not just the world that is socially constructed out of brute reality – so is the self:

> Just as children learn to build their connection to the real by building houses or machines with Legos or Meccanos, the symbolic order is *the mediation through which subjects build themselves while building the real into a «world»*, their familiar «world» where they can live[56].

Part of socialization into human society is to be formed in and into relationships. The child learns how to be son or daughter, sibling and family member. They rapidly identify where, and with whom, they belong. Children acquire a social location along with a physical one. They regularly get «put in their place». Their culture teaches them just *who* they are, they acquire their personal identity through the relationships they form, they see themselves mirrored in the eyes of others.

6. Chauvet's Use of Speech Act Theory

Chauvet, outlining the «performance dimension of the act of symbolization», declares:

> The act of symbolization, we have noted, carries out the essential vocation of language: to bring about an alliance where subjects may come into being and recognize themselves as such within their world. Now, this description corresponds well enough to what J.L. Austin calls *language acts*.[57]

The vagaries of translation turned Austin's *speech* acts into *language* acts, but the description offered suggests that Austin's ideas have also undergone something of a transformation. Austin used the term speech

---

[54] See L-M. CHAUVET, *Symbol and Sacrament*, 85.
[55] L-M. CHAUVET, *Symbol and Sacrament*, 85.
[56] L-M. CHAUVET, *Symbol and Sacrament*, 86 (emphasis his).
[57] L-M. CHAUVET, *Symbol and Sacrament*, 130 (emphasis his).

act as a catch-all for the various things that could be done by an utterance. He comes close to a definition with the phrase «what precise act it is that we are performing when we issue an utterance»[58]. It includes such actions as: stating, warning, ordering, promising, reprimanding, declaring, insulting, apologising, naming, welcoming, describing, identifying, and referring. Austin also declares that «the doctrine of the performative/constative distinction stands to the doctrine of locutionary illocutionary acts in the total speech act as the *special* theory to the *general* theory»[59]. Thus «speech act» refers to all that an utterance accomplishes, including locutionary, illocutionary and perlocutionary acts. The points of correspondence between this and bringing «about an alliance where subjects may come into being and recognize them as such in their world»[60] are not immediately obvious. Chauvet's treatment of some related concepts will show the development of Austin's ideas.

6.1 *Constative and Peformative*

Chauvet dedicates a section of his work (Chapter 4, II, 2 b) to presenting, Austin's distinction between *declarative* and *performative*. Unhappily, the translators have erred by rendering Chauvet's use of «*constatif*» as «declarative», perhaps unaware of Austin's neologism. Chauvet gives examples of constative statements («I wagered»), which describe an event, and performative utterances («I wager»), which constitute the performance itself. Chauvet defines a performative utterance as «an act really changing the position of the subjects by the very fact of the enunciation»[61]. In his example of making a bet, the change of position is to enter into an obligation with the interlocutor. Chauvet clearly means social relationship by «position». He goes on to declare:

Declaration and performance activate two different *functions* of language: the first is its declarative function; the second, its communicative or «allocutive». However, neither ever exists in a pure state; they always subsist in dialectical tension as the two poles of language. «It is a fact that performa-

---

[58] J.L. AUSTIN, «Performative Utterances», 232.
[59] J.L. AUSTIN, *How to Do Things with Words*, 148 (emphases his).
[60] L-M. CHAUVET, *Symbol and Sacrament*, 130.
[61] L-M. CHAUVET, *Symbol and Sacrament*, 131.

tive utterances always say something at the same time they do something»,
Austin remarks[62].

The translator has obscured the Austinian pairing of «constative and
performative» that open this quotation (and are clear in the French
text). Despite explicitly citing Austin in support, Chauvet is in flat dis-
agreement with him on the «two poles of language». Two pages after
the sentence quoted, Austin says:

> We have here not really two poles [performative and constative utterances],
> but rather an historical development. Now in certain cases, perhaps with
> mathematical formulas in physics books as examples of constatives, or with
> the issuing of simple executive orders or the giving of simple names, say,
> as examples of performatives, we approximate in real life to finding such
> things[63].

As we saw above[64], a major result for Austin was that speech is fundamentally performative and hence constative utterances are a special
class of performatives. Chauvet's two functions of language may therefore not be in such dialectical tension as he suggests. His first function
– the declarative function – is to convey information, to describe. His
second function, called «communicative or allocutive»[65], aligns with
the performative role of speech and therefore could be styled as the *relationship-affecting* function of language.

This interpretation of the allocutive function is supported by the example Chauvet gives:

> «I order you to close the door»: this statement presupposes the fact that
> there is a door and that it is open; but of course, as a language act, it «signi-

---

[62] L-M. CHAUVET, *Symbol and Sacrament*, 131; being the translation of *Symbole et
Sacrement*, 138: «Constatif et performatif mettent en œuvre deux *fonctions* différentes
du langage: le premier, sa fonction informative; la second, sa fonction communicative
ou allocutive. Pourtant, ils n'existent jamais à l'état totalement pur. Ils sont toujours
en tension dialectique comme deux pôles du langage. "C'est un fait que les énoncia-
tions performatives disent quelque chose en même temps qu'elles font quelque
chose", remarque Austin».

[63] J.L. AUSTIN, *How to Do Things with Words*, 146-147.

[64] See Ch. I 6.8 above.

[65] The word «allocutive» gave the translators difficulty because they have not
translated it but have put speech marks around it. Both English and French have the
word «allocution» and share the senses of «an exhortation by a general to his troops»
and «a formal address». In French, the word has an additional specialized linguistic
sense: «Communication entre un locuteur et un allocutaire; acte de parole d'un locuteur». *Le Robert*, « Allocution » 1, 266.

fies» to the other his or her subordination (real or simply desired), it puts the other in his or her place (as we say), it instates or reinstates, it creates or reinforces the authority of the speaker over the other[66].

The explicit performative contains information that could have been delivered in a constative utterance: «This is an open door». The performative verb is «to order». A command assumes or creates a relationship between the speaker and the hearer. The invoking of any relationship always affects that relationship – strengthening it by the exercise of it, or undermining it by engendering frustration[67].

Accepting Austin's assertion that performatives are primary, it would follow that Chauvet's «allocutive» function of language is prior to the declarative/informative/constative function, rather than being in dialectical tension with it. Logically, language is about relationship before it is about conveying descriptive information. Even something close to a purely constative utterance «This is red» involves the speaker being in some kind of relationship to the hearer (colour consultant, giver of information, one who states the obvious, driving instructor, helpful provider of an example).

Chauvet then connects his «allocutive» function to Austin's illocutionary dimension of language. He asserts that the illocutionary act – «the act effected *in* saying something»[68] designates an action that

> is strictly intra-linguistic, whose achieved expression is found in a class of performative verbs in the strict sense, such as «I promise you», «I bet you», «I commit myself to you», «I order you» ... : *the relation between the subjects* is not same after as it was before[69].

Following Austin, Chauvet distinguishes the illocution from the perlocution:

---

[66] L-M. CHAUVET, *Symbol and Sacrament*, 131.

[67] John Searle notes that institutional realities operate differently from physical realities: «as several social theorists have pointed out, institutions are not worn out by continued use, but each use of the institution is in a sense a renewal of that institution. Cars and shirts wear out as we use them but constant use renews and strengthens institutions such as marriage, property and universities. [...] each use of the institution is a renewed expression of the commitment of the users to the institution. Individual dollar bills wear out. But the institution of paper currency is reinforced by its continual use». J. SEARLE, *The Construction of Social Reality*, 57.

[68] L-M. CHAUVET, *Symbol and Sacrament*, 132.

[69] L-M. CHAUVET, *Symbol and Sacrament*, 132.

What the illocutionary carries out in the language act itself, the *perlocutionary* achieves as a *consequence* of the latter; for it designates the effect of the language act «on the feelings, the thoughts, the behavior of the audience or the speaker or still other persons»[70].

The speech act «I order you to close the door» can have the perlocutionary effect of the hearer closing the door, as a consequence of the illocutionary effect of their accepting the authority of the speaker.

Chauvet acknowledges that perlocutionary effects can be achieved by utterances that are apparently purely constative, and he gives as example Mary's statement at Cana, «They have no wine». (John 2:3) Why this constative functions, in context, as a performative is able to be shown using Grice's maxims for communication. According to Grice, to comply with the Cooperative Principle it must fulfil the maxim of Quantity (to be neither more nor less than is required) and of Relation (to be appropriate to the immediate needs at each stage of the transaction)[71] – therefore this is information that Mary considers Jesus needs to know. It can only be relevant if there is an implicature (Grice's term) that he ought do something about the situation. A significant aspect of context is the mother-son relationship between speaker and hearer. In his reply Jesus shows he understands this, challenging both the relevance («What is that to me?») and the relationship (in his use of the title «Woman»).

Chauvet adds to Austin's definitions by claiming that illocutionary effects are *intra*-linguistic, while perlocutionary ones are *extra*-linguistic. He extends his earlier example:

> «I order you to close the door» affects primarily either the intra-linguistic (the relation between the superior and the subordinate) or the extra-linguistic (the door is closed or not; or the sentence might engender a feeling of fear, irritation, or pleasure in the one hearing it)[72].

The sense that Chauvet is giving to the intra/extra linguistic distinction is not obvious from this example. The closure of the door is a physical action and clearly extra-linguistic. Irritation at being bossed around is an interior world phenomenon which, according to Chauvet, needs to be labelled linguistically to be known. Yet here, he classes feelings as

---

[70] L-M. CHAUVET, *Symbol and Sacrament*, 133 (emphasis his); J.L. AUSTIN, *How to Do Things with Words*, 101.

[71] H.P. GRICE, *Studies in the Way of Words*, 28.

[72] L-M. CHAUVET, *Symbol and Sacrament*, 133.

extra-linguistic. What *is* intra-linguistic for Chauvet is the relationship between superior and subordinate. In Habermas's terms this is a social world reality. It can be observed and commented on by others, it will affect the objective world behaviours of both parties, and a component of the relationship is the associated (internal world) attitude (e.g. subservience). It is not obvious why this effect is classed by Chauvet as *within* language – it seems as much a part of the linguistically mediated world the speaker and hearer live and move in as the closed door and the upset feelings.

In his division intra/extra Chauvet distinguishes relationships from external world events (the door being closed) and internal world states (feelings and attitudes). It may be paralleled to the class of reality Habermas termed the social world[73] – the totality of all legitimately regulated interpersonal relations[74]. Both Chauvet and Habermas associate Austin's illocutionary force with this aspect of reality.

> As Bourdieu and F. A. Isambert have stressed, the «illocutionary force» of this language is not to be sought in a «magic power of words» or some «verbal mana», but rather in *«the consensus that validates them»*. Thus, an «I promise» has value only as a pact between my partner, myself, and the collectivity which governs the conditions for the validity of promises or as a «relation between the properties of the discourse, the properties of the one who pronounces it, and the properties of the institution that authorizes one to pronounce it». The power of words in the illocutionary act, notably as a performative ritual manifestation, resides in the fact that they are not pronounced by an individual as an individual, but rather as the proxy of the group, as the *representative* of its «*symbolic capital*». Thus, this shows clearly what is going on in all language: a relation of places between subjects, a recognition, an identification, within a social and cultural world[75].

What Chauvet is taking from Bourdieu and Isambert[76] is in line with what Habermas established. Illocutions gain their force from the normative power of social relationships. A teacher's instruction to close the door normally has more illocutionary force that a classmate saying the same thing, because of the existing relationship of authority. The

---

[73] See Ch. II 6.1.4 above.

[74] J. HABERMAS, *The Theory of Communicative Action*, I, 52.

[75] L-M. CHAUVET, *Symbol and Sacrament*, 134 (emphases his).

[76] Pierre Bourdieu (1930-2002), author of *Ce que parler veut dire*, Paris 1982, and François-André Isambert are sociologists. Isambert has been president of the French Association of Religious Sociology and is the author of *Rite et Efficacité*, Paris 1979.

«Other» of society is involved in all performatives. Speaker and hearer can make a bet only if they both belong to a communicative community that has the conventions of betting, and the social reinforcements that promote and police this behaviour (e.g. social mechanisms – such as gossip – that penalize people who welsh on bets.) As Chauvet concludes, «this shows clearly what is going on in all language: a relation of places between subjects, a recognition, an identification, within a social and cultural world»[77]. When a teacher says «close the door» and a student obediently does so, not only is the relationship between those two individuals expressed and strengthened, but also the status (i.e. «place») of the teacher with respect to the class is enhanced. By a tiny increment this would eventually affect the status of teachers and students «in general» in that culture. Each conversation relies on and expresses the cultural background and, in doing so, reinforces or diminishes its values and norms.

6.2 *The Springs the Illocution Releases*

One of the authorities that Chauvet refers to above in support of his theory of symbolic efficaciousness is the sociologist Pierre Bourdieu. In doing so Chauvet does not address the criticisms that Bourdieu levels at Austin:

> This is the essence of the error which is expressed in its most accomplished form by Austin (and after him, Habermas) when he thinks that he has found in discourse itself – in the specifically linguistic substance of speech, as it were – the key to the efficacy of speech. By trying to understand the power of linguistic manifestations linguistically, by looking in language for the principle underlying the logic and effectiveness of the language of institution, one forgets that authority comes to language from outside, a fact concretely exemplified by the *skeptron* that, in Homer, is passed to the orator who is about to speak[78].

---

[77] L-M. CHAUVET, *Symbol and Sacrament*, 134.

[78] P. BOURDIEU, *Language and Symbolic Power*, 107; on 193, Bourdieu explains the *skeptron* (origin of our kingly sceptre) «In Homer this *skeptron* is the attribute of the king, of heralds, messengers, judges, and all persons who, whether of their own nature or because of a particular occasion, are invested with authority. The *skeptron* is passed to the orator before he begins his speech so that he may speak with authority». The *skeptron* is a «big stick» and, as Ulysses use of Agamemnon's staff in the *Iliad* shows, it also authorizes the holder to strike those who do not listen (*Iliad* 2:250 ff.).

Bourdieu sees distinguishing between language and the social use of language as a fundamental error. If one looks for the power of words within words, which is what Bourdieu claims Austin and Habermas were doing, then one will never find it. This ignores Austin's connection between illocutionary force and social conventions, and Habermas's analysis of the double structure of speech[79].

A key concept for Bourdieu is *habitus*. The term goes back to Aristotle, and Bourdieu uses it to describe those dispositions that incline persons to act and react in certain ways. They condition how people perceive and respond to the world. Social inculturation – largely early childhood experiences – ingrain these dispositions into the person so that they «literally mould the body and become second nature»[80]. Support for his assertion that cultures shape the body is provided by Ronald Grimes:

> Effective ritual knowledge lodges in the bone, in its very marrow. This metaphor first struck me with force while in a discussion with an archaeologist. He was explaining how certain values and social practices can be inferred from ancient bone matter. An archaeologist can deduce from bone composition that the men of a particular society consumed more protein than the women. On the basis of bone size and shape, it may also be evident that in some cultures women habitually carried heavier loads than men. Certain social practices are literally inscribed in the bones. Even though we imagine bone as private and deeply interior to the individual body, it is also socially formed[81].

The myriad of mechanisms in the process of being brought up, repeated injunctions like «Sit up straight!» and «Take your hands out of your pockets!» coupled with the example of parents and older siblings, create enduring effects at the level of habitus.

> The power of suggestion which is exerted through things and persons and which, instead of telling the child what he must do, tells him what he is, and thus leads him to become durably what he has to be, is the condition for the effectiveness of all kinds of symbolic power that will subsequently be able to operate on a habitus predisposed to respond to them[82].

---

[79] See Ch. II 6.4 above.
[80] P. BOURDIEU, *Language and Symbolic Power*, 12.
[81] R.L. GRIMES, *Deeply into the Bone*, 7.
[82] P. BOURDIEU, *Language and Symbolic Power*, 52.

Members of the upper classes are the recipients of a linguistically rich childhood. They tend to acquire a considerable share of what Bourdieu calls «linguistic capital»[83], which is not merely an extensive vocabulary but also the speech patterns and accent and unconscious confidence of the dominant social class. Socialisation ensures that members of other classes have the habitus to identify and to respond appropriately to those tones. Without reference to what is said, or the intention behind saying it, the upper class accent establishes a relation of domination.

Bourdieu criticizes Austin for using expressions like «ordinary language». Bourdieu points out that this blanket phrase covers a widely differentiated reality. Linguistic competence varies with age, education, social class, intellectual ability and place of origin. To idealize and pretend there is a completely homogeneous language community is what Bourdieu provocatively calls «the illusion of linguistic communism»[84]. As the example above shows, the linguistic playing field is not level; it is tilted in favour of the powers that be. Rather than the ideal he criticizes, Bourdieu envisages the world of language in terms of class struggle:

> Thus through the medium of the structure of the linguistic field, conceived as a system of specifically linguistic relations of power based on the unequal distribution of linguistic capital (or, to put it another way, of the chances of assimilating the objectified linguistic resources), the structure of the space of expressive styles reproduces in its own terms the structure of differences which objectively separate conditions of existence[85].

The structures of a society are reflected in the manifold shades of language use within it. For example coarse language is used by young poorly-educated males as a way of distinguishing themselves from the «prissy» speech of more highly-educated and better paid members of society. Authority figures use a different style of language from those under authority. This is simply one of the many symbols used to indicate and sustain the stratification of society.

According to Bourdieu the power of performative utterances to name ships, to close meetings, to warn, to dominate is not to be found inside the utterance but in the *habitus* inculcated into members of the society and the existing relationships of power and domination within that so-

---

[83] P. BOURDIEU, *Language and Symbolic Power*, 66.
[84] P. BOURDIEU, *Language and Symbolic Power*, 5.
[85] P. BOURDIEU, *Language and Symbolic Power*, 57.

ciety. He disagrees with Habermas's conclusion that illocutionary force «consists in the fact that it can move a speaker to rely on the speech-act typical commitments of the speaker»[86]. This is too conscious and reasonable for Bourdieu, he sees the force operating at a much more subliminal level, and relying on existing class structures.

Bourdieu is a classic Marxist using class-struggle as the interpretive key to all social realities. He misses the subtlety in Habermas's analysis of the origins of illocutionary force. Habermas does not present the force of an illocution as being a property of the utterance, rather he shows how speech acts draw on the power of social relationships and norms. Bourdieu identifies one aspect of socialization, class-distinction within language use, but there are many more legitimate social relationships than upper class domination over the workers. Parent-child, teacher-pupil, doctor-patient, peer group-member, husband-wife are all examples. Moreover, «habitus» is a label for a process that itself is achieved through communicative action rather than a separate mechanism in its own right. «Get your hands out of your pockets» is an utterance. If the utterance does not act in some way, how is the habitus established? Habermas would agree with Bourdieu that the power of language is not intrinsic in the words, but is about how society uses language.

6.3 Applying Speech Act Theory to Rituals

6.3.1 Rituals are Stagings of Illocutions

Austin had stressed that illocutionary acts involve the invoking of conventions[87]. Chauvet acknowledges the conventional nature of performatives and notes that «the paradigmatic examples of illocutionary acts are to be sought in the verbal or gestural language acts of *rituals*»[88]. Indeed, Austin's first examples of performatives (which were later to be restated as illocutionary acts) were the naming of a ship, taking marriage vows, and making a bet. As well as the utterances which were his focus, Austin drew attention to associated ritual actions: the

---

[86] J. HABERMAS, *Communication and the Evolution of Society*, 62.

[87] J.L. AUSTIN, *How to Do Things with Words*, 117: «We have said that many illocutionary acts invite by convention a response or a sequel»; and 119: «Strictly speaking, there cannot be an illocutionary act unless the means employed are conventional, and so the means for achieving it non-verbally must be conventional».

[88] L-M. CHAUVET, *Symbol and Sacrament*, 134 (emphasis his).

breaking of the champagne bottle on the stem of the vessel[89], the marriage ceremony[90], the handshake that seals the bet. Austin inferred from these examples that language is performative. Chauvet discerns another significant related implication: «Rituals are stagings which unfold the illocutionary-performative dimension of language»[91]. If Chauvet is correct, then *the force that provides ritual efficacy is the same illocutionary force whose basis has been identified in social relationships*. He explicitly adverts to this conclusion:

> At these different levels we are in the order of ritual (in the broad sense) and, even more obviously, in the order of the *«illocutionary which alone breaks the duality between saying and doing»* and brings about symbolically, on the sole basis of the statement, a transformation in the relations between the subjects, under the authority of the social Third (the law) to which they necessarily refer – and refer in an explicit manner in the great instituted rituals. «It is only within this framework that the performative takes on meaning. . . . It has all the characteristics of a rite, and its performance is exactly of the order of symbolic efficacy»[92].

The relationship-affecting power of speech is itself a form of ritual – illocutionary force relies on conventions. The relationship-affecting powers of ritual are *not* a separate, different phenomenon. Both speech and ritual are communicative acts that draw on the social Third – which is much more culture than law. Evoking the normative force of social relationships, both ritual and speech, through the same illocutionary force, change the way persons relate to each other and to objects in their world.

This connection between ritual action and performative utterances had been adverted to by Evans in the first published work that applied speech act theory to theology:

> Sometimes an institutional act can be performed not only verbally but non-verbally. I acknowledge status by bowing or saluting; I welcome by shaking hands; I bless by laying on of hands; I marry by mingling blood. Each action, like a performative utterance has a performative force[93].

---

[89] J.L. AUSTIN, *How to Do things with Words*, 5.

[90] J.L. AUSTIN, *How to Do things with Words*, 17.

[91] L-M. CHAUVET, *Symbol and Sacrament*, 134.

[92] L-M. CHAUVET, *Symbol and Sacrament*, 135; (emphasis his), his quotations are from F.A. ISAMBERT, *Rite et efficacité symbolique*, 94 and 99.

[93] D.D. EVANS, *The Logic of Self-Involvement*, 75.

He sums up these cases where the invoking of social conventions is done by an action instead of by words as: «In doing *p* which has the force of saying «*q*» I do *q*. (In shaking hands I welcome.)»[94] To welcome is an illocutionary act, it can be achieved by *either* an utterance *or* by the simple ritual of a handshake. So, for at least the cases where the ritual is an equivalent to an utterance, it is the same illocutionary effect which is achieved. Chauvet, who must have been aware of the work of Evans, makes no explicit reference to him[95].

Chauvet, Isambert and Evans make an identification between Austin's efficacy of speech acts and the efficacy of rites. The ability to bring about symbolically «a transformation in the relations between subjects» is what Chauvet means by symbolic efficacy. Chauvet gives examples from anthropology: a shaman assisting at a birth by singing a myth, a village transformed from its animosity by a ritual involving the extraction of a tooth, a healing ritual. He then concludes:

> These three examples show us the same thing: the ritual «acts on the real by acting on the representations of the real». If there is actually a physical healing – an extra-linguistic perlocutionary effect – it is *by the intermediary of a symbolic efficacy*, of the illocutionary order, that it is obtained. The ritual acts performatively: from the sole fact of its enunciation by an «authority» recognized as qualified to carry it out, it restores the health of the sick person through reestablishing his or her troubled relations with the members of the community and with the culture of the group[96].

In the healings described there were perlocutionary effects, but the fundamental change that the rituals sought to bring about was an «intra-linguistic» one. The authorized person with great drama, and considerable investment of time and effort, was aiming to change the sufferer's «social location» – from ostracized to included, from controversial to accepted. The shaman represented the group. The community and the individuals involved in the rituals accepted his authority. The changes he brought about in the social order were real enduring changes, and were what the rites aimed to achieve. The objective world consequences were the result of these real social world effects.

---

[94] D.D. EVANS, *The Logic of Self-Involvement*, 76.

[95] Chauvet makes considerable use of Jean Ladrière's *L'Articulation du Sens* which frequently quotes from and refers to Evans's *The Logic of Self-Involvement*. See Ch. III 6.4 below.

[96] L-M. CHAUVET, *Symbol and Sacrament*, 138-9 (emphasis his); citing P. BOURDIEU, *Ce que parler veut dire*, 124.

Following Isambert, Chauvet describes symbolic efficacy as a function «of the consensus created around the representatives on one hand, and of the symbolic connection between the representations and what is at issue, on the other»[97]. He goes on to assert that such efficacy cannot be identified with the scheme of cause and effect, and specifically rejects seeing it as a kind of psycho-somatic activity. Chauvet understands the intended relationship change to be a «symbolic effect» of a different order («intra-linguistic») from any secondary physical effects.

Thus symbolic efficacy involves the uses of symbols («the representations») and authorised ministers («the representatives») of the community consensus. The symbols are accepted as having a connection with the issue and the minister is understood as having the power to activate the symbols in this case.

6.3.2 The Illocution, the Conventions and the Social Other

Chauvet and Habermas agree that illocutionary force comes from the network of social relationships and norms. A person needs to be thoroughly inculturated into a society before they are acknowledged as able to appreciate and use these conventions. Children are not permitted to enter into a contract, because they are not mature enough to realize the full implications of what they are doing. A recent convert is not permitted to make profession in a religious order. Until neophytes have fully imbibed the culture of a community they are not trusted to operate in accord with its conventions. That trust will be extended sooner in small matters than it is in great.

When a performative ritual is invoked – a bet made, vows exchanged, a contract signed – then in addition to the two main parties involved there is always a third. That third is society – the social Other. It is the expectations and customs of society that establish the conventions of betting. The more serious the bet the more formalised it becomes. A trivial bet needs no witnesses other than the participants. A higher stakes bet is often done before an audience of mutual friends (representatives of the social Other whose good opinion both parties wish to retain). Sometimes a single person will be asked to take the role of the social Other. A bartender may be asked to hold the stakes and declare who is the winner.

---

[97] L-M. CHAUVET, *Symbol and Sacrament*, 139; F.A. ISAMBERT, *Rite et efficacité symbolique*, 83-85.

A meeting is an institutional reality – while the meeting is in session the participants are in a particular social place, a special relationship to the others. The chairperson of the meeting has the role of speaking «for the meeting» – he or she expresses the community consensus. When the chairperson says «I declare this meeting over», it is a performative utterance; the social place of everyone involved in the meeting changes. If any other participants said those same words, it would not be a happily accomplished performative because they are not authorised by the group to exercise this function.

Marriage vows must involve the social Other. You cannot marry in private. Witnesses must be present; the public has theoretic right of access. Moreover there is always a registrar, a celebrant, a ship's captain or a minister who takes on the role of the social Other in declaring that the conventions have been duly carried out. The rite by its very nature assigns different levels of authority to those roles. One dimension of the role of the priest in liturgy is to be *in persona ecclesiae*. He speaks and acts as the authorized representative of the entire communicative community of the Church. Liturgy is official *public* worship, and as such automatically includes a ministerial role. A private prayer group, for example gathering to recite the rosary, does not require a person in that role.

6.4 *Self-Implication*

As has been shown above, Chauvet makes direct explicit use of speech act theory in the material he draws from Austin. In addition there is another set of ideas Chauvet invokes which owes something to Austin's insights. This connection is obscure, because Chauvet does not mention a critical link – Donald D. Evans.

The above mentioned Evans was the first student of Austin to publish a book on speech act theory[98]. His 1963 work, *The Logic of Self-Involvement* was overshadowed by the posthumous publication of Austin's *How to Do Things with Words* (1962). In 2001, Richard Briggs commented «Evans's 1963 book is, one suspects, more footnoted than read»[99]. Briggs may have been unaware of the reception of Evans's work in the French-speaking world. The philosopher Jean Ladrière had

---

[98] See Ch. I 7.5.1 above. Evans worked for three Oxford terms under Austin and described him as «exacting, stimulating and kind».

[99] R.S. BRIGGS, «The Uses of Speech-Act Theory», 238.

done more than simply read Evans; he had based his major work on Evans's ideas. In his two volume *L'Articulation du Sens* (1984) he refers explicitly to Evans on 35 of the pages, making him Ladrière's most frequently cited author; Austin and Wittgenstein share second place, each with 27 references. Ladrière contrasts the «words of faith» with «scientific discourse», asserting that each is a different language game. The words of faith are not understood or evaluated appropriately if they are judged by the rules of the wrong game. In his introduction Ladrière describes the texts that he is to address:

> Thereafter come three texts which concern the different interpretations of certain «language games». The first concerns the interpretation of scientific language proposed by neo-positivism and its attitude towards metaphysical propositions. It questions the adequacy of the image of science thus proposed. The second constitutes a presentation of the work of Mr. Donald Evans dedicated to the language of self-implication. The theory of religious language elaborated by Evans on the basis of Austin opens extremely interesting perspectives for the interpretation of the language of faith[100].

Evans had asked the question: «In what ways is language self-involving? That is, what are the logical connections between a man's utterances and his practical commitments, attitudes and feelings?»[101] He gave examples of utterances that he considered self-implicative:

> (1a) In saying, «I submit to your authority», I *commit* myself to various future *actions*.
> (1b) In saying, «Thank you for your kindness», I *imply* that I have an *attitude* of gratitude.
> (2) In saying, «Glorious», I *express* my *feelings*.
> (3) In saying, «I look on life as a game», I *express* my *attitude* towards life[102].

---

[100] J. LADRIÈRE, *L'Articulation du Sens*, I, 13-14; «Viennent ensuite trois textes qui concernent des interprétations diverses de certains "jeux de langage". Le premier concerne l'interprétation du langage scientifique proposée par le néo-positivisme et l'attitude adoptée par lui à l'égard des propositions métaphysiques. Il s'interroge sur l'adéquation de l'image de la science ainsi proposée. Le second constitue une présentation de l'ouvrage de M. Donald Evans consacré au langage de l'auto-implication. La théorie du langage religieux élaborée par M. Evans sur la base des idées de Austin ouvre des perspectives extrêmement intéressantes pour l'interprétation du langage de la foi».

[101] D.D. EVANS, *The Logic of Self-Involvement*, 11.

[102] D.D. EVANS, *The Logic of Self-Involvement*, 12 (emphases his).

All the utterances given involve self-revelation. An implication (sincere or insincere) is being made about the subjective world of the speaker. His example (1a) is of particular interest, it reveals an internal commitment which is orientation towards future acts. It also involves a shift in the social place of the speaker. In publicly declaring that he submits to another's authority, the speaker is performatively affecting his social location and the relationships he is involved in.

Evans applied his theory to the Christian use of language about God as Creator. Ladrière picks up these ideas and applies them across a wide spectrum of religious language, particularly in the area of liturgy. He claims that the language of faith is characterized by self-implication – which is not to say that self-implication is *only* found in this language game.

> The real task consists in characterising the semantic articulation specific to the language of faith. In the mean time, here it is necessary to recall that it is a completely different thing from a speculative language because it is at the same time a language of truth, a language of engagement. The intervention of the clause «I believe» indicates the presence of a process which is a recognition but, at the same time, a position which shows, only insofar as it ratifies, where the will in consequence, intervenes conjointly with the apperception of what shows itself. It is only by the mediation of the engagement, which it expresses, that the language of faith reveals the reality which it evokes[103].

Engagement is crucial in the language of faith. Making a faith statement automatically involves taking a position. The utterer of such a statement shows where he or she stands; part of their inner world is revealed. Declaring «I believe *x*» is a different class of statement from «I know *x*», because there is an element of choice in the former. The will is involved. Ladrière finds in Evans's work a philosophical tool – the self-implicating nature of some performative utterances – for analyzing this act of personal engagement.

---

[103] J. LADRIÈRE, *L'Articulation du Sens*, I, 237; «Le véritable travail consiste à caractériser l'articulation sémantique propre au langage de la foi. Or ici il faut se rappeler qu'il est tout autre chose qu'un langage spéculatif, parce qu'il est, en même temps qu'un langage de vérité, un langage d'engagement. L'intervention de la clause "je crois" indique la présence d'une démarche qui est une reconnaissance mais en même temps une position, qui ne fait voir que dans la mesure où elle ratifie, où la volonté, par conséquent, intervient conjointement avec l'aperception de ce qui se donne. C'est seulement par la médiation de l'engagement qu'il exprime que le langage de la foi fait apparaître la réalité qu'il évoque».

When Chauvet is looking for a philosophical and theological context to explain sacramental efficacy, he finds Ladrière's conception fits well with his approach. Like him, Ladrière is drawing on Wittgenstein and Austin. Following Ladrière, Chauvet expounds the view that the language of faith, through its self-implicating illocutionary effect, «*renders present* the realities of which it speaks»[104]. Declaring that «Jesus is Lord» is an act of submission to the lordship of Christ, a self-implicating act. In making the utterance the reality is not only affirmed *but also made present*. Lordship exists where there are subjects acknowledging it. Lordship is relational; it is a social reality. Chauvet clarifies:

> It is not faith which makes God Father or Jesus Lord. But the identity of God as Father or of Jesus as Christ and Lord would be reduced to nothing if none named it by confessing it and thus acknowledging themselves *at the same time* as children of God and disciples of Jesus[105].

Lordship necessarily implies discipleship; without anyone acknowledging their subject status the term «Lord» would be hollow of meaning. Chauvet goes further, perhaps too far, in asserting the same for historical events: «Christ cannot be alive if none claim to belong to him: his resurrection is inseparable from the witness people – first, those who form the Church – give of him»[106]. In this Chauvet moves from an institutional fact, which requires community support to be true, to an objective fact, which does not. Money is not valuable if no-one believes it, but iron is still magnetic.

6.4.1 Self-Implication in Liturgy

Chauvet characterises liturgy as a pragmatic discipline. It does not set out to explain theology, to codify ethical norms, or to transmit information. Its basic mode is not constative, but rather illocutionary. Liturgy sets out to *do* something:

> It is always the establishment of a new relation of place between the community and God which it seeks to accomplish and purports to achieve [...] [I]t aims not at discursively thematizing the criteria of the community but *at constituting* it by enunciating them. The «we» used in the present tense,

---

[104] L-M. CHAUVET, *Symbol and Sacrament*, 428; (emphasis his) quoting J. LADRIÈRE, *L'Articulation du Sens*, I, 232.
[105] L-M. CHAUVET, *Symbol and Sacrament*, 428; (emphasis his).
[106] L-M. CHAUVET, *Symbol and Sacrament*, 428.

characteristic of Christian liturgical prayer, even when it is said by a priest (who then acts as the bearer of the «symbolic capital» of the ecclesial assembly), truly functions as the illocutionary agent of the community[107].

Christians come together, not to share information, but *to make themselves into the Church*. In gathering for public worship they declare themselves to be Church and to make that relational reality present[108]. In their daily lives they will be many things – family member, worker, citizen, commuter – but when, on the day that they *make* into the Lord's day by treating it as holy, they gather and say «Amen» to prayers like «we praise you, we bless you, we thank you», they are constituting themselves as members of the Church in faith, and, in so doing they are making the Church present on that day, in that place, in their very bodies.

Liturgical language lifts the self-implication of the language of faith to a new level. The «I» of an individual believer becomes the «we» of the Church community and that «we» is more than an aggregation of I-statements by those present. The «we» is we-the-entire-Church. In joining in with we-statements, if only through the concluding «Amen», the participants identify themselves with, and *render present*, something greater than themselves. In that concrete historical situation, in those particular persons the Church of Christ is to be found, present and *active*.

The work of Donald Evans, largely unnoticed for thirty years, was received and developed by Ladrière, thereby influencing readers of French theology. The taking up of this current of thought by Chauvet is now enabling it to make a new and wider impact on the academic and religious world.

6.4.2 Self-Implication in Sacraments

In this notion of self-implication Chauvet finds the key to what is distinctive about sacraments. In his work he considers three elements of Christian existence – scripture, sacrament and ethics[109]. God and grace are at work in all three aspects of the Christian life, all three areas require faith and sanctify the believer. Chauvet's question becomes

---

[107] See L-M. CHAUVET, *Symbol and Sacrament*, 429.

[108] See L-M. CHAUVET, *The Sacraments*, 34: «The primary locus of the Church is the celebrating assembly».

[109] See Ch. III 2.2 above.

«How shall we understand the originality of Sacrament with regard to Scripture and Ethics?»[110] His answer, in which he shifts from talking of broadly defined «Sacrament» to «the sacraments», is that «the original-ity of the sacraments comes only from *the Church* which radically in-volves itself and puts into play its whole identity»[111].

Religious ritual is about communication with God, the gods, or the spirits, and, according to Chauvet, it does this «*through the simple fact that it is carried out according to the social norms of legitimacy and va-lidity*»[112]. It has to be legitimate and proper to belong truly to the group. The sacraments, as symbolic actions, are not aiming «like technological action, at bringing about a transformation of the world, but at working upon the subjects in their relations with God and with one another»[113]. Given Chauvet's definition of «world», affecting subjects and their re-lations would seem to be a transformation of the world, thereby col-lapsing the distinction he wishes to make. The distinction can be recov-ered by using Habermas's categories. Technological action affects the *objective* world while symbolic action affects the *social* world.

Chauvet selects four components of rituality that «clearly show the *concrete modality* according to which the Church sees itself as radically involved in the sacraments»[114].
– The Symbolic Rupture (Heterotopy)
– Symbolic Programming and Reiteration
– A Symbolic Economy of Sparseness
– An Indexical Symbolism
As can be seen, the concept of *symbolism* is central to his understanding of the process of religious ritual.

1. *The Symbolic Rupture* (Heterotopy = other place): Place, time, ob-jects and language of religious ritual are always set apart from the ordi-nary and the profane. This apartness can be carried either too far, or not far enough. Going beyond the upper bound of heterotopy to where the sacred becomes merely foreign, perhaps out of a cultic conservatism, is what Chauvet calls «hieratism». To avoid this, the symbolism of the ritual must be in «contact with the expressed or latent cultural values of

---

[110] L-M. CHAUVET, *Symbol and Sacrament*, 321.
[111] L-M. CHAUVET, *Symbol and Sacrament*, 322 (emphasis his).
[112] L-M. CHAUVET, *Symbol and Sacrament*, 325 (emphasis his).
[113] L-M. CHAUVET, *Symbol and Sacrament*, 329.
[114] L-M. CHAUVET, *Symbol and Sacrament*, 330 (emphasis his).

the group»[115]. Going below the lower bound of heterotopy leads to a trivialization of ritual. Appropriately negotiating between these extremes ought to create «*an empty space with regard to the immediate and utilitarian*»[116] where participants can experience the «otherness» of God and paradoxically be thereby assisted with their particular needs and wants.

> The liturgy thus creates a *symbolic disconnection* which places the assembly in another, non-utilitarian world. As a consequence, there is symbolically room for God; there is a space of gratuitousness where God can come[117].

For Chauvet it is important that all of this is not fully under the control of the participants. They freely choose to enter into ritual and to take part, but they do not master it; they let it master them. Religious ritual, in its otherness, mediates the otherness of God. The participants, through experience of the sacred, the timeless, and the solemn, for a period step out of their ordinary lives and wait upon God. This *liminal* role of ritual has been of particular interest to the sociologist Victor Turner[118].

2. *Symbolic Programming and Reiteration*: Ritual is never invented, it is always «received from a tradition». It is regularly repeated and is understood as having been done since the founding days of the group. Religious rites evoke the origin, the historical founder:

> They function according to the symbolism of *metonymic elision*. They thereby form the prime reservoir of the collective memory of the group. In an anamnestic re-immersing of the group into the primordial time where it was born, ritual erects a barrier against the forces of death which relentlessly threaten to destroy the group's identity and the significance of the world[119].

Metonymy is when the symbol is used as if it were the symbolized. An elision is an omission or a running together. Ritual slices away the time

---

[115] L-M. CHAUVET, *Symbol and Sacrament*, 332.

[116] L-M. CHAUVET, *Symbol and Sacrament*, 337 (emphasis his).

[117] L-M. CHAUVET, *The Sacraments*, 106 (emphasis his).

[118] Chauvet makes several references to Turner's work with the Ndembu people, all in relation to the 1972 French translation of his 1968 work *The Drums of Affliction: A Study of Religious Processes among the Ndembu of Zambia*, Oxford 1968. Turner focuses on liminality in *The Forest of Symbols*, New York 1967, and *The Ritual Process: Structure and Anti-Structure*, London 1969.

[119] L-M. CHAUVET, *Symbol and Sacrament*, 340 (emphasis his).

between the foundation – the *illo tempore* (in those times – the privileged time of the origins[120]) – and today. The acceptance of it as coming from the founder enables it to bridge between his time and the present. The group is re-experiencing its foundation in the action of the liturgy.

Mircea Eliade claims that liturgy achieves this connection with the time of the beginnings by way of a mythic «Great Time» – the time of the heroes and gods – which ritual accesses and which is outside the usual passage of events:

> Christianity, *by the very fact that it is a religion*, has had to preserve at least one mythic attitude – the attitude towards liturgical time; that is, the rejection of profane time and the periodical recovery of the Great Time, *illud tempus* of «the beginnings». [...] For the Christian, Jesus dies and resurrects before him *hic et nunc*[121].

The otherness and repetition of ritual mean that it does not feel like part of everyday life. It carries a flavour of archaism and of eternity. It was like this last year and it will be like this ten years hence. This is important to the ritual participants and a partial explanation of the depth of negative feelings that are evoked when change is introduced.

By self-implication those celebrating in the present bond with the founding community *and* the generations between then and now. Chauvet connects the *apostolicity* of the Church with this metonymic elision[122].

> The programming of the Christian liturgy expresses that it is indeed Jesus of Nazareth who is the Lord. We take bread and wine *as* he did and *because* he did, and we repeat the words he said. [...] In this eminently symbolic act, we *let* Jesus of Nazareth be our Lord[123].

In repeating the ritual the Church is obeying its founder, recreating its origins, keeping continuity with its past, and affirming its identity.

The regular repetition of ritual increases its illocutionary force and enables it to penetrate the human person in a way that a «one-off» event cannot. Something that happens regularly through the stages of life has a defining effect on worldview and structures of personality. The repetition means that ritual is reassuringly predictable unlike the random

---

[120] See L-M. CHAUVET, *Symbol and Sacrament*, 340.

[121] M. ELIADE, *Myths, Dreams, and Mysteries*, 30-31 (emphasis his).

[122] See L-M. CHAUVET, *Symbol and Sacrament*, 342.

[123] L-M. CHAUVET, *The Sacraments*, 109.

events of life. Given the Vatican II call for «full and active participation»[124], it is refreshing to see how affirmatively Chauvet presents this aspect of the human response to ritual:

> It must leave to the rite its function of *protection* in relation to the personal involvement of the participants: it is one of the positive effects of ritual programming to allow the participants to be carried by this programming, that is, not to be constrained all the time to actively carry or support the rite by a participation at the level of the consciousness and intelligence[125].

The space created by the ritual is not only one of freedom for God, it also one of freedom for the participant. They choose their level of involvement.

3. *A Symbolic Economy of Sparseness*: Rituals are economical formalizations of behaviour that use «small means» to symbolize great things. The symbol is naturally much less than the reality it reveals – a basket of vegetables standing in for the entire harvest (but it should be a basket of the *best* examples). Theologically interpreted this is part of the «*eschatological not yet*» of the life of the Church. The sparseness of the symbols (Chauvet warns against letting this slip from sparse into insignificant) is a necessary part of mediation. It is an aspect of absence accepted to find presence[126].

4. *An Indexical Symbolism*: Rite is digital rather than analogue. It is not a sliding scale; it involves quantum leaps: «One cannot be half-baptized, no more than one can make a half-Communion»[127]. The ritual establishes boundaries or limits about the group. It integrates members into the group, and it assigns different roles. In ritual the group recognizes itself as present. It is under this last category that Chauvet reprises his earlier treatment of self-implication. Liturgy must be recognized by the participants as being legitimate and valid – without this «*social consensus*»[128] the rite will not be happily accomplished, it will lack illocutionary force. He quotes Bourdieu and Isambert:

---

124 *SC* 14 «In the restoration and promotion of the sacred liturgy the full and active participation by all the people is the aim to be considered before all else, for it is the primary and indispensable source from which the faithful are to derive the true Christian spirit. Therefore, in all their apostolic activity, pastors of souls should energetically set about achieving it through the requisite pedagogy».

125 L-M. CHAUVET, *The Sacraments*, 108.

126 See L-M. CHAUVET, *The Sacraments*, 102.

127 L-M. CHAUVET, *Symbol and Sacrament*, 347.

128 L-M. CHAUVET, *Symbol and Sacrament*, 348.

This is why «the belief of all, which exists before the ritual, is the condition for the efficacy of the ritual» and «the first efficacy of the rite» is to «cause people to believe in the rite itself»[129].

Liturgy assumes and encourages faith in God, but also in the efficacious action of the Church in liturgy. If a particular expression of a sacramental ritual departs from what is recognizable to the participants as being truly that of the Church then they will suspend the faith which is required for them to feel part of what is going on.

Chauvet's four components of rituality, and his theological applications of them, reflect a sociological and anthropological viewpoint. He is approaching the sacraments «from below». He does not see the seven sacraments as a unique reality utterly divorced from any other human activity. He treats them as rituals with features akin to other human rites. Characteristics like the ability to function «*ex opere operato*», being seen as instituted by Christ, apostolicity, and the limited freedoms of the Church with respect to the sacraments, all have analogies with rituality in general.

7. Symbolic Exchange

Adult members of a society know themselves and their culture and its relationships well, though often at an unconscious level. In knowing their social place they will also be familiar with socially approved mechanisms for enhancing their status. Chauvet assigns particular significance to one of these mechanisms – symbolic exchange.

7.1 *In Traditional Societies*

Chauvet draws on the work of the comparative anthropologist Marcel Mauss[130] on forms and functions of exchange in traditional societies. Mauss studied material from Polynesia, Melanesia, and North West America, and then compared it with literary and linguistic evidence of ancient societies in India and Europe. He found elaborate systems of

---

[129] L-M. CHAUVET, *Symbol and Sacrament*, 348-349, citing P. BOURDIEU, *Ce que parler veut dire*, 133, and F.A. ISAMBERT, «Réforme liturgique et analyses sociologiques», 84.

[130] Marcel Mauss (1872-1950), French sociologist and anthropologist. His work on gift transactions is «Essai sur le don, forme archaïque de l'échange», *Sociologie et anthropologie*, 143-279; first published 1925.

exchange functioning in societies which had no money or barter economy, even between entirely self-sufficient tribal groups:

> In the systems of the past we do not find simple exchange of goods, wealth and produce through markets established among individuals. For it is groups, and not individuals, which carry on exchange, make contracts, and are bound by obligations; the persons represented in the contracts are moral persons – clans, tribes, and families; the groups, or the chiefs as intermediaries for the groups, confront and oppose each other. Further, what they exchange is not exclusively goods and wealth, real and personal property, and things of economic value. They exchange rather courtesies, entertainments, ritual, military assistance, women, children, dances, and feasts; and fairs in which the market is but one element and the circulation of wealth but one part of a wide and enduring contract. Finally, although the prestations and counter-prestations take place under a voluntary guise they are in essence strictly obligatory, and their sanction is private or open warfare[131].

What characterized these prestations[132] was that, even though the object of exchange was offered as if it were a free gift, it was understood by all parties involved that it was not disinterested. The givers acquired status through lavish giving. The recipient has to accept the «gift» and in so doing takes on the obligation to provide a return-gift at some future time. Moreover the return-gift should be of greater value than the gift received. In North American tribes, with the custom of *potlatch* (an extravagant and ceremonial feast at which a chief gives away presents or destroys them to enhance his status), Mauss asserts «the potlatch must be returned with interest like all other gifts. The interest is generally between 30 and 100 percent a year»[133].

This kind of exchange system is quite distinct from money-based market transactions between individuals. Such a commercial transaction involves the exchange of goods or services for money with the assumption that once value has been received and full payment made then there are no more obligations on either vendor or purchaser. The satisfied customer may well return in future but is not under any obligation to do so. The prestations of traditional societies are very different. Mauss explains it thus:

---

[131] M. MAUSS, *The Gift*, 3.
[132] «Prestation» is a term from anthropology that, according to the OED signifies «a gift, payment, or service that fulfills some traditional function in a society».
[133] M. MAUSS, *The Gift*, 40.

Tamati Ranaipiri, one of Mr. Elsdon Best's most useful informants, gives quite by chance the key to the whole problem. «I shall tell you about *hau*. *Hau* is not the wind. Not at all. Suppose you have some particular object, *taonga*, and you give it to me; you give it to me without a price. We do not bargain over it. Now I give this thing to a third person who after a time decides to give me something in repayment for it (*utu*), and he makes me a present of something (*taonga*). Now this *taonga* I received from him is the spirit (*hau*) of the *taonga* I received from you and which I passed on to him. The *taonga* which I receive on account of the *taonga* that came from you, I must return to you. It would not be right on my part to keep these *taonga* whether they were desirable or not. I must give them to you since they are the *hau* of the *taonga* which you gave me. If I were to keep this second *taonga* for myself I might become ill or even die. Such is *hau*, the *hau* of personal property, the *hau* of the *taonga*, the *hau* of the forest. Enough on that subject»[134].

Tamati, a New Zealand Maori of the 1800s, was trying to explain the spirit (*hau*)[135] of the forest, and in the process described how the spirit of a gift controlled the exchange process. Gifts, even stone ones, are *not* inanimate in his understanding – they have an *animus*, a *spiritus*, a *hau*[136]. This spirit in the gift does not lose its link with the original owner. It impels the recipient to make a return-gift. Yet, by introducing a third person and a different valuable item (*taonga*), Tamati makes it clear that this spirit is not a magical property of that particular gift. It can return to the originator by means of a different return-gift «the product of the *hau* of the *taonga*». There are various ancient Maori proverbs which assert that *taonga* can destroy the person who receives them if he does not make an appropriate return-gift[137].

---

[134] M. MAUSS, *The Gift*, 8-9, incorporating a citation from E. BEST, «Forest-Lore» in *Transactions of the New Zealand Institute*, I, 431 and 439.

[135] P.M. RYAN, *The Reed Dictionary of Modern Maori*, (1995) 46, gives «*hau*, wind, atmosphere, famous, fraction remainder (maths), soul, essence», whereas H.W. WILLIAMS, *A Dictionary of the Maori Language*, (1844) 47, has «*hau*, return present by way of acknowledgement for a present received».

[136] See M. MAUSS, *The Gift*, 90, where he recounts the Maori myth of Te Kanava which tells how spirits took the shadows of the *pounamu* (greenstone, a form of jade) displayed in their honour.

[137] G. GREY, *Ko Nga Whakapepeha*, (1857) 112-113, gives the legend of Tokoahu who wandered widely receiving *taonga* but never making return-gifts. Eventually a frustrated giver cried «*Nau ra e te taonga. E kai ra koe i au*». (Come, come oh my valuables, destroy this fellow for me.) Tokoahu died of the effects of this curse. Anyone who is avaricious risks having applied to them the proverb «*Nga waewae*

The information from Tamati is key for Mauss because here he discerns the underlying principle for this system of exchange that predates ordinary trade and barter. In this primeval system, major life-events call for communal celebration. These celebrations normatively involve everyone – those who come bring a blessing gift; anyone omitted can curse the event. The exchanges between rival groups are one step away from warfare. Maori welcome visitors with a *haka* which is a *war* dance. The challenge ritually asks the question: «Do you come to celebrate or to fight?» Opting for celebration does not remove the element of conflict, because the exchanges themselves are a type of conflict for status and honour. The giver of prestations gains status and honour and puts the recipients under the obligation to make future return-gifts. The *mana* of a tribe – and Mauss considers that «wealth» is one of the best translations of that word – is based on how much they are owed by their surrounding tribes. The notion of credit existed long before the money economy. Prestations are given in the expectation of greater future returns. In such cultures, sacrifices are understood as prestations given either to the gods or the dead. A gift made to the gods will certainly be repaid with interest through good fortune, abundant crops and the like. To give to all your relatives and not to the departed would lead them to feel excluded and therefore likely to inflict a curse.

According to Mauss this dynamic of relating to other groups through symbolic exchanges characterised by obligatory generosity, the compulsion to receive the gifts, and the necessity of making a greater return-gift, was to be found in ancient societies throughout the world. He points to European myths and legends that indicate the prior existence of the same value system – the bad fairy that is not invited to the christening, and «the theme of the fateful gift, the present or possession that turns to poison, is fundamental in Germanic folklore. The Rhine Gold is fatal to the man who wins it, the Cup of Hagen is disastrous to the hero who drinks of it»[138].

This system of prestations was universal and may be the origin of commercial trade. In some cultures the two existed side-by-side, the celebration, with gifts given by the chiefs, accompanied and contrasted by a market in which commoners haggled over price. That the exchanges involved the gifting of women suggests that the biological im-

---

haororere o Tokoahu, kei tua, kei tua». (The wandering legs of Tokoahu, which were here, there and everywhere.)

[138] M. MAUSS, *The Gift*, 62.

perative to exogamy is a factor. Mauss asserts that the motives for these exchanges were more social than utilitarian. They expressed and brought about relationships within and between communities. The gift transactions are not disinterested. The coin used to pay for them is the intangible one of social position and influence. The one who gives freely receives honour and prestige in return. In traditional societies these are not an inconsiderable reward.

Chauvet's summary of Mauss's idea of prestation exchanges omits any mention of the sanction of warfare and downplays the elements of conflict. He emphasises their paradoxical nature and the importance of relationship.

> There is much evidence that these «free» exchanges are «obligatory», that this «generosity» is «mandatory», that this «liberality» pushed to the extreme of not wanting even to seem to desire a gift in return is really quite «interested». But «their notion of "interest" is only a rough analogue to the interest that drives us». It has to do first with the desire *to be recognized as a subject*, not to lose face, not to fall from one's social rank, and consequently to compete for prestige[139].

Chauvet sees in this pattern of gift–reception–return-gift a logic of relationship that can be applied to how God relates to humanity. He emphasises the liberality – the «lack of counting» – in the gift given, how it must be received appropriately and how the dynamism of the exchange compels a return-gift. He stresses that such gifts must be prodigal, because they symbolize the giver. They both establish and express the relationship between giver and recipient. The ideal outcome is a kind of mutual munificence.

7.2 *In Contemporary Western Society*

Chauvet claims that the system of gift exchange which exists in traditional societies is still a component of all human exchanges throughout the world. Western thinking is dominated by commercial metaphors but it is this system of symbolic exchanges which «*allows us to live as subjects and structures all our relations in what they contain of the authentically human*»[140]. Chauvet goes on to outline four «logics» of value:
1. *Utilitarian* value – a car is valuable as a rapid means of transport.

---

[139] L-M. CHAUVET, *Symbol and Sacrament*, 102 (emphasis his), citing M. MAUSS, *Sociologie et anthropologie*, 201 and 271.
[140] L-M. CHAUVET, *Symbol and Sacrament*, 103 (emphasis his).

2. *Exchange* value – a car is worth a particular dollar amount in economic terms.
3. *Sign* value – a car is a sign of social standing, has a certain social cachet.
4. *Symbolic* value – which cuts right across the first three. What is exchanged, for example a lock of hair, may have *no* utilitarian value, *no* exchange value and *little* sign value. The object exchanged has only symbolic value, what it symbolizes is precisely the relationship it expresses. «*The true objects being exchanged are the subjects themselves*»[141].

Chauvet makes a significant connection between ritual and speech acts by linking symbolic exchanges with language transactions: «What is transpiring in symbolic exchange is of the same order as what is transpiring in language [...] In both cases, it is a matter of a reversible recognition of each other as fully a *subject*»[142]. Thus, sending a greeting card is making an assertion about «who I am for you and who you are for me»[143] and exactly the same dynamic underlies a *spoken* greeting. Illocutionary force capable of affecting relationships is at work in symbolic exchanges.

Chauvet contrasts *business* exchange and *symbolic* exchange. Business exchange is based on sign value, the third of his values, which subsumes the utilitarian and exchange values[144]. Businesses set prices according to socially perceived desire for the services or commodity on offer. This is contrasted with the «non-value» of symbolic exchange. Chauvet asserts that business exchange and symbolic exchange are «thus to be understood as *two poles*, the tension between them being constitutive of every human society. But these two poles in dialectical tension belong to *two different levels* of exchange»[145]. His first metaphor suggests a continuum between two equal opposing forces, with every exchange having elements of both, being located somewhere on the globe connecting the poles. His second metaphor does not readily fit with the first. Different levels can move in different directions without tension. As with Chauvet's suggestion that constative and performative are in dialectical tension, an alternative possibility would be to

---

141 L-M. CHAUVET, *Symbol and Sacrament,* 106 (emphasis his).
142 L-M. CHAUVET, *Symbol and Sacrament,* 106-107 (emphasis his).
143 L-M. CHAUVET, *Symbol and Sacrament,* 107.
144 See L-M. CHAUVET, *Symbol and Sacrament,* 104.
145 L-M. CHAUVET, *Symbol and Sacrament,* 106 (emphases his).

assert the primacy of the symbolic. Given the connection of symbolic exchange with illocutionary force this would be more consistent with Austin's insights.

Taking symbolic exchange as primary implies every business exchange, no matter how alienating, is a recognition of the existence of another subject. There may not be much of a relationship with a check-out operator in a supermarket, but taking money for goods can be seen as a symbolic exchange as well as a business one. The operator speaks to the buyer, minimally announcing the total price, and this involves acknowledging there is some*one* who can comprehend what is being said and who will pay. This is difficult to recognize in Chauvet's lyrical description of symbolic exchange:

> *It is subjects who exchange themselves* through the object; who exchange, *under the agency of the Other*, their *lack-in-being* and thus come before each other in the middle of their absence deepened radically as otherness because of their exchange[146].

When a symbol is exchanged – and *a sentence is a symbol* – then a process is set in motion of gift–reception–return-gift. If the exchange is happily completed then the giver has declared «this is who I am for you and who you are for me»[147]. This has been received, endorsed or modified and responded to with «this is who you are for me and who I am for you». With the interchange of personal pronouns there is always a consciousness of being before the «them» of the social Other. The giver and recipient are asserting the legitimacy of the relationship between them – it belongs to the type of which «they» approve.

Chauvet's motivation for his extensive treatment of symbolic exchange is revealed when he gives this quasi-definition: «The sacraments are the ecclesial mediations of the exchange between humanity and God»[148]. Given that he understands sacraments in that fashion, this assertion makes the connection to speech act theory:

> Since the original space of symbolic exchange is language, more exactly communication by speech between subjects, we are led to understand the efficacy of the sacraments in relation to the *efficacy of speech*[149].

---

[146] L-M. CHAUVET, *Symbol and Sacrament*, 107 (emphases his).
[147] L-M. CHAUVET, *Symbol and Sacrament*, 107.
[148] L-M. CHAUVET, *The Sacraments*, 123.
[149] L-M. CHAUVET, *The Sacraments*, 123.

Chauvet has embarked on his enterprise of sketching the symbolic order so as to establish a framework for the understanding of the efficacy of speech, of symbolic exchange and ultimately of sacraments. This order is a framework for understanding the world. It is one in which the key transactions are not one-way cause-and-effect relationships but the bi-directional relations of symbolic exchange.

8. The Act of Symbolization

In an extended example[150] about two secret agents in Second World War France independently given a recognition key – the two halves of an irregularly torn five-dollar bill[151] – Chauvet distinguishes six features that characterize the act of symbolization:

1. the act of joining,
2. distinction,
3. relation to the other,
4. non-value,
5. revealing,
6. agency.

1. The symbol is intended to *do* something. It is not merely conceptual; its goal is practical. The spies have the notes so that they can *be joined* and their counterpart can be securely *identified*.
2. «We symbolize only distinct elements»[152]. The two halves of the note are necessarily distinct, but so too is the spy distinct from the torn note. There is a distinction, a distance, between the symbol and the symbolized.

---

[150] L-M. CHAUVET, *Symbol and Sacrament*, 128-130. Chauvet revisits this in *The Sacraments*, 83-85, where he identifies four «moments» in the act of symbolization: «(a) Symbolization is an act and not an idea. [...] (b) Each of the elements of a symbol is relevant *only in its relation to the other*. [...] (c) The monetary *value* of the bill *does not matter* [...] (d) The act of symbolization is *simultaneously a "revealer" and an "agent."*»

[151] The French text has it as «un billet de banque découpé en puzzle» (L-M. CHAUVET, *Symbole et Sacrement*, 136) and speaks of it not mattering whether it is of 50 or 100 francs. Translating this into US currency ignores the fact that the story is set in *occupied France*. A 50 franc note was a commonplace there, whilst a $5 bill could have aroused fatal suspicions. A symbol is deeply embedded in its cultural context. Therefore, translation into another culture is hazardous.

[152] L-M. CHAUVET, *Symbol and Sacrament*, 129.

3. The recognition symbols have value *only in relation* to other. If one is destroyed the other is useless. The spies have to keep possession of the notes – the relation between the note and them – so as to make the identification possible. Taken in isolation the symbol is meaningless.
4. The currency denomination is unimportant – a piece of newspaper would do as well. The symbol draws its value from the symbolized, not from itself. Its worth is not intrinsic.
5. The symbol *reveals* identity – when the two half-notes are reunited the spies recognize their partner. The symbol does not hide the symbolized but shows it forth.
6. Through revealing, the symbol is an *agent*. The moment of joining the notes bonds the spies in an alliance. Before meeting, the pieces reassured them they were not alone. They signalled «there is another like me out there». Symbols *do* things.

Chauvet's critique of metaphysics is preparation for his theory of how a symbol works:

> We can truthfully speak here of the *efficacy* of the symbol, and efficacy which touches reality itself. The whole question is to know *what reality* we are speaking about. If we represent it on a model of a *hyperkeimenon*, a «substrate», an ontological «substance», then such an efficacy becomes unthinkable. But as we have explained we are not dealing with such an unprocessed reality. It is a reality always already culturally processed, speaking only because spoken, that happens to us; and this reality is *the most real*[153].

It is not some underlying level of reality that makes symbols effective. There is no secret magic contained within them. Their effectiveness is *given* to them. They are powerful only when embedded in the matrix of a culture. Symbols do not stand isolated; they are always part of a web-work of interrelated symbols and associations. A magnet attracts iron filings through a field of electromagnetic force. A masterpiece like Michelangelo's *Pietà* attracts people through the myriad interconnec-tions of culture – books, films, sermons, photographs, tee-shirts, art his-torians, and trinket sellers all collude to assure people that *this* is a «must-see». The *Pietà* is a cultural icon, a symbol, and like all symbols it draws on *other* symbols. It evokes images of motherhood – the beau-tiful young mother with her son in her lap. It also calls up images of

---

[153] L-M. CHAUVET, *Symbol and Sacrament*, 130 (emphases his).

death – alluding to the horror of the crucifixion by the showing of its aftermath. Somehow it brings beauty, birth, death and grief together in the perception of many viewers, and, in contemplating it, their views of those realities are subtly changed. Since, in Chauvet's terms, human beings do not experience the real-as-it-is-in-itself, but the world-as-it-is-for-them, to change a person's view is to change their world.

> Such is without a doubt one of the major functions of the symbol: it allows all persons to situate themselves as subject in their relation with other subjects or with the worlds of these other subjects (with the meaning we have previously given to the term world) or with their own worlds. An instance of this would be the evocation of one's childhood world[154].

While accepting Chauvet's point that symbols affect relationships and social location, it is noteworthy how many significances the word «world» has in his writings. He uses «world» frequently, both in its common sense referring to external reality, and «with the meaning we have previously given» – a subject's interpretation of external reality, and the shared social space, humanly constructed, in which subjects inter-relate. This is one area where the distinctions incorporated into Habermas's three worlds of discourse would benefit Chauvet's theorizing.

9. The Corporality and Particularity of Sacraments

The believer who participates in liturgy does so in a very corporeal fashion. They are physically present, they adopt various postures, make particular ritual gestures, and touch objects and people in ways that the rite dictates. In eucharist the host is tasted and eaten. As Chauvet points out «faith cannot be lived in any other way, including what is most spiritual in it, than *in the mediation of the body*»[155]. This is self-implication in the most concrete of fashions; the embodied self is involved. Watching the celebration of a mass on television may be uplifting, but it is *not* participation in the liturgy. Liturgy is not celebrated alone. The believer gathers with a community, which has certain members and particular presiders, in a physical location which is within a diocese which has a bishop (who is *named* in every eucharist). The Church has a particularity, a history, a concrete presence in the world. The Roman Catholic Church has a defined set of members, and a

---

[154] L-M. CHAUVET, *The Sacraments*, 73.
[155] L-M. CHAUVET, *The Sacraments*, xii.

documented history. It is *not* an ahistorical reality. Catholic liturgy does not link the participants to some platonic ideal of the Christian community – it incorporates them into the real community – defects and all. Even the communion of saints, which connects to symbolic programming and reiteration as discussed above (we celebrate as they did), connects believers to real saints from particular countries, times and cultural contexts.

Just as the place of the liturgy is the particular body of the believer, so that believer finds their place (social, cultural, state of life, role in worship) in the particular body of the Church. The eternal is mediated in temporal corporality.

10. «Vatican II» Model of Sacraments

Chauvet asserts that, in the period prior to the second Vatican Council, sacraments were understood as «channels, or even very narrow ducts»[156].

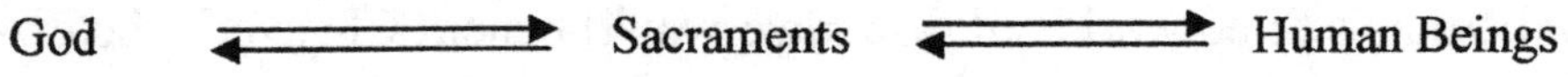

God   ⇄   Sacraments   ⇄   Human Beings

Figure 24: Chauvet's "Diagram 1"

In this vision, salvation was perceived as available only through the sacraments, with the Reign of God and the Church being understood as coterminous. Chauvet interprets the Council as replacing that model with this triangular scheme:[157]

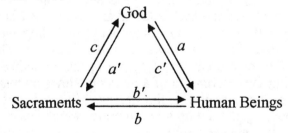

Figure 25: Chauvet's "Diagram 2"

---

[156] L-M. CHAUVET, *Symbol and Sacrament*, 410.
[157] The diagram is a translation of that found in the French text, *Symbole et Sacrement*, 425. The one on page 415 of the English text lacks the letters and has two of the arrows transposed.

The Council texts were not illustrated. This diagram is a summary and interpretation by Chauvet. It refers to several theological teachings, in which Chauvet distinguishes two distinct «cycles» at work. He asserts strongly that the two only operate together, but for the sake of clarity, here they are separated:

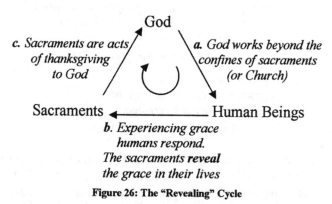

Figure 26: The "Revealing" Cycle

The first part of the outer cycle (a.) corresponds with Council teachings such as «[The Church] knows that man is constantly worked upon by God's Spirit»[158] and:

> Those who, through no fault of their own, do not know the Gospel of Christ or his Church, but who nevertheless seek God with a sincere heart, and, moved by grace, try in their actions to do his will as they know it through the dictates of their conscience – those too may achieve eternal salvation[159].

The third part of this cycle is incontestable – the very name of the sacrament of the Eucharist reveals it as an act of thanksgiving, and this element is present to a greater or lesser extent in the other sacraments.

Part (b.) however, is an emphasis that comes from Chauvet rather than from the fathers of the Council. They do say that sacraments «express faith»[160] but that is not the same as «reveal the grace in their

---

[158] GS 41.

[159] LG 16.

[160] SC 59 «The purpose of the sacraments is to sanctify men, to build up the Body of Christ, and, finally, to give worship to God. Because they are signs they also instruct. They not only presuppose faith, but by words and objects they also nourish, strengthen, and express it. That is why they are called "sacraments of faith". They do, indeed, confer grace but, in addition, the very act of celebrating them most effectively

lives». Conciliar teaching is far clearer on sacraments conferring grace, part of the other cycle of Chauvet's model.

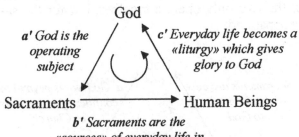

Figure 27: The "Operating" Cycle

The inner cycle (a', b', c') which runs the other way, picks up the traditional teaching, affirmed throughout the liturgy, that God is at work in the sacraments and they provide resources for daily life. They sanctify and lead human beings to glorify God.

For Chauvet, these two cycles are *not* separable. Both must operate simultaneously – sacraments operate by revealing and reveal by operating. Chauvet's aim is «to open up a path that will allow us to think of the sacraments simultaneously as both "revealers" and "operators"»[161]. He has prepared for this with the example of the two spies with the torn halves of the note[162]. Joining the parts of the five-dollar bill *causes* the alliance, but it does so by *revealing* that they are already allies. To open this path of understanding, which he reminds us, is only one approach and not *per impossibile* a resolution of the mystery of the sacraments, Chauvet lists some of his stepping stones:

> In understanding the sacraments as «effective symbolic expression», we are obviously in direct continuity with what we have said about language and symbol throughout the first part of this book. We base ourselves especially on the concept of «expression» and on the notions of the «illocutionary», the «performative» and the «symbolic efficacy of rites». [...] If the rites of traditional religions aim at a verifiable empirical efficacy (for example,

---

disposes the faithful to receive this grace to their profit, to worship God duly, and to practice charity». See also *SC* 33.

[161] L-M. CHAUVET, *Symbol and Sacrament*, 416.

[162] See Ch. III 8 above.

healing), they obtain it through the intermediary of a symbolic efficacy, that is, through setting up a new relation between subjects or between subjects and their socio-cultural «world» or both. Now, the end of Christian rites is of another order, beyond the realm of value, one designated by the term «grace»[163].

Underpinning Chauvet's sacramental understanding is his concept of the always-already of language, its role in mediating reality, and the power of language to do things. This is the same power that he sees at work in rites, a power that finds its basis in relationships within society. It involves a causality that depends on a sign being received and understood. This leads Chauvet to say:

> The sacraments are revealers (insofar as they are operators) which make symbolically visible what identifies as Christian human existence anterior to them; that consequently they manifest the «already-there» of grace in the experience of faith; that they therefore have an expressive function of response to what God has done, and of gratitude for what God has done[164].

Christians are never without grace. The Holy Spirit is constantly at work in the lives of every human person. «The Spirit *prepares* men and goes out to them with his grace, in order to draw them to Christ»[165]. So when people come to receive a sacrament, that will show and celebrate the fact that God has been at work in their lives.

In the Gospel account of the encounter between Jesus and a woman «who had a bad name in the town» in the house of Simon the Pharisee (Luke 7:36-50), Jesus declares: «I tell you that her sins, her many sins, must have been forgiven her, or she would not have shown such great love», and then he says to her «Your sins are forgiven» (7:47-8). Jesus both forgives the woman her sins *and* declares that they must already have been forgiven. Her action in coming to him and showing her love for him revealed her as forgiven. She was already restored to a life-giving relationship with God when she entered Simon's house; indeed it was that which motivated her coming – she was acting out of gratitude. However, in showing her love for the Lord she was also strengthening that relationship. The celebrating of the rapport had a positive effect on that same bond. Arriving in a graced state, the encounter with Jesus was still an occasion of grace for her. Given the social nature of

---

[163] L-M. CHAUVET, *Symbol and Sacrament*, 425.
[164] L-M. CHAUVET, *Symbol and Sacrament*, 431.
[165] *CCC* §737.

sin and forgiveness, the public declaration by Jesus would also affect her name in the town, and thereby redeem her social standing. His declaration is a performative utterance changing her social place.

When he goes on to speak of the sacraments as operators «(insofar as they are revealers)», Chauvet makes it clear that the rites set out to bring about what they express. He warns of the dangers implicit in translating liturgical language into theological language: «No more than an illocutionary act can be changed to a declaration, can religious language, especially ritual language, be rendered into theoretical language»[166]. Moreover, Chauvet declares:

> What happens here is not of the physical, moral, or metaphysical but of the symbolic order. This kind of symbolism, we have said, is the most «real». [...] Clearly the whole problem here lies in the manner in which one thinks of *reality*: it is not of the order of subsistent entities, but of the order of the on-going transformation of subjects into believers[167].

Sacraments operate on human beings and their relationships with God and to each other. Becoming a child of God in baptism does not mean a physical change to the DNA, even less that the baptized becomes a «godling». The change that takes place is *social*, not *physical*. The community of the Church accepts the sibling status of the baptized and encourages him or her to live accordingly. The faithful believe that God both initiates and accepts this change of status. Saint Paul five times uses the metaphor of adoption for what takes place in baptism[168]. Adoption is most clearly a social reality.

10.1 *Penance – a good fit to Chauvet's model*

Chauvet takes seriously Prosper of Aquitaine's dictum *lex orandi, lex credendi*[169] and bases his theology of the sacrament of penance on an analysis of the rite. He identifies four important realities – the Church and the three key elements of his model of Christian existence:

1. *The Church*: As with every sacrament, penance is «an event of the Church: it is within the ecclesial character shown by the linguistic "we"»[170]. It takes place «*in the Church*» as the introduction to the rite

---

[166] L-M. CHAUVET, *Symbol and Sacrament*, 437.
[167] L-M. CHAUVET, *Symbol and Sacrament*, 438.
[168] Rom 8:15, 8:23, 9:4 , Eph 1:5, Gal 4:5.
[169] *Epistle* 217. His precise words were: «*legem credendi lex statuat supplicandi*».
[170] L-M. CHAUVET, *Symbol and Sacrament*, 431.

makes clear: «the Church, having sinners in its midst, is at the same time holy and in need of cleansing, and so is unceasingly intent on repentance and reform»[171]. Moreover, it involves the other members of the Church who are all affected when any member sins. «Penance always therefore entails reconciliation with our brethren and sisters who remain harmed by our sins»[172]. According to Chauvet, this ecclesial dimension reveals that «the grace of forgiveness received by sinners in their most personal acts of repentance is not reducible to a purely individual matter: it is mediated by the Church»[173] – which is what the recent liturgical reforms of the rite of penance have demonstrated in the communal forms of the celebration of the sacrament.

2. «*Word*» (reading, homily, examination of conscience): There is a dimension of intellectual contemplation and understanding in the sacrament. The scriptures are read that the penitent might see their life in the light of the gospel. Chauvet strikingly asserts:

> The Church does not profess its belief in sin, but in the forgiveness of sin – so much so that none discover themselves to be sinners unless they discover themselves to be *pardoned sinners*[174].

Grace has already been at work in the lives of those who come to be reconciled. In acknowledging their sinfulness the penitents also see the evidence of God at work in their lives. His action precedes and overflows the sacrament.

3. «*Sacrament*»: With respect to the central part of the rite, Chauvet draws attention to a further three points:
- it is *ecclesial* – «the whole Church, as a priestly people ... intercedes for [sinners]»[175];
- it is *personal* – the individual avows their sin, an expression of their subjective world;
- it is *ministerial* – the performative announcement of absolution is made by the priest «acting as the servant of the Church's action, as the bearer of the assembly's "symbolic capital" [...] as an authorized representative of the Church and in God's name»[176].

---

[171] *The Rites* I, 527, §3.
[172] *The Rites* I, 528, §5.
[173] L-M. CHAUVET, *Symbol and Sacrament*, 432.
[174] L-M. CHAUVET, *Symbol and Sacrament*, 433.
[175] *The Rites* I, 531, §8.
[176] L-M. CHAUVET, *Symbol and Sacrament*, 435.

4. «*Thanksgiving and Ethical Practice*» which conclude the celebration are called for as a return-gift. «The sacrament comes into its truth only when we become what we have celebrated and received»[177]. The reconciliation must be both expressed and lived out – in praise of God and in ethical praxis.

10.2 *Eucharist – a challenge for Chauvet's model*

Penance fits Chauvet's model well. The sacrament of reconciliation is all about changing a relationship. It is eminently social. Baptism, which Chauvet describes as one of «the two paradigmatic sacraments» is also well suited to his model. As with Penance there is a central performative utterance («I baptize you» and «I absolve you»), where it is clear that the *object* of the utterance is an individual human person whom the rite is acting upon. Their «place» changes from candidate to Christian, from penitent to reconciled. However, the other «paradigmatic» sacrament provides some difficulties for Chauvet's approach.

In Eucharist the central performative utterances are in the words of institution: «This is my body [...] This is my blood [...] Do this in memory of me». The utterances are addressed to the congregation but the *objects* referred to are the bread and the wine. What changes in the celebration of the eucharist is not a relationship but the elements themselves. The bread and wine become the body and blood, humanity and divinity of Jesus Christ. The scriptures, the liturgy and the teachings of the Church all agree in affirming that what is bread and wine as the eucharist commences becomes something quite different. This is not a change in name, or a change in function, it is a change at the level of being. The classic teaching is that given by the Council of Trent:

If anyone denies that in the sacrament of the most holy Eucharist the body and blood together with the soul and divinity, of our Lord Jesus Christ and, therefore the whole Christ is truly, really and substantially contained, but says that he is in it only as in a sign or figure or by his power, *anathema sit*[178].

The real presence of Christ in the consecrated elements is not presented in the tradition as a subjective phenomenon, but as objective reality. Chauvet responds by drawing attention to the fact that «presence» is a relational reality. Being present is less about location in space than it is

---

[177] L-M. CHAUVET, *Symbol and Sacrament*, 435.
[178] Council of Trent (1551) DzH 1651; ND 1526.

about who is being related with. «Present to someone» is the basis of presence for Chauvet:

> In the symbolic order, presence and absence are not two complete realities that would be dialectically inseparable, a little like two sides of a piece of paper – they do not form two countable entities. They are not bivalent but form one ambivalent reality [...] *It is the very concept of «presence»* – in what it contains that is essentially symbolic and human at the philosophical level [...][179]

Moreover, in Chauvet's «symbolic order» the deepest level of reality is not *esse* (being) but *ad-esse* (being for)[180]. He recalls Heidegger's treatment of what constitutes a pitcher and the conclusion that «the "thingness" of the pitcher does not reside at all in the matter that makes it up, but in the emptiness it holds». «It is of the pitcher's essence to be shaped for this possibility of pouring out»[181]. Objects as well as people can have a socially defined «place» – and that place can be changed by ritual, as for example the consecration of vessels for liturgical use.

Bread is meant to be shared. The reality of bread is every bit as symbolic as it is biological. Bread and wine are very different from apples and water, because they are «the work of human hands». They were invented, named, and defined by their human use. They have a social location that is part of their reality – bread as the dietary staple and wine with its overtones of feasting and the sacred. In the symbolic order what is *real* is the socially constructed world, not brute facts. What is perceived is more *sign*ificant than the sensation.

Chauvet resists any reduction of the eucharist to merely the words of institution and the elements. He sees the Eucharistic presence of the Lord as one part of the dynamic interplay of the Church making itself present to the Christ as Christ makes himself present to the Church.

> «Christ is here», we continually say throughout the liturgy. [...] He is here, not like a «thing», but in the gift of his life and his coming-into-presence. The *adesse* of a presence is of a different order from the simple presence of a mere thing. The concept of «coming-into-presence» precisely marks the absence with which every presence is constitutively crossed out: nothing is

---

[179] L-M. CHAUVET, *Symbol and Sacrament*, 404.
[180] See L-M. CHAUVET, *Symbol and Sacrament*, 393.
[181] L-M. CHAUVET, *Symbol and Sacrament*, 395.

nearer to us than the other in its very otherness [...] nothing is more present to us than what in principle escapes us[182].

As the people gather in his name, Christ is becoming present to them. They are greeted by the priest with the words «The Lord be with you». These words both acknowledge and invoke the reality of which they speak, as does the response of the congregation. The Lord Jesus is petitioned for mercy in the penitential rite – acknowledged as present and acting. The Word of God is acclaimed and listened to when the scriptures are read. The congregation stands in honour of the good news of Jesus Christ. Like the torn five-dollar note of the secret agents, the communion host is an unfulfilled symbol until, in the very act of joining, it reveals the greater reality. The *Church gathered* is the other half of the eucharistic symbol.

> «Be what you see and receive what you are»; we have pointed out how much this symbolic language of Augustine, which demands that Christians give Christ, through their ethical practice this body of humanity implied by their reception of his Eucharistic body, brings us closest to the mystery. It is indeed the risen *Christ* himself who is received in Communion; but he is received for what he *is*, that is, *gift* from God's very self, only when he is joined to his ecclesial body. The symbol requires the radical distinction of the two, but it also requires their indissoluble intrinsic relation. Is not the *res* («ultimate effect») of the Eucharist the *Christus totus*, Head *and* members[183]?

Even when received there is an incompleteness to the sacrament until it is lived out in ethical practice.

Despite the beauty and profundity of his theologizing about the social place of bread and wine, and the relational reality of Christ's presence, Chauvet does not affirm what the scriptures, the tradition and the liturgy teaches; that Christians eat the body of the Lord and drink his blood. The eucharist transforms not mere perception but absolute reality. Chauvet's philosophy is phenomenological and the question arises as to whether it has the «*genuinely metaphysical* range, capable, that is, of transcending empirical data in order to attain to something absolute, ultimate and foundational in its search for truth»[184].

---

[182] L.-M. CHAUVET, *Symbol and Sacrament*, 404.
[183] L.-M. CHAUVET, *Symbol and Sacrament*, 407 (emphases his).
[184] *FR* 83.

The suggestion that Chauvet's approach struggles to express the objectivity of the eucharist does not imply that it has nothing to offer. Pope John Paul II called for philosophy of a metaphysical range, but as the philosopher Karol Wojtyla wrote:

> With all the phenomenological analyses in the realm of the assumed subject (pure consciousness) now at our disposal, we can no longer go on treating the human being exclusively as an objective being, but we must also somehow treat the human being as a subject in the dimension in which the specifically human subjectivity of the human being is determined by consciousness[185].

Wojtyla argues that classic scholasticism has been reductive of the human being to an object in the world and that there is a need to attend to «subjectivity [...] a kind of synonym for the irreducible in the human being»[186]. Chauvet addresses precisely this issue, beginning from the subject and viewing the world as evoked by that subject.

Phenomenological and linguistic approaches may struggle to express completely the Church's faith with respect to the Eucharistic presence of the Lord, but they are suited to addressing the subjectively understood reality of the believer; what it means to *have* faith.

11. Conclusion

Louis-Marie Chauvet succeeds in bringing speech act theory to bear on the issue of sacramental efficacy. He abandons traditional categories used to explain the operation of the sacraments. He goes to some lengths to justify his break with tradition and, as has been shown above, even overstates the differences between the traditional view and his own. For the power of symbols and performative utterance to be appreciated, an appropriate worldview is required. In his treatment of the «symbolic order» and the necessary mediation of language Chauvet has provided such a view. He makes the crucial connection between speech acts and rites, asserting that rituals are stagings of illocutions – settings that enhance the performative power of the utterances contained within them. Drawing on Bourdieu, Chauvet finds the source of illocutionary force to be in the consensus of the community involved. He draws out the significance of the role of the minister as the authorized representative of this community consensus, the bearer of the «social capital».

---

185 K. WOJTYLA, «Subjectivity and the Irreducible», 210.
186 K. WOJTYLA, «Subjectivity and the Irreducible», 211.

From anthropology Chauvet presents the significance of symbolic exchange, the role that central symbols can play in a rite. He shows how the object can stand for the subject who gives it, how it can call forth a return-gift, how the social relationships thereby expressed are affected and give power and value to that symbol. He made a further significant connection in making it clear that utterances are symbolic exchanges. In his analysis of liturgy in terms of self-implication and the way the language of faith makes present the realities of which it speaks, Chauvet has picked up a development of speech act theory which was neglected by writers in English.

All these elements and more are brought together against the backdrop of his symbolic order in his models of the structure of Christian existence and sacraments as operators-revealers. Louis-Marie Chauvet provides precisely what he claimed to offer – *«une relecture sacramentelle de l'existence chrétienne»*[187].

---

[187] The subtitle of Chauvet's work is translated as «a sacramental reinterpretation of Christian existence». It carries overtones such as «a re-reading in a sacramental key of Christian existence».

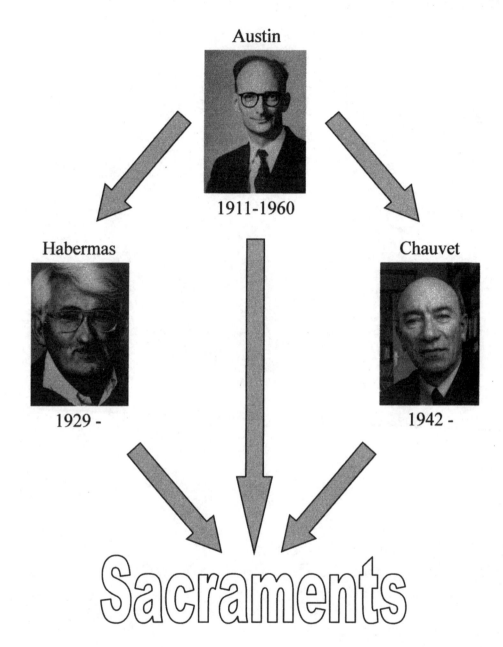

Austin

1911-1960

Habermas

1929 -

Chauvet

1942 -

Sacraments

CHAPTER IV

Sacraments within a Catholic Lifeworld

1. Introduction

The three preceding chapters of this thesis present an exposition of
the ideas of Austin, Habermas and Chauvet. Both Habermas and Chauvet incorporate the ideas of Austin, but worked independently of each
other. Only Chauvet wrote about sacramental theology. This chapter
applies the ideas of all three authors to that field, so as to use speech act
theory to analyse what happens in ritual sacraments along the lines established by Chauvet, by drawing on Habermas's development of Austin. The seven sacraments are being considered as communicative actions within a Roman Catholic culture. This model is applied to
problems from the tradition and tested against dogmatic definitions.

2. The Roman Catholic Communicative Community

A contention of this thesis is that the Roman Catholic Church can be
considered as a single communicative community, which is to say that
it has a shared set of beliefs, a symbolic system, distinctive rituals,
authority structures and a clear membership system. A challenge to
seeing it as a communicative community is that it includes many
different language groups and operates within different cultures.
Communicative communities normally share the *same* language and
culture. However, the Roman Catholic Church has been singularly
successful in maintaining cohesion and its characteristic identity while
also implanting itself in different countries. *Liturgiam Authenticam*
asserts:

> Characteristic of the orations of the Roman liturgical tradition as well as of the other Catholic Rites is a coherent system of words and patterns of speech, consecrated by the books of Sacred Scripture and by ecclesial tradition, especially the writings of the Fathers of the Church[1].

Liturgy both forms and expresses the community which takes part in it. Roman Catholics throughout the world share this «coherent system of words and patterns of speech», identify the Pope as their leader, treat the same texts as sacred and authoritative, use some of the same gestures, honour the same saints, follow the one liturgical calendar, enjoy an artistic heritage, and consider each other as belonging to the same group.

This assertion of the Roman Catholic Church as a single communicative community carries the corollary that there is a «Catholic Lifeworld» – a backdrop of worldview knowledge and «more or less diffuse, always unproblematic, background convictions»[2] that Catholics share and which makes communication among them possible. For example, all Catholics accept the Scriptures as sacred, but many have only a vague idea as to what is in them. Nonetheless, an argument presented as «biblical» is accepted as carrying weight.

Habermas established that «the lifeworld also stores the interpretive work of preceding generations»[3] which is of interest to systematic theology as a mechanism of the tradition within Christianity. The Church is constituted in response to God's self-revelation, and «in His gracious goodness, God has seen to it that what He had revealed for the salvation of all nations would abide perpetually in its full integrity and be handed on to all generations»[4]. Part of the mission of the Church is the continual interpretation and conservation of what God has revealed. Revelation is for the salvation of all nations, and thus it aims to put all into a right relation with God. Previous generations have lived their response to this revelation and taught their children by their example. This orthopraxis and orthodoxy have formed the lifeworld of the Roman Catholic Church.

> Now what was handed on by the Apostles includes everything which contributes toward the holiness of life and increase in faith of the People of

---

[1] CONGREGATION FOR DIVINE WORSHIP, *Liturgiam Authenticam* 49.

[2] J. HABERMAS, *The Theory of Communicative Action, I*, 170.

[3] J. HABERMAS, *The Theory of Communicative Action, I*, 70.

[4] *DV* 7.

God; and hands on to all generations all that she herself is, all that she believes[5].

The «Deposit of Faith» is not merely the content of theological libraries; it is the life and faith experience of the Church: «all that she herself is». It is communicated by all the mechanisms that communicate culture: preaching, teaching, conversation, bed-time stories, songs, hymns, jokes, writing, scriptures, art, witness, ritual, festal times and seasons. The teachings about *sensus fidelium*[6] make sense against a dynamic understanding of tradition and a Catholic lifeworld which provides the knowledge, attitudes and life-skills of living the faith.

2.1 *Personality Structures*

Different societies call for different skills and attitudes from their members. A capitalist society needs entrepreneurs, and «the patterns of motivation and the stock of competencies for speech and action»[7] which are required to produce them are embedded in the lifeworld of such a society. Scrooge McDuck is a sympathetic character in American children's comic books unlike his Victorian namesake. American culture presents children with inventors and industrialists as heroes and role models. Creativity, independence of spirit, desire for riches, and the ability to overcome setbacks, are valued and promoted. Communicative communities socialize juvenile members towards roles that will contribute to the success and survival of the community.

One of the first challenges that the early Church encountered was persecution. Borrowing liberally from surrounding cultures, whilst also drawing on the Old Testament and the example and teaching of Jesus, the Church assembled the supports to a personality structure that it needed to endure and to witness to the very crowds who persecuted it. The role the times called for was that of *martyr* – one who would face torture and death rather than reject faith in Christ Jesus. The *acta* of the martyrs were collected, sermons were preached about great martyrs, stories written («The passion of St. *X*». the literary genre developed), artworks designed, songs sung, and feast days celebrated. The oldest

---

[5] *DV* 8.
[6] For example *LG* 12.
[7] H. BAXTER, «System and Lifeworld», 47.

liturgical calendars are lists of the anniversaries of martyrs[8]. Celebrating the memory of martyrs is a way to prepare others to follow in their steps. The motivations and competencies for martyrdom are still maintained in the Catholic lifeworld and continue to be expressed by heroic individuals.

In other, less dramatic, ways the lifeworld of Catholic Church holds components of personality structures that serve the mission of the Church. Celibacy, commitment, and attitudes of service are valued. The Pope, bishops and parish priests are held in esteem. Catholic liturgy teaches people how to pray. It offers scripture passages for reflection, guides meditation, gives times of silence, and provides exemplar prayers of the faithful. The Church teaches holiness. It promotes charity and social justice. Much of the way the Catholic culture communicates is so subtle as to be almost subliminal; its values are presented in names, gestures, turns of phrase, associations of ideas, and uncontested assumptions. The subtlety of the Catholic lifeworld becomes apparent when dealing with converts who have acquired an adult, conscious knowledge of the faith, but lack the instinctive responses of «cradle Catholics».

The personality structures that the Catholic lifeworld carries and promotes are relevant to sacraments. The person raised in the Catholic culture is formed to be sacramental, to have attitudes about grace, authority, fellowship, and communion. A well-formed Catholic desires the assistance that sacraments offer, and trusts their efficacy. They have been brought up, for example, to label certain behaviours as sinful, and to identify particular internal world phenomena as the experience of guilt, and others as the experience of forgiveness. A person without these abilities would have difficulty engaging with the sacrament of reconciliation. The Church not only developed rituals appropriate for the work of redemption, it also promoted the personality structures that can benefit most from those rites. Liturgy shapes the mindset of those who participate. Tradition carries not only the order of the sacraments but also the set of competencies, abilities, and felt needs, that enable Catholics to fruitfully experience them. «Devotions» can promote the attitudes that increase the fruitfulness of sacraments. Eucharistic devo-

---

[8] For example the so-called Philocalian Kalendar dating from 336 AD. See W. FRERE, *Studies in Early Roman Liturgy*, I, 8. The Coptic Church still has its own calendar beginning with the «Era of the Martyrs»; i.e. the date of the military election of Diocletian as Emperor (AD 284).

tion encourages reverence for, and recognition of, the eucharistic presence of Christ, thus strengthening the subjective experience of receiving the eucharist.

According to Habermas, when a theme is addressed it ceases to be part of the unconsidered background of the lifeworld and is brought forward as part of the world to be understood in terms of the validity claims to truth, truthfulness and sincerity. If this is true of every communicative action then it can be expected to apply to the central performatives of the sacraments.

2.2 Sacraments and the Three Validity Claims

A common teaching of sacramental theologians is summarised by Johann Auer:

> Thus, within the space of temporal history in the Church, the sacramental sign is a *signum memorativum* (for it remembers Christ's work of salvation), a *signum representativum* (for it makes present the advent of grace in Christ), and a *signum prognosticum* (for it anticipates eternal salvation). By virtue of this its triple character, the sacramental sign points to the eternal mystery of God, to the mystery of Christ that has occurred within time, and to the mystery of eternal bliss that is to begin at the end of time[9]

The sacraments are understood as pointing in three different temporal directions. They point back in time to the Christ-event, in particular to his saving death and resurrection. They point to something happening at the present moment where the sacrament is bringing about that right relationship with the Trinity which is called grace. Finally they point to the future, towards the *eschaton*, where all God's promises will be realized in the glorious *parousia*.

A context for appreciating this set of characteristics of the sacramental sign is provided by Habermas in his treatment of the threefold validity claim of a communicative action. He asserts that every utterance is connected, at least implicitly, to his three worlds – the objective world, the social world and the subjective world. Utterances have the power to move the hearer because each of these connections is cognitively testable. The three validity claims are to truth, rightness and truthfulness.

---

[9] J. AUER, *A General Doctrine of the Sacraments*, 67.

– *Truth*, in this sense, is correspondence with the objective world. If the utterance has a historical reference then this validity claim will direct attention to the past.
– *Rightness*, is to do with norms of behaviour and legitimate relationships in the social world. This is a present reality. The social world validity claim concerns the existing normative context that gives the speaker his conviction his utterance is right.
– *Truthfulness*, or sincerity, since it involves the subjective world of the speaker is the only validity claim not able to be «redeemed» in the present. Only the speaker has access to his internal world. The corresponding speech-act obligation is *to prove trustworthy*. This is particularly evident in the case of *promising*. The sincerity of a promise is only finally validated when it is carried out. Thus this validity claim involves the future.

So, if a lecturer says to his class «I will return your essays tomorrow», then his sentence points in three temporal directions in its validity claims. It is a performative utterance, there is an implicit «I promise» at the beginning of the statement. For it to be a successful communicative action the students must understand the objective world meaning. It refers to essays the class submitted in the recent past. The utterance is part of the social dynamic of a class. The students are to understand the word «your» as applying to them. They are in a relationship where the lecturer has a right to expect attention and assessable work from them, and they have a right to expect communication and assessment from him. This utterance expresses and makes real that present social reality. The students may also choose to trust the sincerity of the lecturer and plan their next day in the expectation that he will prove reliable.

There are evident parallels between the sign structure of sacraments and the validity claims of the communicative actions as is shown in the diagram on the next page. An acknowledged theological interpretation of the sacraments shows significant commonalities with Habermas's validity claims. This is the point of intersection of major themes of this thesis. Sacrament being understood as sign and communication. The efficacy of a communication being understood, not only in terms of truth, but also as establishing right relationship and leading to future ethical action. The sacraments as *signs* do share characteristics with other communications.

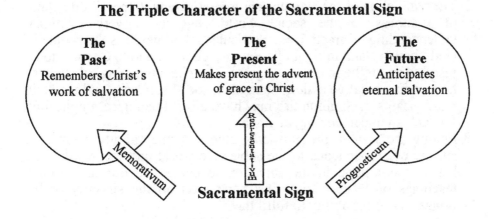

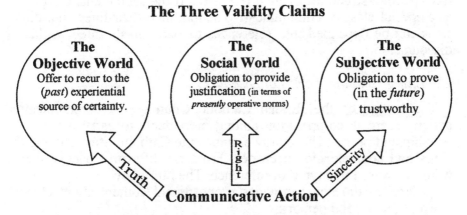

Figure 28: Parallel structure of sign nature and validity claims

This could be interpreted as all communication having a kind of sacramentality, an assertion that this thesis would affirm. Here it is advanced as evidence of a «fit» between the theory of communicative action and sacramental theology.

This similarity of structure suggests avenues for exploration:

1. If the *signum memorativum* is a special case of relating the validity claim of truth to the objective world, how much of the *meaning* of the sacramental sign is tied to the past and to tradition/lifeworld? If the sacrament did not recall the Christ-event, would it have meaning? Would it cease to be a sacrament? If Jesus or his disciples baptized during his public ministry, was this a sacrament?

2. The paralleling of the *signum representativum* with the validity claim of rightness to the social world suggests a very relational understanding of grace. If the particular social world is the people of God, then to stand in right relation to each other and to Christ is to be justified and to be in a state of grace. The phenomenological study of how communicative actions strengthen social solidarity and maintain relationships in communities may have direct theological implication for such an understanding of grace.

3. Putting the *signum prognosticum* alongside the validity claim of a sincere correspondence to the subjective world underscores the link between our hope in the salvation to come and our faith in the teachings of Jesus Christ. Our hope rests on the sincerity of his promises and his ability to fulfil them.

Communicative actions and sacraments have both been considered to have parallel structures of time reference. If the sacraments are treated as a special class of communicative action, then their three sign directions can be expanded into references to Habermas's three worlds of discourse.

2.3 *Liturgy and the Worlds of Discourse*

The liturgy of the Roman Catholic Church is a communicative action. There is co-operation among individuals to carry out acts of worship and praise. The liturgy assumes the Catholic lifeworld and the skills and competencies it carries. From the lifeworld background it brings forward three types of reference. The liturgy by

– *constative statements* provides propositional content about objects, events, texts, and persons;
– *illocutionary verbs*, explicit and implicit, performatively draws on relationships within and beyond the Church;
– *expressive utterances* makes public the subjective worlds of the participants.

Implicitly all three worlds of reference are involved in every utterance and communicative gesture. By standing *for the gospel* a participant in eucharistic liturgy has make a gesture with propositional content. It has a different meaning than standing after a meal. Context and convention establish the content of the gesture. The standing also relates to the social world of all those in the congregation who have stood at the same time. A relationship of solidarity is reinforced. The standing is also expressive of the inner world of the person who stands, showing at least their attention to what is required of the moment. The belated, reluctant slouch of an inattentive teenager is even more expressive.

If this is true of every communicative act in a liturgy, then *a fortiori* it is true of the central performative utterance (or gesture) of a sacrament. Consider the paradigmatic sacrament of baptism and the Trinitarian baptismal formula, as an example of a performative. Austin presented the utterance of the baptismal formula in its conventional context by an authorized person as a clear case of an utterance that, when happily accomplished, *does* something rather than merely *describing* it. He identified two levels to the utterance – its meaning and its force. In Habermas's theory of communicative action, these are understood in terms of the objective world of entities that are referred to by the propositional content of utterances and the social world of legitimate relationships whose normative power accounts for the force of a performative. Habermas discerned a third level by also relating the utterance to the internal world of the speaker. All utterances express something of the privileged inner world of the one who makes them.

Applying Habermas's three worlds model to the utterance of the baptismal formula gives the structure pictured on the next page. Compare and contrast this illustration with «I warn you, smoke a pipe» on page 121 above. This is the theory of communicative action applied to what happens in the celebration of a sacramental rite. The baptism ritual contains many references to the objective world. The communicative gesture that accompanies the utterance – immersion or the pouring of water – has propositional content; someone gets wet[10]. Water is an objective reality. The meaning of the word «baptize» includes connotations of past events – the baptism of Jesus by John the Baptist, the death and resurrection of Jesus. Without knowledge of these things the utterance cannot be fully understood, and the rite attempts to ensure that the participants do understand it. When the baptismal formula is uttered there are certain social world realities involved. The people gathered for the baptism represent the Church. The minister of baptism is authorized by the Church to make this utterance and his authority is recognized. The candidate for baptism has already taken up a relationship with the Church. Standing behind all these relationships is the Trinity. The persons of the Trinity, themselves in relation, are the underpinning for the normative force that empowers this utterance. The

---

[10] See Ch. I 7.4.1 above.

minister is acting *in persona Christi*. The Father is sending the Holy Spirit to make the person undergoing baptism into an adopted son or daughter in the Son. The force of the utterance, which gives meaning and power to the words «I baptize you», is this web of connections which are recognized in the Church. Since the greatest of these relationships are with the Trinity, more than social conditioning is involved. These relationships are grace-filled and life-giving.

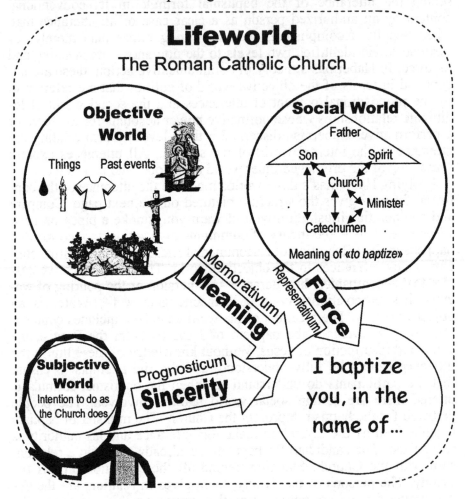

Figure 29: Worlds and Sacramental Utterance

Gerald O'Collins, in his discussion of the nature of Christian faith, identifies «three distinguishable, if inseparable dimensions in the one act: confession, commitment and confidence or trust»[11]. It can be seen how these three dimensions of the act of faith, which is the response expected of the recipient of baptism, respond precisely to the three dimensions of the action of the sacrament. The confession corresponds to the objective world, this is the *fides quae* («believing that»), the acceptance of facts. The commitment involves accepting the personal relationship with Christ within the Church, this is the *fides qua* («believing in»), and corresponds to the social world of right relationships. The confidence or trust is in the promise of salvation made by Jesus Christ, and communicated in his name by the priest.

The happy outcome of the formula of baptism includes relational change. The Catechism describes the effects of baptism:

> The fruit of Baptism, or baptismal grace, is a rich reality that includes forgiveness of original sin and all personal sins, birth into the new life by which man becomes an adoptive son of the Father, a member of Christ and a temple of the Holy Spirit. By this very fact the person baptized is incorporated into the Church, the Body of Christ, and made a sharer in the priesthood of Christ[12].

Forgiveness involves a change of status from sinner to forgiven. Adoption and membership are clearly relational. Becoming a temple of the Holy Spirit is the relationship of indwelling. The triad of adoptive Son, member, and temple are biblical expressions of a new relationship with each person of the Trinity. Incorporation into the Church which is the Body of Christ is a human social reality backed by a divine mandate. Leaving aside for the present the issue of an ontological change undergone in baptism, there is abundant evidence of an illocutionary effect; «the relation between the subjects is not the same after as it was before»[13].

The sincerity of the performative utterance of the minister involves not just his subjective world, but also, since this is an institutionally bound action, the definitions and sincerity of those on whose behalf he intends to act.

---

[11] G. O'COLLINS, «Believing in the Risen Christ», 68. See also his *Fundamental Theology*, 137-39.

[12] *CCC* §1279.

[13] L-M. CHAUVET, *Symbol and Sacrament*, 132.

2.4 *Sacraments as Institutionally Bound Speech Acts*

When a speaker utters a promise, one of the requirements for its happy outcome is what Searle called the «sincerity condition»[14]; the speaker must intend to do the future act which he promises. This intention is a subjective world reality. With respect to serious matters, an existing relationship of trust is usually called for before a promise will be accepted. A private promise between individuals is categorised by Habermas as «institutionally unbound»[15]. There is no institution that enforces the interpretation or carrying out of private promises. In contrast, the utterance of a judge in a court of law: «I sentence you to three years in prison» is an institutionally bound statement. The justice department and the penal system have precise rules and procedures for interpreting the judge's dictum. So long as he is intending to pronounce sentence, that is, to act as a judge, then the meaning of what he has uttered does not depend on any evident sincerity, enthusiasm, or other subjective world reality. The courtroom context is carefully defined and staged. The expression used by the judge conforms to a legal formula. He is acting in a circumscribed manner and using stock phrases because the meaning of his utterance is defined for him and his hearers by the institution to which he belongs. The institution provides the interpretation of his utterance and carries it out. It could be argued that his sentence was too severe, and it could be overturned, but, once uttered, sentence has indisputably been passed, and no-one will be in reasonable doubt as to what it *entails*. Similarly the central performative utterances of sacramental liturgies depend for the interpretation and effect on the institution of the Church, not on any subjective world reality of the minister beyond the intention to do as the Church does.

One effect of the happy performance of the formula of baptism is the promise of salvation. The formula is uttered by the minister of the sacrament, but it is not *his* subjective world which provides the sincerity condition which makes this a true promise. Just as the peace offer depends on the sincerity of the president rather than that of his ambassador, so the promise of salvation depends on the risen Christ who declared: «Go out to the whole world; proclaim the Good News to all creation. He who believes and is baptised will be saved». (Mark 16:15-16) The recipient of a sacrament requires faith in Christ rather than

---

[14] See Ch. I 7.1 above.
[15] See Ch. II 6.3.2 above.

faith in the minister of the sacrament. It is Christ's word which is to be trusted. The role of the Church is to ensure a faithful understanding of that word. The Church makes Christ and his promises known to each generation. The interpretation of his words is of ultimate significance, hence the institutional binding of this interpretation particularly in the case of sacraments.

2.5 *The Intention of the Minister of a Sacrament*

In the debate between Derrida and Searle context was the disputed topic[16]. For Derrida the context of an utterance is infinitely variable and what characterizes language signs is that they are iterable: they can be used in different contexts to mean the same thing. Austin and Searle, in contrast, privileged the «normal context» of discourse, distinguishing it from «non-serious» contexts such as in a play, or poem, or joke. Part of what is particular to each context, and what distinguishes the serious from the non-serious is the *intention of the speaker*. For Grice the «meaning» of an utterance involves saying something with «the intention of inducing a belief by means of the recognition of this intention»[17].

In the history of sacraments the question of context and the intention of the minister arose in the debate about what constitutes a sacrament. In his *Historia Ecclesiastica*, Rufinus of Aquileia (*c.* 344-410) recounts the story of Bishop Alexander of Alexandria (d. 326) seeing a group of youths on the beach *playing* at baptism. One of them was the future bishop, St Athanasius. The young Athanasius was play-acting the role of bishop for his friends. Having summoned the young people and questioned them about the «scrutiny» and «ceremony» they had undergone, Bishop Alexander singled out Athanasius for future ordination and enrolled the other youths in the ranks of the baptized *without* any other baptismal ceremony than what they had experienced at the hands of Athanasius! Rufinus has Alexander accepting the mock baptism as valid. This patristic tale, associated with two saints, ensured that «baptism done in jest» has been often discussed in the tradition.

Augustine (354-430) writing against the Donatists sets up a discussion of all aspects of the issue:

---

[16] See Ch. I 7.1 above.
[17] H.P. GRICE, «Meaning», 384. See Ch. I 7.2 above.

The question is also commonly raised, whether baptism is to be held valid which is received from one who had not himself received it, if, from some promptings of curiosity, he had chanced to learn how it ought to be conferred; and whether it makes no difference in what spirit the recipient receives it, whether in mockery or in sincerity: if in mockery, whether the difference arises when the mockery is of deceit, as in the Church, or in what is thought to be the Church; or when it is in jest, as in a play[18].

Augustine identifies the questions of the ecclesiastical status of the minister of the sacrament, the intention of the recipient, the intention of the minister and the context of the event. His central answer is:

All people possess baptism who have received it in any place, from any sort of men, provided that it were consecrated in the words of the gospel, and received without deceit on their part with some degree of faith[19].

For the situation where «there was no society of those who so believed, and when the man who received it did not himself hold such belief, but the whole thing was done as a farce, or a comedy, or a jest»[20], Augustine recommends praying to God for a sign as to whether this was true baptism.

Hugh of St Victor (1096-1141) excludes this last case by demanding that the minister manifest an unequivocal intention to act[21]. Praepositinus (d. 1210) clarified this as the «intention to do what the Church does»[22], and this became the common teaching of theologians, picked up by Thomas Aquinas[23], and authoritatively taught by the Councils of Florence (1439) and Trent (1547)[24]. The Council of Trent also advised

---

[18] AUGUSTINE, *De Baptismo contra Donatistas*, 53:101; *PL* 43, 212.

[19] AUGUSTINE, *De Baptismo contra Donatistas*, 53:102; *PL* 43, 213.

[20] AUGUSTINE, *De Baptismo contra Donatistas*, 53:102; *PL* 43, 213.

[21] HUGH OF ST VICTOR, *De Sacram*. II, 6, 13: *PL* 176, 460. «Vide ergo et considera quod rationale esse oportet opus ministeriorum Dei, nec propter solam formam praejudicare ubi intentio agendi nulla est».

[22] Praepositinus of Cremona, «Intentio faciendi, quod facit ecclesia».

[23] *ST* III, 64, 8, ad. 1. Aquinas adds the refinement «to intend to do what Christ and the Church do».

[24] The Council of Florence taught in the *Bull of Union with the Armenians*: «All these sacraments are made up of three elements: namely, things as the matter, words as the form, and the person of the minister who confers the sacrament with the intention of doing what the church does. If any one of these is lacking, the sacrament is not effected». A-T I, 542. The Council of Trent's teaching is in the canons on the sacraments: ND 1321; DzH 1611.

Figure 30: Intention and its Recognition

penitents they would be negligent about their salvation, «if, knowing that a priest absolved one jokingly, one would not diligently seek another who would act seriously»[25].

Trent thus requires the minister of reconciliation to have the intention of doing what the church does, and expects the recipient of the sacrament to recognize the seriousness of the priest's intention. We might recall Grice's definition of meaning:

> We may say that «A meant [in the non-natural sense] something by x» is roughly equivalent to «A uttered x with the intention of inducing a belief by means of the recognition of this intention»[26].

If we substitute a sacramental utterance for his variables we can read it as:

---

[25] ND 1628; DzH 1685.
[26] H.P. GRICE, «Meaning», 384.

We may say that «*A priest* meant something by *the formula of absolution*» is roughly equivalent to «*A priest* uttered *the formula of absolution* with the intention of inducing a belief by means of the recognition of this intention».

The Council of Trent offers teaching about both the intention of the minister and the recognition of the minister's intention by the penitent, declaring the sacrament to be lacking in effectiveness if either is lacking. According to Grice, both the intention of the speaker and the recognition of that intention by the hearer are required for the happy outcome of a performative speech action.

A priest-teacher could role-play the sacrament of reconciliation for a group of seminarians using all the words and gestures of the rite of which he was a valid minister, but this would not be the sacrament. He does not intend to celebrate the sacrament, merely to teach about it. Similarly the dress rehearsal for a wedding differs from the real thing, not in who is present, nor (possibly) in the utterances used, but in the intention of the couple. *Rehearsing* vows is not the same as *making* them.

Intention is an internal world reality. Ultimately only the person concerned knows their own intentions. The assumption that underlies communication is that utterances of intention are sincere. According to the Thomistic philosopher, John Owens:

> Speech does not relate indifferently to the possibilities of truth and falsehood, but has a primitive relation to truth, a relation which is presupposed in speaking both truths and falsehoods. Talk is not a neutral art, equally available for truth and lies. We could imagine a language which is used exclusively for truths; we cannot imagine a language which is used exclusively for lies. A working language assumes a primitive trust that a speaker is not seeking to mislead or manipulate[27].

This is not to say that lies are not told, but for them to succeed as lies they have to be taken as true. Lies rely on this assumption; they have to pass themselves off as trustworthy statements to be effective as lies. Sincerity is signalled in numerous other ways than the words themselves. Human beings are highly skilled at communicating intention. The wedding rehearsal will be different from the wedding in many ways. Even if it were a full dress rehearsal and the text of the wedding ceremony were adhered to, it would have been announced as a rehearsal and the participants will be light-hearted or perfunctory, or in

---

[27] J. OWENS, «Dissenting from Reality», 136.

any one of a myriad ways they will clearly flag that they are not serious.

Human communication has many levels of seriousness: jokes, satire, stories, teasing, fantasizing, and levity of various forms, in contrast to formal discourse, profundity, and weighty solemnity. One aspect of liturgy is that it moves the register of discourse to the heavy end of this scale[28]. Liturgy is public; it is held in a sacred place; the language is structured and formal. The demeanour of the participants may be joyous but it does not encourage frivolity. If ritual is a staging for an illocutionary act, then part of how it achieves that effect is by establishing a context of utter seriousness and importance. To invoke the institutional backing of the Church – to act *in persona ecclesiae* – is no light matter. The *sincerity* of the priest celebrant, beyond the intention to do as the Church does, is not required for validity. His utterances are institutionally bound, they are backed up by the Church, not by him. A valid baptism celebrated in one small parish will be recognised throughout the world. While not required for validity, the sincerity of the priest – faith in the words he utters – is certainly encouraged! Sincerity is called for from those who receive sacraments; from those who make promises and vows in baptism, confirmation, marriage and ordination; from those who profess their contrition in reconciliation; from those who respond «Amen» to the Eucharistic prayer and in recognition of the real presence of the Lord as they receive the Eucharist. Sincerity cannot be forced but ritual and liturgy are designed to evoke it.

2.6 *The Effect of the Sacrament and the Holiness of the Minister*

A key effect of sacraments is sanctification. Holy things and holy people are accepted as being conducive to this process. There is a natural desire and expectation for the minister of holy things to be a holy person. Sadly, there are times when this expectation is not fulfilled, raising the issue of how effective the sacraments are when the minister of them is not in a state of grace, or is a cause of public scandal. Augustine addressed this issue with respect to the sacrament of baptism, in the context of his debates with the Donatists:

---

[28] Neil Postman, in *Amusing Ourselves to Death*, points out the difficulties inherent in televising liturgies. He notes: «I believe I am not mistaken in saying that Christianity is a demanding and serious religion. When it is delivered as easy and amusing, it is another kind of religion altogether», 121.

And we learn that the baptism is holy in itself, because it is of God; and whether it be given or whether it be received by men of such like character, it cannot be polluted by any perversity of theirs, either within, or yet outside the Church[29].

He is presenting the sacrament as being «of God» – its holiness and effectiveness derive from God, not from the minister or the recipient. Elsewhere he asserts that the effect of the sacrament is not dependent on the minister because it is Christ who baptizes:

Therefore, whoever the man be, and whatever office he bear who administers the ordinance, it is not he who baptizes, that is the work of Him upon whom the dove descended[30].

In the terminology of speech act theory, this is deputized discourse with the primary agent being Christ and the minister as the deputized secondary agent.

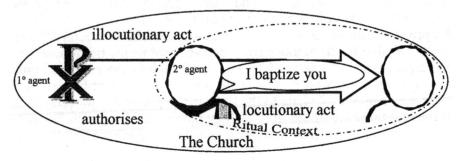

Figure 31: Sacrament as double-agency discourse

Notice that the Church is not another entity between the minister of the sacrament and Christ. Christ belongs to the church as its head (or rather the Church belongs to Christ), the minister represents the Church (and usually belongs to it). Even in the case of baptism, which incorporates those who receive it into the Church[31], the recipients as catechumens «are already joined to the Church, they are already of the household of

---

[29] AUGUSTINE, *On Baptism against the Donatists*, V, 21; *PL* 43, 192: «per se ipsum, quia Dei est, sanctum esse cognoscimus, et sive tradatur sive accipiatur a talibus, nulla eorum perversitate violari, sive intus, sive foris».

[30] AUGUSTINE, *Ep.* 89, 5; *PL* 33, 311: «Proinde homo quilibet minister ejus qualemcumque sarcinam portet, non iste, sed super quem columba descendit, ipse est qui baptizat».

[31] See *CCC* §1279.

Christ»[32]. Thus the Church provides the matrix and mechanism of the discourse. From the Church the minister gains his authorisation to speak for the Church, *in persona ecclesiae,* and on behalf of Christ, *in persona Christi.* From his or her connection with the Church the recipient learns the import of what is said and done. The Church contains the context of the ritual, not only in the physical sense, but also in the sociological sense – it gives the ritual its meaning and cultural setting. The minister speaks the words, the locution, but it is Christ who provides the illocutionary force which enables the sacrament to act effectively.

A non-sacramental parallel would be the president, who sincerely desires peace, instructing his hawkish ambassador in the capital of the enemy country to present a peace proposal. The illocutionary force of the peace offer does not depend on the ambassador who utters it, but on the intention of the one in whose name he speaks. The primary agent of the offer is the president. The ambassador is an intermediary. His own views may be bellicose, but that is irrelevant to the peace proposal. It is not his offer, he is simply the proxy who presents it on behalf of his head of state. Wolterstorff describes the process:

> If the ambassador was deputized to say what he did say in the name of his head of state, then the head of state speaks (discourses) by way of the utterings of the ambassador; locutionary acts of the ambassador count as illocutionary acts of the head of state[33].

The moral state and warlike views of the ambassador do not fundamentally affect the offer he presents, but his status as «duly deputized» is significant. If it turns out that he was not authorized to present the offer, then its status is thrown into doubt.

Similarly, the moral state and views of the minister do not determine the efficacy of a sacrament. A non-Christian midwife, baptizing a dangerously ill newborn at the request of its incapacitated mother, may only have the intention of doing what its mother wants, but, in so doing, she has been authorized by the mother. The mother is exercising her right as a member of the Church, thus it is the Church which authorizes the minister in this limit case[34]. The sacrament does not rely on the faith, ecclesial status, or virtue of the midwife. She pours the water

---

[32] *AG* 14 § 5.
[33] N. WOLTERSTORFF, *Divine Discourse,* 45.
[34] See *CCC* §1256, §1284. Even someone not baptized can baptize.

and says the words (the locutionary act), the illocutionary agent is Christ. The Church accepts the child as a validly baptized member on the basis that God acts through the midwife.

2.7 *Sacramental Character*

Austin in describing performative actions made it clear that their effectiveness depended on the authority of the one making the utterances:

> Suppose, for example, I see a vessel on the stocks, walk up and smash a bottle hung at the stem, proclaim «I name this ship the *Mr. Stalin*» and for good measure kick away the chocks: but the trouble is, I was not the person chosen to name it (whether or not – an additional complication – *Mr. Stalin* was the destined name; perhaps in a way it is even more of a shame if it was). We can all agree that the ship was not thereby named[35].

Very frequently a communicative action will be made on behalf of another authority who is not physically present. Italian translates the word «spokesman» with «*portavoce*», which literally means «one who carries the voice» of another. The delegate or vicar speaks «in the name of» or «by the authority of» another person. The illocutionary effect of such an utterance depends not on the power of the utterer, but on the authority *vested* in them by the other.

On February 6, 1840, at Waitangi in New Zealand a treaty *was made*. Treaty-making is a clear example of a performative action. The document, which records and symbolizes this event, bears many signatures, crosses, and copies of tattoos, which are the personal marks of the chiefs of Maori tribes. As chiefs they had the *mana*, the authority, to speak and to make a treaty on behalf of their tribe. The document also bears the signature of Captain William Hobson. Captain is not an exalted rank, but Hobson was not signing on his own behalf. As the appointed delegate of Queen Victoria, he signed for «the Crown» – that social and legal entity which stands behind the government of the United Kingdom. This treaty was a foundational event in the history of New Zealand. Its provisions were not always honoured, but it created a relationship between the Maori people of New Zealand and the English Crown. It gave legitimacy to a fledgling colony. As the wording of the Treaty had it:

---

[35] J.L. AUSTIN, *How To Do Things with Words*, 23.

> Her Majesty the Queen of England extends to the Natives of New Zealand Her royal protection and imparts to them all the Rights and Privileges of British Subjects[36].

The chiefs had their own authority, Hobson's was delegated. His signature on the treaty is an example of what Wolterstorff characterized as «deputized discourse»[37]. In Habermas's analysis of what constitutes illocutionary force it would be reliance on the commitment of Queen Victoria (the Crown) to her subjects that gave the «social world meaning»[38] and binding power to this communicative act. The Treaty of Waitangi has endured as a moral and legal commitment well beyond the lifetimes of the original signatories. A social reality came into existence in 1840 backed by the Maori peoples of New Zealand and the English Crown. Delegated individuals established the covenant (and this was the term missionaries used in explaining the treaty prior to its signing), but what was effected was beyond their competence as individuals. They acted with an authority greater than their own and achieved something which has endured, because they belonged to collectives which honour the communicative actions of authorized individuals.

The level of illocutionary force of a communicative action depends on the authority of legitimate social relationships. If a religious priest were to be warned by his community superior about the content of his teaching, then he would have truly been warned. Yet, if the superior were to say «I am conveying this warning to you from the superior-general», then even though the content was the same, the *force* of the warning would be greater. If, the superior were to go on to say: «the Congregation for the Doctrine of the Faith, speaking with the authority of His Holiness in these matters, has asked you to be warned» then the force of that warning would be the highest that exists in this particular authority structure. The higher the authority, the greater the illocutionary force.

When a priest validly baptizes «in the name of the Father, and of the Son, and of the Holy Spirit», he does so *in persona Christi*, as the authorised delegate of Jesus Christ. The illocutionary effect of his ut-

---

[36] *Treaty of Waitangi*, English version (a Maori version was also signed) third article. http://www.govt.nz/en/aboutnz/?id=77737fd3275e394a8ed9d416a72591d0 [Accessed 11.6.2004].

[37] See Ch. I 7.5.3 above.

[38] See Ch. II 6.4 above.

terances is backed by the authority of God. There is no higher court of appeal. This is the fundamental authority of the universe. What is effected in this sacramental action is done, as unrepeatable, by God. It is true and effective to the deepest level of reality – hence the teaching that baptism confers a «special character» that cannot be removed. Patristic authors likened this character to a *sigillum,* the impression from the signet ring; the mark of an authority. A legal document takes effect when it has been signed and sealed, but the authority of the document comes from the person, not the wax impression.

2.8 *Subjective Requirements for the Recipient of the Sacraments*

Sacramental theology is largely written by clerics for clerics to read, perhaps even more so in the past when the language of discourse was Latin. In such discourse attention naturally focuses on the minister of the sacraments. The ontological approach, anxious to identify what is necessary for validity, encourages this tendency. Validity is binary; it has two values. A rite is either a valid sacrament or it is not; there are no shades of grey. Excessive emphasis on sacramental validity can lead to a minimalist approach to the celebration of the sacrament whereby only that which is required for validity is done.

Adopting a communicative model of sacraments *requires* the role of the recipient and their subjective experience be addressed. The philosophers of communication whose work we have addressed show how active the recipient of communication is. Hearing, understanding and uptake are dynamic rather than passive. Austin has shown that communication can be impeded in many ways. The binary pair of truth and falsity is only one component in his range of infelicities[39]. Communication can have a happy outcome despite hitches and flaws. For example: A husband asks his wife «Get me the "thingummy" out of the "whatsit"», and she understands exactly what he means and does what he intends! Yet, infelicities can vitiate a communication. An insincere apology is still an apology but is quite different from a sincere one. An expression of gratitude can be warm and convincing or merely proforma. Human communication is rife with nuances and shadings; it is far from being binary in its operation, there is almost always room for improvement. Viewing sacraments as communicative actions will lead to concern for their fruitfulness.

---

[39] See Ch. I 6.3 above.

Communicative actions, to achieve a happy outcome, require *uptake* on the part of the hearer. Given the freedom of hearers to refuse, this uptake can be blocked in four ways (language, plus the 3 validity claims):

1. A lack of comprehension: the hearer does not understand the words of the speaker.
2. Refusal of the truth claim of the speaker: A hearer denies what the speaker affirms.
3. Rejection of the rightness of what the speaker claims: «You can't ask me to do that!»
4. Non-acceptance of the sincerity of the speaker: considering him to be lying or manipulative, not open about his intentions[40].

Sacraments find their realization in the recipient. Even Eucharist fulfills its meaning when received. Hence it seems appropriate to construct a parallel set of requirements for the happy reception of a sacrament by an adult, conscious participant:

1. They should comprehend what is being said to them or spoken over them. This would not necessarily involve understanding every word of, for example, the formula of absolution, but they ought to recognize that it *is* a formula of absolution and know what absolution is.
2. An acceptance of the truth of the gospel, the claims of Jesus, his saving death and resurrection. A comprehensive knowledge is not demanded, nor even integral objective orthodoxy. For example marriage between two Protestants is accepted by canon law as being a valid marriage. Sacraments presuppose a certain faith in the recipient – not necessarily a total or dogmatically correct one, but the recipient ought not to be someone totally ignorant or entirely without faith.
3. For the sacrament to be effective from a communicative point of view, the recipients must be prepared to enter into the relationship that the sacrament implies. They need to accept, even if only in a limited fashion, the rightness of the sacrament and the authority of the minister over them at that moment.
4. The recipient ought to recognize the intention of the minister to sincerely celebrate the sacrament. This sincerity can be assumed unless there is evidence to the contrary. This provides a context to the ad-

---

[40] See J. HABERMAS, *Communication and the Evolution of Society*, 2, and Ch. II 6.6.2 above.

vice of the Council of Trent that a penitent should seek another con-
fessor if they were absolved jokingly.

Augustine requires that baptism be received: «without deceit on their
part with some degree of faith»[41]. One who received a sacrament de-
ceitfully would lack the conformative attitude required to accept the
rightness claim; they would be rejecting the relationship that is offered
in the sacrament. One who does not want to become a child of God and
a member of the Church is not going to be open to what baptism gives.
The «some degree of faith» corresponds with the degree of knowledge
and belief required to understand and accept the truth of what is happening in the sacrament. This is consistent with the teaching of the
Council of Trent that sacraments confer grace on those «who place no
obstacle in the way»[42]. «*Obex*» (bolt, bar, barrier, obstacle) in the active
sense means a positive action against something; «to reject it». In the
passive sense it can be taken as a lack of a necessary «disposition».

This consideration of the normal conditions for the reception of sacraments – an adult, conscious subject – brings into relief the cases
where these conditions do not apply, when the recipient is a child or is
not conscious of what is happening to them.

2.8.1 The Baptism of a Baby

Nicholas Wolterstorff presented the role of the secretary in deputized
discourse[43]. This example could be extended: as well as acting in proxy
for the boss in writing and signing a letter, the secretary can *hear* on the
boss's behalf, and sign that documents have reached him. The speaker
trusts that the import of the utterance will be conveyed to the boss at a
later time or date. Meanwhile, if the authority of the secretary is
deemed sufficient, matters can proceed on the basis that the boss has
been notified. Similarly the ambassador sent with a peace proposal
might be asked by the head of state to *negotiate* a peace settlement on
his behalf, whereupon he does not simply speak for the head of state, he
listens and responds for him as well. Just as there can be a proxy on the
speaker's end of a communication, so too there can be proxies at the
receiving end.

---

[41] AUGUSTINE, *De Baptismo contra Donatistas*, 53:102; *PL* 43,213.
[42] ND 1316; DzH 1606: «non ponentibus obicem».
[43] See Ch. I 7.5.3 above.

Some speech acts depend more on the speaker than on the hearer for their happy fulfillment. Expressive utterances like «I am angry» do not require the acceptance by the hearer to be an effective self-expression, though if the hearer rejects the truth of the remark the purpose of *communicating* the anger has been defeated. A declaration before an audience like «I promise, to you little child, that I will care for you as you grow up» is ostensibly made to the child, but is for the ears of those present who can understand. The truth and sincerity of the promise will be conveyed to the child as he or she grows up, and the speaker could declare: «I kept the promise I made to you when you were too young to understand». A key witness to a promise is the one who utters it. Vows are solemn promises that call on God as witness and guarantor.

The act of adopting a baby is a kind of communication with them. An adult or even an adolescent cannot be adopted without him or her giving their consent. In the case of a child their birth parent, or the State, is accepted by the law as speaking for them in consenting to the adoption.

A baby comes to baptism in the arms of someone, usually a parent, who will be responsible for their upbringing. The requirements for the recipient of the sacrament are transferred to them – they must understand what they are asking on their child's behalf, they must have some faith. They stand as proxy for their child. For the sacrament to achieve its full fruitfulness, the recipient needs, eventually, to understand, appreciate, and choose, what was done on their behalf. The effects of the sacrament do not wait or depend on this. Augustine speaks of the Church standing in for the child:

> Mother Church has no doubt that [spiritual enlightenment] takes place in little ones by means of the sacrament; she offers them her maternal heart and lips so that they may be initiated into the sacred mysteries, because they cannot yet believe unto righteousness with their own heart or make profession with their own lips unto salvation. And no believer hesitates to call them believers – a name which is, of course, taken from believing. And yet, it was not these little ones themselves, but others who made the responses for them during the sacred rites[44].

---

[44] AUGUSTINE, *De peccatorum meritis et remissione*, I, 25; CSEL 60, 36: «Quod per sacramentum in parvulis fieri non dubitat mater ecclesia, quae cor et os maternum eis praestat, ut sacris mysteriis inbuantur, quia nondum possunt corde proprio credere ad iustitiam nec ore proprio confiteri ad salutem. Nec ideo tamem eos quisquam

Augustine has those who offer the act of faith for their child acting *in persona ecclesiae*, so that the faith of the Church, rather than that of the parents, is what stands in for the as yet absent faith of the babe. The domestic church is called «the Church in miniature» and John Paul II comments: «the Christian family is grafted into the mystery of the Church to such a degree as to become a sharer, in its own way, in the saving mission proper to the Church»[45].

What has been done in infant baptism and what is yet to happen is well summed up in the introduction to the Lord's Prayer in the concluding part of the rite:

> My dear brothers and sisters, this child has been reborn in baptism. He is now called the child of God, for so indeed he is. In confirmation he will receive the fullness of God's Spirit. In holy communion he will share the banquet of Christ's sacrifice, calling God his Father in the midst of the Church. In the name of this child, in the spirit of common sonship, let us pray together in the words our Lord has given us[46].

The adoption as a child of God has been accomplished but there is much still to come. The child will grow to full membership within the Church; he will not enter it from outside. For now the congregation present speak on behalf of the newly baptised by praying, *in the name of the child*, the Our Father.

2.8.2 Anointing *in extremis*

There are communications that require little response: applause for victory, a touch on the shoulder in sympathy, silently being present to another. Gestures that involve physical contact can have high levels of illocutionary force: a hand on the chest in warning, a touch on the brow in concern for sickness, a lover's caress. Bodily contact communicates at levels below the rational.

In an anointing rite the celebrant is advised to «become acquainted with the family, friends, and others who may be present», and if possible to involve them in the preparation and celebration of the rite[47]. The

---

fidelium fideles appellare cunctatur, quod a credendo utique nomen est, quamvis hoc non ipsi, sed alii pro eis inter sacramenta responderint».

[45] *Familiaris Consortio*, 49.

[46] *Rites* I, 441 §181.

[47] *Rites* I, «Introduction to the Rite of Anointing Outside Mass», 819 §112.

central performatives of the rite are the laying on of hands in silence; then, while anointing head and hands, the words:

> Through this holy anointing may the Lord in his love and mercy help you with the grace of the Holy Spirit. May the Lord who frees you from sin save you and raise you up[48].

The Church is being present to the sick person. The sacrament seeks to communicate care and concern. It does it through human contact and powerful gestures of help – the warmth of a hand, the smooth coolness of oil. The words call on God to help and declare that the Lord is at work to forgive and to save. Christian hope in divine mercy is affirmed. What is not sought is any response from the sick person.

«Consciousness» is a relative term. People apparently unconscious have been known later to recount what was said in their presence. Someone who cannot respond is not necessarily unaware of what is said to them. After words no longer seem to be understood, physical contact is a form of communication that can still be available. An otherwise non-communicative sick person may clutch the hand that is put in theirs. Thus it is hard to define a point at which the sacrament of anointing would cease to be a communication that is received *at some level* by the sick person. The gestures of the sacramental rite have been chosen for their simplicity and profundity. It is well-suited for communicating its message even to someone who is «far gone».

As at baptism the recipient of the sacrament is usually accompanied by care-givers. They understand the message of the sacrament on behalf of the recipient – perhaps being able to reassure the sick person in a later moment of lucidity that the anointing has indeed been done. Those family, friends, and care-givers have a particular connection to the sick person. They share in the sacrament as of right. The message of the sacrament is also for them and they receive it. They also receive it *in the name of* the sick one.

In short, even at the beginning and at the end of life sacraments *communicate*. They communicate the love and grace of God to those who receive the sacraments and to those who stand with and for them.

---

[48] *Rites* I, 825 §124.

2.9 *The Total Sacrament in the Total Sacramental Situation*

Austin spoke of the importance of «the total speech act in the total speech situation». An appreciation of how rituals are stagings of illocutions and how much the illocutionary force determines the fruitfulness of the sacramental encounter, will encourage attention to the totality of the ritual act in its context. The central performative of a ritual draws force, seriousness and weight from its context. The participants in ritual are affected by the whole of the ritual, not merely by the utterances at its heart. Even remote preparation, like the rehearsal for a wedding, the choosing of suitable attire, is not unconnected with the illocutionary force of the sacrament. It is part of what makes that day and that moment special. It helps evoke the deepest level of sincerity from the participants.

Context includes location, architecture, art, vestments, music, tones of voice, and all the perceptible symbols. The effect of the context will depend on how much the participants have been socialized into the church culture from which these symbols are drawn. Richard Fenn points out that context includes social factors:

> Where authority is clear and strong, and where members know what distinguishes them from non-members, these rituals are performed with a seriousness and power that is downright «magical». To believe in the saints' power to intercede and intervene in this world, for instance, or to believe in the transforming power of the sacrament, requires – and is made possible by – the most solemn and eventful words and gestures in acts of worship. The force of religious language is greatest in the context of ritual[49].

Confused messages from Church officials, and any lack of clarity, diminishes the effectiveness of liturgy. A community with defined social boundaries and strong identification of themselves as belonging to the group enters more deeply into a ritual.

The past is part of the ritual context. The ritual is identified with that which previous generations have celebrated. Continuity with the past is important for *legitimating* the sacrament in the eyes of the recipients. Garish discontinuity can hamper the confidence in the rite itself which is an element of the faith that the sacrament calls for in the recipient. Slavish repetition of past forms can also, as Chauvet notes, vitiate the

---

[49] R. FENN, «Recent Studies of Church Decline: The Eclipse of Ritual», 126.

experience of the ritual by disconnecting it entirely from the present day[50].

2.10 *Historical Continuity*

A survey of the history of any of the seven sacraments[51] will reveal variations in how it has been celebrated across the centuries. This gives rise to the question of the identity of the sacrament in its different forms. Is the plunging of an adult beneath the flowing water of a river «in the name of the Lord Jesus»[52] the *same* sacrament as the sprinkling of the head of a babe above the font of a cathedral, whilst saying «I baptize you, in the name of the Father, and of the Son, and of the Holy Spirit»? A related question is posed by Kenan Osborne:

> The uniqueness of each and every baptism or eucharist bears eloquent witness to sacramental *Haecceitas*. No actual baptism can ever be repeated; no actual eucharist can ever be repeated. The reality of baptism can only be found in the singularized happenings of these existential baptisms and eucharists. Outside of these actualized and singularized baptismal and Eucharistic events the very terms baptism and eucharist have at best some generic, non-realistic, linguistically conventional meaning[53].

For Habermas, «linguistically conventional» meaning is the only kind of meaning there is. To speak of the world is to use language and its conventions. The dichotomy that Osborne is trying to set up between «realistic» and «linguistic» collapses when the phenomenological approach of Habermas and Chauvet is applied. The physical world consists entirely of singulars, each particle is distinct from its neighbour, each instant different from the one before, but the lifeworld, which human beings experience, is overlaid with conventions, concepts and symbols. A new item of furniture is happily identified as «a chair», without existential concern about the existence or non-existence of the essence of «chairness» or any platonic ideal chair. What constitutes a chair is embedded among the unquestioned certainties of an English-speaking lifeworld. The same is true for less tangible social realities. A

---

[50] See Ch. III 6.4.2 above.

[51] The work that is credited with opening up these issues, with respect to the present form of a sacrament and its historical variations, is H.C. LEA, *A History of Auricular Confession and Indulgences in the Latin Church* (1896).

[52] See Acts 2: 38, 8: 16, 10: 48, 19: 5.

[53] K. OSBORNE, *Christian Sacraments in a Postmodern World*, 58.

«greeting» is perhaps harder to define, but members of the same communicative community identify and respond to greetings without difficulty.

Institutional facts (in Searle's sense) are human creations, but this does not make them any less factual. When the chairman declares «this meeting is adjourned», then the meeting *is* over. The chairman had the authority to make that performative declaration and the social reality of the group changes when he does so. When the performances are of significance to a social group they can be institutionally bound – systems will be put in place to ensure their «correct» interpretation. The Treasury declares what is legal tender, and what is not. The Justice System backs up the sentences uttered by judges. The Office of Births, Deaths and Marriages records the natural entries into, the significant change of state within, and the departures of persons from, New Zealand society.

The institution that defines a social reality can change its definitions, and the reality will accordingly change. Decimal currency is introduced, and the old notes are no longer legal tender. What was money is so no longer. What is money, and does the task that the old did, looks different. The Totalisator Agency Board introduces a new bet called a «Trifecta», and that term, and the associated practises, enters use in the betting fraternity.

Sacraments are institutionally bound social realities. The primary institution they are bound to, and interpreted by, is the Church. A particular water ritual *is* a baptism only when the Church accepts it as the initiation of a new member, a new disciple of Jesus Christ. In the name of – with the authority of – Christ, the Church claims the person and declares them to be a child of God and a member of the faithful. As the institution that binds the reality of baptism, the Church has the authority to change wording and conditions, to set new limits on what is acceptable. If the Church says «this is a baptism», then it *is*. If a competent authority within the Church declares it invalid, then it *is not* a sacrament.

Viewing sacraments as institutionally bound communicative actions of the Church makes it clear that their nature is intimately bound up with that of the Church itself. Sacraments do not make sense in isolation from the Church.

Marriage as a social reality has two institutions concerned in defining it. It is institutionally bound by both the Church and the government. In a multi-faith society there can also be a variety of religions with differing definitions of the married state – for example whether or not polygamy is acceptable. Controversy arises when the institutions binding the reality disagree on its definition. The New Zealand government passed a Civil Unions bill on 9 December 2004 which «allows same sex and de facto couples to formally register their relationships under the Births, Deaths and Marriages Act. It is intended that they will have the same rights, entitlements and obligations as married couples»[54]. Among the groups who opposed the bill were the Anglican and Roman Catholic Bishops of New Zealand. They were concerned that what constitutes a marriage in New Zealand society is being redefined into something quite different from the Christian understanding[55]. New Zealand Catholics belong to the communicative community of the nation as well as to the communicative community of the Church, and are influenced by both.

2.11 *The Institution of the Sacraments*

According to Chauvet, it is part of the nature of ritual that it be understood as coming from the founder:

> Programming is constitutive of the religious rite insofar as one acts there *as the ancestors acted, as the founder* (mythic, historicized, or historical) acted. Even more, one does this *because* they (supposedly) acted this way[56].

The ritual functions to slice away time between the present and the «*illo tempore*» of the origins[57]. In the action of the ritual the group understands itself as re-experiencing the foundational events. Chauvet leaves open the question of whether in a particular case that ritual does actually go back to the founder. The Council of Trent anathematized anyone who asserts, «the sacraments of the New Law were not all instituted by Jesus Christ our Lord»[58], and they listed the seven sacraments.

---

[54] *The Press* (the newspaper of Christchurch, New Zealand) 10 December 2004, 1.

[55] In February 2005 similar legislation was tabled in the Canadian parliament. Archbishop Brendan O'Brien, writing as president of the Canadian Conference of Catholic Bishops to the Canadian prime minister on 31 January, stated that the prelates «stand united in their opposition to legislation that would *redefine* marriage in such a way that it is no longer recognized as the unique, essential and fundamental relationship of a man and a woman», (emphasis added).

[56] L-M. CHAUVET, *Symbol and Sacraments*, 340 (emphases his).

[57] See Ch. III 6.4.2 above.

[58] Canons on the Sacraments, ND 1311; DzH 1601.

During his ministry the historical Jesus: was baptized, engaged in Jewish ritual worship in synagogues and the Temple, pardoned sinners, exorcized demoniacs, healed the sick, shared in ritual meals, blessed children, performed signs and wonders, and ultimately was crucified, died and rose in glory. There are parallels that can be drawn between features of the ministry and the work of the sacraments. They can truly be claimed to be a continuation of the work of the historical Jesus in the world.

John Searle identifies the paradigm for establishing an institutional fact (instituting a new social reality) as «"*X* counts as *Y*" and its variants»[59]. Something new becomes part of the social fabric, when a competent authority declares «this is legal tender» or «this is the process you must go through to remain in the country» or «two long rings on the bell means there is a phone call for the superior». Rituals are social realities – they are institutional rather than brute facts. Birth is a brute fact but baptism is an institutional one, depending on the institution of the Church for its significance. According to Searle institutional facts are made so by a performative utterance. The chairman declares «This meeting is now open», and the institutional reality of a meeting comes into existence.

Studies in the history of liturgy suggest that, unlike the clarity of Searle's model, the actual historical beginning of a ritual may be difficult to identify, because rituals often develop organically and gradually with the same actions being given different interpretations, or variations on the actions being understood as being the same reality. The Eucharistic words of Jesus «This is my body» (Matt 26:26) and «This is my blood» (Matt 26:28) interpreted in a weak fashion constitute the establishment of an institutional fact – from now on in these circumstances the bread and wine *count* as the body and blood of the Jesus. An orthodox interpretation has them as a performative declaration bringing about at change at the level of brute fact. These two expressions and the imperative «Do this as a memorial of me» (1Cor 11:25b) are sufficient to assert that, during his lifetime, Jesus instituted a ritual involving bread and wine (and *the ritual* is an institutional fact). The eucharistic ritual celebrated today claims identification and continuity with that celebrated by the Jesus of the ministry. What enables this identification and continuity is the existence of an institution which defines what this ritual is. The Church defines the Eucharist and it itself is

---

[59] J. SEARLE, *The Construction of Social Reality*, 34. See Ch. I 7.1 above.

defined by it. The existence of reference texts, like 1Cor 11, is important, but the Eucharist is an institutionally bound communicative action. The sacrament does not stand alone from the Church. Jesus could not have instituted the Eucharist without instituting the Church (or an equivalent institution) – an enduring ritual requires participants and a body to say what is, and is not, that ritual.

The command to baptise all nations in the name of the Trinity is presented as being from the *risen* Christ (Matt 28:19). Kenan Osborne provides a summary of «the history of the origins of the seven sacramental rituals»[60]:

> The sacraments of baptism and eucharist seem to go back to the time of Jesus, or at least to the time of the apostolic church. It is in the writings of Hermes (140-50) that we have the first clear reference to a rite of reconciliation after baptism. [*The Shepherd*, Commandment, 4.3.] The Apostolic Tradition of Hippolytus (c. 215) gives us the first extant indication of ordination and its ritual. [1,2-4; 7-9.] In the same work we have the first clear evidence of a blessing of oil for the sick. [5,1.] We have reliable historical data that church officials began to enter into the marriage celebration around 400. However, only from the time of Peter Lombard (1150) do we have a clear indication that marriage was accepted as a true sacrament in the Western church. In the year 1000 there is clear evidence that confirmation, generally and only in the West, was celebrated as a rite separate from baptism.

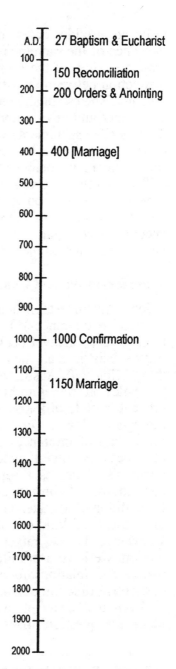

A.D. 27 Baptism & Eucharist
150 Reconciliation
200 Orders & Anointing
400 [Marriage]
1000 Confirmation
1150 Marriage

---

[60] K. OSBORNE, *Christian Sacraments*, 8-9. The diagram is an adaptation of his.

Osborne provides dates from the earliest clear extant evidence of the existence of the sacramental rites, which could well be somewhat later than the origin of the rites. As he shows with marriage there is also a distinction between the rite itself and when it is given the title of «sacrament». The establishment of the sacraments and their distinction from each other and other activities of the Church was a slow and complex process. The sacraments were presented as continuations of the works of the Lord during his ministry, but the institution of the complete seven sacraments belongs to the time of the risen Lord and his Church.

The rites that evolved into our modern sacraments have always been seen as taking their power and effectiveness from Christ and as being in connection with him. They are understood as works of Christ, and as encounters with him. The *structure* of the rite is of the Church, but the *person* encountered therein is Jesus Christ.

3. **Performative and Constative**

John Austin established that language was not merely descriptive (constative utterances), but also *did* things (performative utterances). Louis-Marie Chauvet declared that «[constative and performative] always subsist in dialectical tension as two poles of language»[61], thereby disagreeing with Austin who maintained that «we have here not really two poles but rather an historical development»[62]. This is not an insignificant issue to differ on; it is the key result that Austin argued toward throughout *How to Do Things with Words*. Austin set out to characterize a class of utterances that he thought existed alongside constative utterances. He investigated performatives and found that he could not distinguish them as a separate class because performatives *included* constatives. All constatives can be made into explicit performatives by the addition of «I state» at the beginning of them. To state something is to do a special kind of action, and to present something to another as knowledge. Hence, rather than two poles of language in a dialectical tension, we have a primitive level of communication which is performative and relationship-affecting, and on this foundation is built the descriptive function of language, constative utterances.

Given that Chauvet makes considerable effective use of Austin's ideas, the question arises as to what would be the consequences for

---

[61] L-M. CHAUVET, *Symbol and Sacraments*, 131.
[62] J.L. AUSTIN, *How to Do Things with Words*, 146.

Chauvet's sacramental theology of accepting the priority of the performative over the constative. We will explore the implications of taking this as fundamental to communication, first with reference to divine revelation, and then, with respect to the sacraments.

3.1 *Revelation as Primarily Performative*

Christians believe that God has spoken through the events of salvation history «in many and various ways by the prophets, [and] in these last days he has spoken to us by a Son»[63]. Viewing communication as primarily constative has been the dominant paradigm since the time of Aristotle. In the first chapter of *De Interpretatione* he wrote:

> Every sentence is significant [...], but not every sentence is a statement-making sentence, but only those in which there is truth or falsity. There is not truth or falsity in all sentences: a prayer is a sentence but is neither true nor false. The present investigation deals with the statement-making sentence; the others we can dismiss, since consideration of them belongs rather to the study of rhetoric or poetry[64].

Aristotle recognized that statement-making sentences (Austin's constative utterances) were only one part of language. He identified prayer as a form of speech that is neither true nor false. He implied that other forms of non-statement-making speech exist but dismissed them from consideration in his philosophy and assigned them to rhetoric and poetry. Rhetoric deals with the language of persuasion and poetry is concerned with moving the hearer; so both fields are indeed vitally involved with language that does more than make true and false statements. However, since Aristotle focused on constatives, philosophers and theologians have followed his lead. From this perspective the important things that are revealed in all communication are the true or false statements. Divine revelation was thus understood (at least primarily) as the communication of truths; a collection of propositions. If, on the contrary, Austin's perspective of the priority of the performative nature of language is adopted, then divine revelation will be seen, as all performatives are, in the words of Chauvet «an act really changing the position of the subjects by the very act of the enunciation»[65]. In this

---

[63] *DV* 4 citing Heb 1:1-2.
[64] ARISTOTLE, *De Interpretatione*, 17, a 1-5.
[65] L.-M. CHAUVET, *Symbol and Sacraments*, 131.

performative understanding, the primary effect of revelation is to put humanity and the cosmos into a new relationship with God. The key is not the *content* of revelation but that *God has spoken to humankind*. This word being spoken does not return empty, it really changes the world.

Moses was instructed to take off his shoes on approaching the burning bush, because the communicative action of God had made that place holy (Exodus 3:5). Making an area sacred is to literally change its social «place»; it ceases to be part of the profane world and is set apart. Since God has spoken in the world, the world is different – its *place* has changed. This holiness is perceived as concentric on the Christ-event: the Holy Land, the Holy City, the Holy One of God. The holiness is also related to time: the time of the prophets, the ministry of Jesus and his post-resurrection appearances, the apostolic age, and the post-apostolic period. Revelation puts the world into a new relationship and offers to everyone the possibility of actualizing that relationship more fully, by consciously accepting it and whole-heartedly responding to it. The lover cannot *make* his beloved love him back, but he can *woo* her. The *content* of the expressions used in courtship is important, but secondary to the love relationship being offered by those expressions.

In the rare times that New Testament authors write about their own works they do not suggest a priority of propositional content. As the exegete Étienne Nodet and historian Justin Taylor, observe:

> This prologue [of Luke] does not specify any content, even though it is obviously a biography of Jesus, but concentrates solely on the status of the book, of the witnesses and of those to whom it is addressed. According to 1John 1:4, «we are writing to you that your joy may be made perfect», a declaration which puts a seal on a process of reception and transmission, described in terms of bodily senses, resulting in communion between the writer and those addressed[66].

The effects described are performative ones; relationship-affecting. The scriptures, which have a normative role in the transmission of revelation, are written, «so that you may believe» (John 20:31) rather than solely *what* ought be believed.

Vatican I stressed the propositional content of revelation, presenting «a body of divine doctrine furnishing answers to important questions

---

[66] E. NODET – J. TAYLOR, *The Origins of Christianity*, 11.

about God, man and the universe»[67]. The chapter of *Dei Filius* on revelation scarcely mentions Christ; its emphasis is on those *things* which are to be believed:

> Wherefore, by divine and catholic faith all those things are to be believed which are contained in the word of God as found in scripture and tradition, and which are proposed by the church as matters to believed as divinely revealed, whether by her solemn judgement or in her ordinary and universal magisterium[68].

In contrast, the fathers of Vatican II present a *person* who is to be believed:

> The most intimate truth which this revelation gives us about God and the salvation of man shines forth in Christ, who is himself both the mediator and the sum total of Revelation[69].

There has been dogmatic development between 1870 and 1965. The magisterium presents the person of Christ as the completion and summation of revelation. Miracles and prophecies are no longer singled out as «certain signs of revelation»[70]; they are now one aspect, among others, of the presence of the Son of God. What Jesus reveals is not a collection of «things about God» but his very self as the ultimate revelation of the Father:

> To see Jesus is to see His Father. For this reason Jesus perfected revelation by fulfilling it through his whole work of making Himself present and manifesting Himself: through His words and deeds, His signs and wonders, but especially through His death and glorious resurrection from the dead and final sending of the Spirit of truth[71].

From revelation as a set of true statements about God to revelation as the self-manifestation of the person of Jesus Christ, God's Son and our saviour, is a significant development in magisterial teaching. Theologians need philosophical tools adequate to address the issues involved.

---

[67] A. DULLES, *Revelation Theology*, 172.

[68] *Dei Filius* III, 3.

[69] *DV* 2. The contrast is not absolute. Revelation as personal is present in Vatican I. The Council does state that it pleased God «to reveal Himself and the eternal decrees of his will» (DzH 3004), and not only a set of truths about himself.

[70] See *Dei Filius* III, 3.

[71] *DV* 4.

Austin's treatment of communication, as doing far more than making true and false statements, seems peculiarly well-fitted to this task.

If divine revelation, like the utterances of God in the creation account, is seen as primarily performative, then its information content is secondary to its effecting and affecting relationships. Revelation changes the social space of the cosmos and offers to everyone the possibility of relationship with the Trinity, which they can accept by consciously and whole-heartedly responding. Sacraments presume and assume revelation. They are a response to the divine initiative. They are the ritual reception of, and performative response to, that which God is offering.

3.2 Sacraments as Primarily Performative

The rituals used in the celebration of the seven sacraments contain many constative utterances. Facts about God, Jesus Christ and the life of the Christian are presented during the ceremony. More fundamentally, any reporting of a past event is constative («I warn you» is performative, «Yesterday, I warned you» is not), and there is much recalling of salvation history in the rituals. For example, the blessing of the water in baptism contains utterances like «In the waters of the Jordan your Son was baptized by John and anointed with the Spirit»[72]. The scripture readings employed are replete with constative utterances. According to Botha's analysis of the Johannine account of Jesus and the Samaritan woman (John 4:1-42), 41 of the 50 utterances in that passage are constative[73]. The institution narrative in the Eucharistic prayers is a recounting of a past event «On the night before he died, Jesus took bread ...» and is therefore constative in form. Even the clear performative utterances «I baptize you» and «I absolve you» may be deceptive. According to B.R. Brinkmann «the history of the personal or declarative mode for baptism does not clearly take us back to the beginnings»[74].

If constative and performative are two poles of language, then the greater frequency of occurrence of constative utterances in liturgy would suggest that Christian worship is predominantly descriptive. Recognising that constatives are a class of performatives and realizing

---

[72] *Rites* I, 327 §571.
[73] J.E. BOTHA, *Jesus and the Samaritan Woman*, 96-186.
[74] B. BRINKMANN, «On Sacramental Man: I, Language Patterning», 398.

that apparently simple constative statements can be used to perlocutionary effect, enables the nature of liturgical language to be seen differently. Familiar assertions about salvation history and tales of Jesus are not uttered for their information content. The facts given in liturgy are rarely new to the participants. These stories are told because they are foundational to the body. The Church is the group that keeps the memory of Jesus alive and continues his work of salvation. The anthropologist Margaret Mead defined ritual as:

> The repetition of those symbols which evoke the feeling of that primordial event which initially called the community into being with such power that it effects our presence at that event – in other words, represents the primordial event[75].

The utterances in the scriptural texts may be constative, but when the scriptures are *proclaimed* liturgically, they are both a performance and implicitly performative; they are doing something. Declaring how God has acted in the past (constative) prepares people for his action in the present ritual (implicit performative). Part of the performativity of liturgical language identified by Ladrière is its capacity to self-implicate. By attending to the prayers of the celebrant which are couched in the first-person plural, by responding with «Amen», and by praying in unison, participants in liturgy take themselves into the experience of being church. By identifying with «we» statements, they position themselves within the community, implicitly claiming to belong to a group that, in space and time, transcends the congregation gathered with them. Prayer, movement and song in unison unite the group on multiple levels; a congregation is in a socially different space from an audience. The sharing of the eucharistic bread and cup involves a human action of putting oneself into communion with companions as well as the divine response to this ritual gesture. In standing for the gospel and listening reverently, the hearers take up the social place of disciples. Christian ritual has the perlocutionary effect of putting participants into the position of the first followers of Jesus. Their very taking part in liturgy is significant, as Richard Fenn indicates:

> But the point here is simply that to take part in any liturgy is to signify to oneself and others that one is constituting a community and oneself as a member of that community. So to take part in the Christian liturgy is to

---

[75] U. HOLMES, «Ritual and the Social Drama», 197.

take on one's role in a new kingdom: one that «shall have no end». It is the political act of all time and is therefore potentially seditious within the secular politics of a specific time and place. Caesar understood the political nature of the liturgy all too well[76].

Simply attending a liturgy is a communication, a public stance. The action of gathering together and forming a congregation is the first performative act of any liturgy. Both chronologically and logically, sacraments are performative before they are constative. According to *Sacrosanctum Concilium* «the purpose of the sacraments is to sanctify men, to build up the body of Christ and finally, to give worship to God. Because they are signs they also instruct»[77]. Each aspect of the purpose proposed by the Council is performative: «to sanctify», «to build up», «to give worship». The secondary effect «to instruct» is also performative.

Sacraments are very precisely a response to the performative utterances of divine revelation. Communication is a symbolic exchange and revelation is communication. The «*hau*» of a gift[78] acts upon the recipients to enable them to receive the gift and to freely evoke a return-gift. The Holy Spirit acts in divine revelation to prepare humankind to receive the Word of God and to freely enter into the relationship of grace. The sacraments are ritual expressions of that return-gift. In Baptism the candidates' ears are anointed so that they may hear the word of God. God has spoken and they want to be among those who are actively listening and responding. The water ritual and their being named with the authority of the Trinity mean they are *defined* in terms of a relationship with God. They take a *Christian* name, so that they and the world may know of their relationship to Christ, the Word of God.

4. Salvation History as Communicative Action

Sacramental Theology is intimately connected with Ecclesiology, which the Catechism observes when it declares:

The sacraments are «of the Church» in the double sense that they are «by her» and «for her». They are «by the Church», for she is the sacrament of Christ's action at work in her through the mission of the Holy Spirit. They are «for the Church» in the sense that «the sacraments make the Church»,

---

[76] R. FENN, *Liturgies and Trials*, 28.
[77] *SC* 59.
[78] See Ch. III 7.1 above. The *hau* is the spirit of the gift.

since they manifest and communicate to men, above all in the Eucharist, the mystery of communion with the God who is love, One in three persons[79].

This description includes the notions of communication and communion. The sacraments «communicate to men», and the Church itself is a sacrament because Christ's action is at work in her. The encyclical *Ecclesia de Eucharistia* opens with the thematic sentence: «The Church draws her life from the Eucharist»[80], and proclaims that this «recapitulates *the heart of the mystery of the Church*». Both the Church and the sacraments are embedded in the sweep of salvation history, the story of God's interaction with humanity. Does the theory of communicative action have application to this context?

Creation, God's first act of revelation, is presented in the scriptures as being accomplished by utterances. Performatives of unsurpassed force, these mighty statements uttered with divine authority to no audience (except God himself and those who later read of them), effect what they speak of. They display God's primacy over every class of being.

«Covenant» is one of the great themes in the Old Testament. Each of the covenants was initiated by God speaking. Through promise and contract God entered into special relationships with individuals and groups, leading to the formation of a people who considered themselves as God's chosen. The relationship between the people and God is symbolized and concretized in the Law. More than a collection of imperatives, this was understood as how to live in response to God's revelation. In the religious culture of the Old Testament there were a variety of rituals. These have been positively understood in the Christian tradition as types and foreshadowings of the «mysteries» of the new covenant. The liturgical songs that permeated these rituals, the psalms, are still in use in Christian (and Jewish) liturgy. Yet another thread in the tapestry of the salvation history is the Wisdom traditions. Originally appearing as collections of pithy sayings, proverbs, perhaps collected by sages responsible for educating court officials, these developed into paeans of praise for lady Wisdom. They were utterances and teachings intended to discourage folly and to promote skills for good living.

---

[79] *CCC* §1118.
[80] JOHN PAUL II, *Ecclesia de Eucharistia*, 1.

Judaism was a culture characterized by the production and preservation of sacred writings. The laws of the priests, the sayings of the prophets, the proverbs of the sages, and the songs of the psalmists were recorded, ordered, and kept alive by way of texts. The process is reflexive and recursive as these texts shaped the liturgy and the culture, which then re-edited those same texts and produced more to join the canon. David in his dying discourse describes himself as «the singer of the songs of Israel» (2 Sam 23:1). The songs he sang both belong to Israel and form Israel; they may have done more for national unity and identity than his many military successes. Jesus was born and raised within this context of a people of God formed by God's word. This people were the primary recipients of his ministry of preaching, teaching, exorcism and healing. From among their number he called disciples.

In short the story of salvation history can easily be told in terms of communicative action. The perspective promoted by Chauvet can be applied «across the board». Viewing divine revelation as communication is not difficult for that is what it is. The human response is historical, contingent and fallible.

4.1 *Always-Already Speaking*

The Church was not created out of nothing. Its first members did not join as blank slates. They arrived already speaking a language of faith; they were already formed in a culture of belief. The first members of the Church were embedded in the cultural matrix of Judaism. The world view they shared was one in which the scriptures were read, God was worshipped, and revelation and divine authority were accepted as factual. The Church has never forgotten its origins and, against opponents like Marcion[81], it has claimed continuity with the people of the covenant. However, in light of the novelty the Church saw in itself, it came to see also a discontinuity with the «old» covenant.

---

[81] Marcion (d. c. 160) was one of the first to attempt to define a list of the books sacred to the Christians. Gnostic and anti-Semite, he considered the Jewish Creator-God as only the Demiurge, entirely different from the God of Love revealed in Christ. His canon consisted of an edited version of Luke's gospel and ten epistles of Paul.

4.2 *Novelty*

What sets Christianity apart and creates the distinction from Judaism is the person of Jesus of Nazareth whom his disciples hailed as the Christ. Like all points of discontinuity he belongs fully to what comes before him and fully to what follows, yet, because of him, what follows is different from what came before. Jesus spent a period of time as a wandering teacher and people followed him. From among his followers he chose a core group whom he formed more intensively and, by choosing them, set them apart from the others.

The account of the calling of the Twelve, like that of the sending out of the 72, is a chain of performative utterances. Jesus *calls, names* and *sets apart*. Jesus *sends forth*. These are all illocutionary verbs. For them to be happily accomplished by Jesus, the group had to accept his authority over them. The group did accept him as their «Rabbi» and «Master» and accepted his right to:

– name them – «Simon to whom he gave the name Peter» (Mark 3:16);
– call them: «Follow me» (Mark 1:18);
– chastise them: «He rebuked Peter» (Mark 8:33);
– mission them: «He summoned the twelve and began to send them out» (Mark 6:7a);
– vest authority in them: «giving them authority over the unclean spirits» (Mark 6:7b);
– teach them: «"Here is a teaching that is new" they said "and with authority behind it."» (Mark 1:27).

The characteristic saying of Jesus that this group of disciples is to remember, is «(Amen,) I say unto you ...» He uses this expression in teachings, healings and exorcisms. In the understanding of the group each of these types of activity was evidence of the *authority* of Jesus.

A group of people become disciples by choosing to respond to a call to follow a master. The disciples of Jesus all entered into a relationship with Jesus whereby they recognized him as having authority over them. In some situations members of the group exercised authority delegated by Jesus. The group members had their worldview transformed by Jesus. They accepted what he said God was like. They imitated him in calling God «Father». They believed Jesus to be the Messiah sent by the Father. They expected him to have a key role in the end-time judgement.

This group has rituals special to it. They have some kind of meal ritual that is distinctive[82]. They take over the water ritual that John the Baptist has been using and reinterpret it in the name of Jesus. The disciples of the Baptist have a prayer, special to their number, which they pray in addition to their usual Jewish prayers. So the disciples of Jesus ask for, and are given, a distinctive prayer of their own (Luke 11:1-4). The suffering, death and resurrection of Jesus have a transformative impact on the disciples. The post-resurrection encounters, the experience of the Ascension and Pentecost weld them into a new reality which comes to call itself the Church and its members the Christians. In the light of the resurrection their estimation of the authority of Jesus is transformed. He is understood as having authority over life and death. His right to speak on behalf of God is fully vindicated and accepted, *just at the time when he is no longer present to speak*. They proclaim Jesus as Lord, as Christ, and as Son of God. This Church group constitutes a communicative community. They share a culture, a world-view and a language. They have stories of their foundation. They have a day each week when they gather to eat the meal of the Lord together and to keep his memory alive. It is a striking change from celebrating the God-given Sabbath to celebrating the Lord's Day. Their ordinary lives continue: they earn their living, care for their families and try to put into action what they had been taught by the Lord. The very earliest Church was a tiny movement within the enormous Roman Empire. It was only when they gathered that they knew themselves to be Church. In the liturgy of the Lord's meal they rendered present their reality as disciples of Jesus. From that self-understanding they

- taught in the name of Jesus: «those who are working amongst you and are above you in the Lord as your teachers» (1Thess 5:12);
- prayed in the name of Jesus: «all the saints everywhere who pray to our Lord Jesus Christ» (1Cor 1:1);

---

[82] E. NODET – J. TAYLOR, *The Origins of Christianity*, 119-20: «Behind the account of the Last Supper there is indeed a liturgical tradition which is independent of Passover. It is none other than a sort of community meal in which the significant elements are bread and/or wine. This is not a feast, but only the first stage of a complete meal (which may or may not be festive), since the share which each receives is minimal and would not normally be sufficient for food. The central meaning which it symbolized is connected with Pentecost, signifying both the renewal of the Covenant (Sinai) and an anticipation of the Kingdom (first-fruits). It has a weekly expression, linked to the night between the Sabbath and the first day of the week (watching for the dawn). It may also have a daily expression».

– worked «miracles and marvels through the name of your holy servant Jesus» (Acts 4:30);
– healed in the name of Jesus: «Aeneas, Jesus Christ cures you» (Acts 9:34);
– anointed their sick «in the name of the Lord» (James 5:14);
– exorcised in the name of Jesus: «I order you in the name of the Jesus Christ to leave that woman» (Acts 16:18);
– offered reconciliation in the name of Jesus: «We beseech you on behalf of Christ, be reconciled to God». (2Cor 5:20);
– «dedicated their lives to the name of our Lord Jesus Christ» (Acts 15:26);
– exercised authority over their own number in the name of Jesus; «My orders, in the Lord's name, are that this letter is to be read to all the brothers. The grace of our Lord Jesus Christ be with you». (1Thess 5:28);
– commended themselves to Jesus as they died: «Lord Jesus, receive my spirit» (Acts 7:59).

What made the Church the Church was that it acted in the name of Jesus. When church officials uttered a performative they claimed to do so as a proxy for the Lord. The members of that community are precisely those who accepted the authority of their office-holders to do so. The liturgy was where the Church most recognized itself as Church and the liturgy defined the Church as the Church defined the liturgy. The role of the ordained in ordering the Church is connected with their role in liturgy.

Communicative communities can perdure longer than the lifetimes of individual members, so long as the community continues to identify itself with its origins and with the body that existed between that time and this. The Treaty of Waitangi still has normative force, because the New Zealand government sees itself as in continuation with the Crown that authorised Captain Hobson to make and sign the Treaty. Respecting obligations incurred in the past is important for the continuity and legitimacy of communicative communities.

The Church was formed by the performative actions of Jesus of Nazareth and the influence of the Holy Spirit. The Roman Catholic Church understands itself as being in continuity with its foundation by Christ. It claims to be vested with authority by Jesus Christ to act in his name. The sacraments of the Church are ways that the Church defines, preserves, and develops Christ's work of sanctification. The sacraments are done in his name as works of Christ rather than merely parts of Church order. Edward Schillebeeckx describes them as *encounters*:

> From this account of the sacraments as the earthly prolongation of Christ's glorified bodiliness, it follows immediately that the Church's sacraments are not things but encounters of men on earth with the glorified man Jesus by way of a visible form. On the plane of history they are the visible and tangible embodiment of the heavenly saving action of Christ. They are this saving action itself in its availability to us; a personal act of the Lord in earthly visibility and open availability[83].

The actions of Christ are continued and made available by the Church. Christ is the primary agent in each sacramental event. The sacrament, through the mediation of the Church, brings the participant into encounter with the risen Christ.

5. Conclusion

Sacraments clearly *do* things, they are «actions of Christ and his Church»[84]. While communication is understood as merely the exchange of data, then any communication model will appear inadequate to speak of the dynamic reality of sacraments in the life and work of the Church. However Austin has opened up a vista of the performative nature of utterances; according to him we «do things with words»[85]. Habermas developed Austin's ideas into the theory of communicative *action* providing philosophical underpinning to Austin's analytic insights. Sociology has described the power and importance of language and ritual in all human societies. Human beings do not live in unmediated contact with brute reality. They live socialized into a richly symbolic, inter-subjective world overlaid with language. According to Chauvet and Mauss the fundamental transaction of society is not trade but gift-exchange. The gifts range from the huge and outrageously valuable to the tiny and symbolic. Each gift calls for reception and a return-gift. Chauvet includes speech transactions as symbolic gift-exchanges. Combined, these theories provide a way of speaking of sacramental efficacy in terms of communicative action – a communication model of sacraments. Revelation is communication, a gracious self-gift by God. Perceived as communicative actions the sacraments are the ritual recep-

---

[83] E. Schillebeeckx, *Christ the Sacrament of the Encounter with God*, 44.
[84] *CIC* 840.
[85] J.L. Austin, *How to Do Things with Words* – the book title itself.

tion and return-gift to God's self-revelation. The spirit of the gift of divine revelation is the Holy Spirit, who prepares, evokes and enables a response from the human spirit. The central act of this response is the act of faith with its three distinguishable dimensions of confession of facts, commitment to relationship with Christ within the Church, and confidence in the promises of Christ[86]. These three dimensions correspond with those identified by Habermas as part of every human utterance. There is a lesser act of faith in one's fellow human beings in each communication. The full act of faith is expressed and staged in the sacramental rituals. In different areas and aspects of life the Church constitutes itself and exercises its ministry of sanctification by enabling the faithful to express and deepen their faith (and thereby know themselves as «the faithful») through the exercise of the sacraments.

Viewing sacraments as communicative actions involves an emphasis on subjectivity and the fruitfulness of the sacrament. Communication imposes responsibility on both speaker and hearer to ensure a happy outcome. Understood in this light, sacraments call the ministers of the rite to strive in every way to ensure the success and fruitfulness of the communication and they call on recipients to participate actively in full recognition of the intention of the Church. For, in sacraments, the Church intends what Christ did, to save the world.

---

[86] See G. O'COLLINS, *Fundamental Theology*, 137-39.

ABBREVIATIONS

AAS	*Acta Apostolicae Sedis,* Città del Vaticano
ABD	*Anchor Bible Dictionary,* ed. D.N. Freedman, New York 1992
ACR	*The Australasian Catholic Record*
al.	*alii* (others)
AnGr	Analecta Gregoriana
A-T	G. ALBERIGO – *al.,* ed., *Conciliorum oecumenicorum decreta,* 1973^3 – N. TANNER, ed., *Decrees of the Ecumenical Councils,* 1990. «Tanner» preserves the pagination of «Alberigo», while adding an English translation; hence only one page number is given in references.
BBC	British Broadcasting Corporation
BiI	*Biblical Interpretation*
BS	*Biblical Studies*
CCC	*Catechism of the Catholic Church,* Dublin 1994
CDF	Congregation for the Doctrine of the Faith
Ch.	Chapter
CIC	*Code of Canon Law*
CSEL	Corpus Scriptorum Ecclesiasticorum Latinorum, Vienna 1866-
DV	*Dei Verbum,* Dogmatic Constitution on Divine Revelation, Second Vatican Council, 1965
DzH	H. DENZINGER – P. HÜNERMANN, *Enchiridion Symbolorum, definitionum et declarationum de rebus fidei et morum,* Freiburg 1991^{37}
ed.	edited by, editor(s)
FR	*Fides et Ratio,* Encyclical Letter on the Relationship between Faith and Reason, John Paul II, 1998
Fs.	Festschrift (Written in honour of)
Gr.	*Gregorianum*
GS	*Gaudium et Spes,* Pastoral Constitution on the Church in the Modern World, Second Vatican Council, 1965
HeyJ	*The Heythrop Journal*

HTD	J.L. AUSTIN, *How to Do Things with Words*, ed. J.O. Urmson – M. Sbisà, Cambridge MA 1962, 1975[2]
ITQ	*Irish Theological Quarterly*
JAC	*JAC: A Journal of Composition Theory*
JB	*Jerusalem Bible*
JBL	*Journal of Biblical Literature*
JP	*Journal of Philosophy*
JR	*Journal of Religion*
JTS	*Journal of Theological Studies*
LG	*Lumen Gentium*, Dogmatic Constitution on the Church, Second Vatican Council, 1964
MTh	*Modern Theology*
ND	J. NEUNER – J. DUPUIS, ed., *The Christian Faith in the Doctrinal Documents of the Catholic Church*, Bangalore 2001[7]
OED	*Oxford English Dictionary*, ed. J.H. Simpson – E.S.C. Weiner, Oxford 1989[2]
PhP	J.L. AUSTIN, *Philosophical Papers*, ed. J.O. Urmson – G.J. Warnock, Oxford 1961
PhRev	*Philosophical Review*
PL	J-P. MIGNE, *Patrologia completus cursus, Series Latina*, 1844-64
PhRh	*Philosophy and Rhetoric*
RB	*Revue Biblique*
Rites	*The Rites of the Catholic Church*, I-II, study edition, Collegeville MN 1990, 1991
RelS	*Religious Studies*
REP	E. CRAIG, ed., *Routledge Encyclopedia of Philosophy*, London 1998
RStR	*Religious Studies Review*
SC	*Sacrosanctum Concilium*, Constitution on the Sacred Liturgy, Second Vatican Council, 1963
SJL	K.T. FANN, ed., *Symposium on J.L. Austin*, London 1969
SJT	*Scottish Journal of Theology*
ST	THOMAS AQUINAS, *Summa Theologica*
Suppl.	Supplement to
TDNT	*Theological Dictionary of the New Testament*, ed. G. Friedrich, Grand Rapids 1971
TI	K. RAHNER, *Theological Investigations*, London 1961-1992
TS	*Theological Studies*

BIBLIOGRAPHY

1. Magisterial Documents

Ad Gentes, Decree on The Church's Missionary Activity, Second Vatican Council, 1965, A-T 1011-42.

Bulla Unionis Armenorum, Bull of Union with the Armenians, Council of Florence, 1439, A-T 534-59.

Dei Filius, Dogmatic Constitution on the Catholic Faith, First Vatican Council, 1870, A-T 804-11.

Dei Verbum, Dogmatic Constitution on Divine Revelation, Second Vatican Council, 1965, A-T 971-81.

Ecclesia de Eucharistia, Encyclical Letter on the Eucharist in its Relationship with the Church, John Paul II, 2003, *AAS* 95 (2003) 433-75.

Familiaris Consortio, Apostolic Exhortation on the Role of the Christian Family in the Modern World, John Paul II, 1981, *AAS* 74 (1982) 81-191.

Fides et Ratio, Encyclical Letter on the Relationship between Faith and Reason, John Paul II, 1998, *AAS* 91 (1999) 5-88.

Gaudium et Spes, Pastoral Constitution on the Church in the Modern World, Second Vatican Council, 1965, A-T 1069-1135.

Instructio de Ecclesiali Theologi Vocatione, Instruction on the Ecclesial Vocation of the Theologian, Congregation for the Doctrine of the Faith, 1990, *AAS* 82 (1990) 1550-70.

Liturgiam Authenticam, Fifth Instruction «for the right implementation of the Constitution on the Sacred Liturgy of the Second Vatican Council» Congregation for Divine Worship and the Discipline of the Sacraments, 2001, *AAS* 93(2001) 685-726.

Lumen Gentium, Dogmatic Constitution on the Church, Second Vatican Council, 1964, A-T 849-900.

Optatam Totius, Decree on the Training of Priests, Second Vatican Council, 1965, A-T 947-59.

Sacrosanctum Concilium, Constitution on the Sacred Liturgy, Second Vatican Council, 1963, A-T 820-43.

2. General works

ALBUQUERQUE, D., *Truth and Action in Speech Acts: A Study on J.L. Austin's Essays on Truth*, New Delhi 1995.

ALLAN, K., «Speech act theory», in R. ASHER, ed., *Encyclopedia of Languages and Linguistics*, Oxford 1994, VIII, 4127-38.

ALLWOOD, J., «A Critical Look at Speech Act Theory», in Ö. DAHL, ed., *Logic, Pragmatics and Grammar*, Göteborg 1977, 53-99.

AMBROSE, G.P., «Chauvet and Pickstock: Two Compatible Visions?», in L. BOEVE – L. LEIJSSEN, ed., *Contemporary Sacramental Contours of a God Incarnate*, Leuven 2001, 74-84.

ARENS, E., ed., *Habermas und die Theologie: Beiträge zur theologischen Rezeption, Diskussion und Kritik der Theorie kommunikativen Handelns*, Dusseldorf 1989.

ASIEDU, F.B.A., «Illocutionary Acts and the Uncanny: On Nicholas Wolterstorff's Idea of Divine Discourse», *HeyJ* 62 (2001) 283-310.

ATKINSON, J.M., «Refusing Invited Applause: Preliminary Observations from a Case Study of Charismatic Oratory», in T.A. van DIJK, ed., *Handbook of Discourse Analysis*, III, London 1985, 161-81.

AUER, J., *Allgemeine Sakramentenlehre und Das Mysterium der Eucharistie*, Regensburg 1971; English trans., *A General Doctrine of the Sacraments and The Mystery of the Eucharist*, Washington 1995.

AUSTIN, J.L., «*Agathon* and *Eudaimonia* in the Ethics of Aristotle», in J.M.E. MORAVCSIK, ed., *Aristotle: A Collection of Critical Essays*, New York 1967, 261-96.

———, «Are There *a priori* Concepts», in *Proceedings of the Aristotelian Society* 1939, 83-105; *PhP*, 1-22.

———, «The Meaning of a Word», in *PhP*, 23-43.

———, «Other Minds», in *Proceedings of the Aristotelian Society*, Suppl. 20, 1940, 148-87; *PhP*, 44-84.

———, «Truth», in *Proceedings of the Aristotelian Society*, Suppl. 24, 1950, 111-128; *PhP*, 85-101.

———, «How to Talk: Some Simple Ways», in *Proceedings of the Aristotelian Society* 1953-54, 227-46; *PhP*, 181-200.

AUSTIN, J.L., «Unfair to Facts», in *PhP*, 102-22.

————, «A Plea for Excuses», in *Proceedings of the British Academy* 1956, 1-30; *PhP*, 123-52.

————, «Ifs and Cans», in *Proceedings of the British Society* 1956, 109-32; *PhP*, 153-80.

————, «Performative Utterances», in *PhP*, 220-40.

————, «Pretending», in *Proceedings of the Aristotelian Society* 1958, 261-78; *PhP*, 201-19.

————, *How to Do Things with Words*, ed. J.O. Urmson – M. Sbisà, Cambridge MA 1962, 1975^2.

————, *Philosophical Papers*, ed. J.O. Urmson – G.J. Warnock, Oxford 1961.

————, *Sense and Sensibilia*, ed. G.J. Warnock, Oxford 1962.

AYER, A.J., *Language, Truth and Logic*, London 1936, 1964^2.

BAIRD, J.A., *Holy Word: The Paradigm for New Testament Formation*, London 2002.

BAKER, J., «Grice, Herbert Paul (1913-88)», in *REP*, IV, 172-77.

BARRON, R., «Thomas Aquinas: Postmodern», in L. BOEVE – L. LEIJSSEN, ed., *Contemporary Sacramental Presence in a Postmodern Context*, Leuven 2001, 265-78.

BAUERSCHMIDT, F., «The Lamb of God in the Age of Mechanical Reproduction», *Communio* 30 (2003) 581-98.

BAXTER, H., «System and life-world in Habermas's *Theory of Communicative Action*», *Theory and Society* 16 (1987) 39-86.

BeDUHN, J.D., «The Historical Assessment of Speech Acts: Clarifications of Austin and Skinner for the Study of Religions», *Method and Theory in the Study of Religion* 14 (2002) 84-114.

BELLAH, R.N., «Christianity and Symbolic Realism», *Scientific Study of Religion* 9 (1970) 89-96.

BENVENISTE, É., *Problèmes de linguistique générale*, Paris 1966.

————, *Le vocabulaire des institutions indo-européennes: 2. pouvoir, droit, religion*, Paris 1969.

BERGIN, L., *O Propheticum Lavacrum: Baptism as Symbolic Act of Eschatological Salvation*, Rome 1999.

————, «Between Memory and Promise: Sacramental Theology since Vatican II», in L. BERGIN, ed., *Faith, Word and Culture*, Dublin 2004, 80-97.

BERNSTEIN, R.J., ed., *Habermas and Modernity*, Cambridge MA 1985.

BOEVE, L., «The Sacramental Interruption of Rituals of Life», *HeyJ* 64 (2003) 401-17.

BOEVE, L., – LEIJSSEN, L., ed., *Sacramental Presence in a Postmodern Context*, Leuven 2001.

————, ed., *Contemporary Sacramental Contours of a God Incarnate*, Leuven 2001.

BOTHA, J.E., *Jesus and the Samaritan Woman: A Speech Act Reading of John 4:1-42*, Leiden 1991.

BOTTOMORE, T., *The Frankfurt School*, London 1984.

BOURDIEU, P., *Ce que parler veut dire: l'économie des échanges linguistiques*, Paris 1982; English trans., *Language and Symbolic Power*, tr. G. Raymond – M. Adams, Cambridge 1991.

BRACKEN, J.A., «Toward a New Philosophical Theology based on Intersubjectivity», *TS* 59 (1998) 703-19.

BRETSCHER, P.G., «Exodus 4:22-23 and the Voice from Heaven», *JBL* 87 (1968) 301-11.

BRIGGS, R.S., «The Uses of Speech-Act Theory in Biblical Interpretation», *BS* 9 (2001) 229-77.

————, *Words in Action: Speech Act Theory and Biblical Interpretation*, Edinburgh 2001.

BRINKMANN, B.R., «On Sacramental Man: I Language Patterning», *HeyJ* 13 (1972) 371-401.

————, «On Sacramental Man: II The Way of Intimacy», *HeyJ* 14 (1973) 5-34.

————, «On Sacramental Man: III The Socially Operational Way», *HeyJ* 14 (1973) 162-89.

————, «On Sacramental Man: IV The Way of Interiorization», *HeyJ* 14 (1973) 280-306

————, «"Sacramental Man" and Speech Acts Again», *HeyJ* 16 (1975) 418-20.

BROWNING, D.S., – FIORENZA, F.S., ed., *Habermas, Modernity and Public Theology*, New York 1992.

BUSS, M.J., «Potential and Actual Interactions between Speech Act Theory and Biblical Studies», *Semeia* 41 (1988) 125-34.

CALLAHAN, C.A., «Karl Rahner's Theology of Symbol: Basis for his Theology of the Church and the Sacraments», *ITQ* 67 (1982) 195-205.

CAMPBELL, J.G., «Are All Speech-Acts Self-Involving?», *RelS* 8 (1972) 161-64.

CARNAP, R., *Meaning and Necessity: A Study in Semantics and Modal Logic*, Chicago 1947, 1956[2].

CHAUVET, L-M., *Du Symbolique au symbole. Essai sur les sacrements*, Paris 1979.

———, *Symbole et Sacrement: Une relecture sacramentelle de l'existence chrétienne*, Paris 1987; English trans., *Symbol and Sacrament: A Sacramental Reinterpretation of Christian Existence*, tr. P. Madigan – M. Beaumont, Collegeville MN 1995.

———, *Les sacrements. Parole de Dieu au risque du corps*, Paris 1993; English trans., *The Sacraments: The Word of God at the Mercy of the Body*, tr. P. Madigan – M. Beaumont, Collegeville MN 2001.

———, «The Liturgy in its Symbolic Space», *Concilium* (1995/3) 29-39.

———, «The Broken Bread as Theological Figure of Eucharistic Presence», in L. BOEVE – L. LEIJSSEN, ed., *Contemporary Sacramental Presence in a Postmodern Context*, Leuven 2001, 236-62.

CHOMSKY, N., *Syntactic Structures*, The Hague 1957.

CLARKE, W.N., «John Paul II: The Complementarity of Faith and Philosophy in the Search for Truth», *Communio* 26 (1999) 557-70.

DAVIES, O., «The Sign Redeemed: A Study in Christian Fundamental Semiotics», *Modern Theology* 19 (2003) 219-41.

DAVIS, S. – KENDALL, D. – O'COLLINS, G., ed., *The Redemption: An Interdisciplinary Symposium on Christ as Redeemer*, Oxford 2004.

DAWKINS, R., *The Selfish Gene*, Oxford 1976, 1982[2].

———, «Viruses of the Mind», 1991, in B. DALHBOM, ed., *Dennet and His Critics: Demystifying Mind*, Cambridge MA 1993. [On-line text, accessed 11.05.2004] http://cscs.umich.edu/~crshalizi/Dawkins/viruses-of-the-mind.html.

DERRIDA, J., «Signature Event Context», *Glyph* 1 (1977) 172-97.

DETWEILER, R., «Speaking of Believing in Genesis 2-3», *Semeia* 41 (1988) 135-41.

van DIJK, T.A., «Discourse Analysis as a New Cross-Discipline», in T.A. van DIJK, ed., *Handbook of Discourse Analysis*, I, London 1985, 1-10.

DIX, G., *The Shape of the Liturgy*, Westminster 1945.

DOWNING, F.G., «Words as Deeds and Deeds as Words», *BiI* 3 (1995) 129-43.

DREW, P., «Analyzing the Use of Language in Courtroom Interaction», in T.A. van DIJK, ed., *Handbook of Discourse Analysis*, III, London 1985, 133-48.

DULLES, A., *Revelation Theology: A History*, New York 1969.

ELIADE, M., *Le Sacré et le Profane*, Paris 1956; English trans., *The Sacred and the Profane: The Nature of Religion*, tr. W.R. Trask, San Diego 1959.

————, *Mythes, Rêves et Mystères*, Paris 1957; English trans., *Myths, Dreams, and Mysteries: The Encounter between Contemporary Faiths and Archaic Realities*, tr. P. Mairet, New York 1960.

EVANS, D.D., *The Logic of Self-Involvement: A Philosophical Study of Everyday Language with Special Reference to the Christian Use of Language about God as Creator*, London 1963.

FANN, K.T., ed., *Symposium on J.L. Austin*, London 1969.

FARRELLY, C., *Introduction to Contemporary Political Theory*, London 2004.

FENN, R.K., «Recent Studies of Church Decline: The Eclipse of Ritual», *RStR* 8 (1982) 124-28.

————, *Liturgies and Trials: The Secularization of Religious Language*, Oxford 1982.

FERRARA, A., «Pragmatics», in T.A. van DIJK, ed., *Handbook of Discourse Analysis*, II, London 1985, 137-57.

FIORENZA, F.S., «The Church as a Community of Interpretation: Political Theology between Discourse Ethics and Hermeneutical Reconstruction», in R.J. BERNSTEIN, ed., *Habermas, Modernity and Public Theology*, New York 1992, 66-91.

FISH, S.E., *Is There a Text in This Class? The Authority of Interpretive Communities*, Cambridge MA 1980.

FORTIN-MELKEVIK, A., «The Reciprocal Exclusiveness of Modernity and Religion among Contemporary Thinkers: Jürgen Habermas and Marcel Gauchet», *Concilium* (1992/6) 57-66.

FRERE, W.H., *Studies in Early Roman Liturgy: I. The Kalendar*, Oxford 1930.

FRETHIEM, T.E., «Word of God», *ABD*, VI, 961-68.

FUCHS, L.F., «Louise-Marie Chauvet's Theology of Sacrament and Ecumenical Theology: Connections in Terms of an Ecumenical Hermeneutics of Unity Based on a Koinonia Ecclesiology», in L. BOEVE – L. LEIJSSEN, ed., *Contemporary Sacramental Contours of a God Incarnate*, Leuven 2001, 63-73.

GADAMER, H-G., *Wahrheit und Methode*, Tübingen 1960; English trans., *Truth and Method*, tr. G. Barden – J. Cumming, London 1975.

GARRIGAN, S., *Beyond Ritual: Sacramental Theology after Habermas*, Aldershot 2004.

GRADY, H. – WELLS, S., «Towards a Rhetoric of Intersubjectivity: Introducing Jürgen Habermas», *JAC* 6 (1985-6) 3-19.

GRAY, P.T., «Making Us Ourselves: Double Agency and Its Christological Context in the Thought of Austin Farrer», in L. BOEVE – J. RIES, ed., *The Presence of Transcendence*, Leuven 2001, 125-33.

GREY, G., *Ko Nga Whakapepeha me Nga Whakaahuareka a Nga Tipuna o Aotea-roa: Proverbial Sayings of the Ancestors of the New Zealand Race*, Cape Town 1857.

GRICE, H.P., «Meaning», *PhRev* 66 (1957) 377-88.

———, «Utterer's meaning and intentions», *PhRev* 78 (1969) 147-77.

———, *Studies in the Way of Words*, Cambridge MA 1989.

GRIFFITHS, P.J., «How Epistemology Matters to Theology», *JR* 79 (1999) 1-18.

GRIMES, R.L., *Beginnings in Ritual Studies*, Columbia 1982, 1985[2].

———, *Research in Ritual Studies: A Programmatic Essay and Bibliography*, London 1985.

———, «Infelicitous Performances and Ritual Criticism», *Semeia* 41 (1988) 103-22.

———, *Deeply into the Bone: Reinventing Rites of Passage*, Berkeley 2000.

GUZIE, T., *Jesus and the Eucharist*, New York 1974, 1995[3].

HABERMAS, J., *Strukturwandel der Öffentlichkeit*, Neuwied – Berlin 1962, Frankfurt 1989[2]; English trans., *The Structural Transformations of the Public Sphere*, tr. T. Burger, Cambridge 1989.

———, *Theorie und Praxis*, Neuwied – Berlin 1962; English trans., *Theory and Practise*, tr. J. Viertel, London 1974.

———, *Technik und Wissenschaft als Ideologie*, Frankfurt 1968; partial English trans. *Toward a Rational Society*, tr. J.J. Shapiro, London 1971.

———, *Erkenntnis und Interesse*, Frankfurt 1968; English trans., *Knowledge and Human Interest*, tr. J.J. Shapiro, London 1972.

———, *Zur Logik der Socialwissenschaften*, Frankfurt 1970; English trans., *On the Logic of the Social Sciences*, tr. S.W. Nicholsen – J.A. Stark, Cambridge MA 1998.

———, *Toward a Rational Society: Student Protest, Science, and Politics*, London 1971.

———, «The Public Sphere», in M. COHEN – N. FERMON, ed., *Princeton Readings in Political Thought*, Princeton 1996, 709-14.

HABERMAS, J., «Was heisst Universalpragmatik», in K. APEL, ed., *Sprachpragmatik und Philosophie*, Frankfurt 1976; English trans., «What is Universal Pragmatics?», in *Communication and the Evolution of Society*, tr. T. McCarthy, Boston 1979.

——, *Zur Rekonstruktion des historischen Materialismus*, Frankfurt 1976; partial English trans., *Communication and the Evolution of Society*, tr. F. G. Lawrence, Boston 1979.

——, *Theorie des kommunikativen Handelns*. I. *Handlungsrationalität und gesellschaftliche Rationalisierung*. II. *Zur Kritik der funktionalistischen Vernunft*, Frankfurt am Main 1981; English trans., *The Theory of Communicative Action*. I. *Reason and the Rationalization of Society*. II. *Lifeworld and System: A Critique of Functionalist Reason*, tr. T. McCarthy, Boston 1984, 1987.

——, *Moralbewusstsein und kommunikatives Handeln*, Frankfurt am Main 1983; English trans., *Moral Consciousness and Communicative Action*, tr. C. Lenhardt – S. Weber Nicholsen, Cambridge MA 1990.

——, *Der philosophische Diskurs der Moderne: Zwölf Vorlesungen*, Frankfurt am Main 1985, English trans., *The Philosophical Discourse of Modernity: Twelve Lectures*, tr. F. Lawrence, Cambridge MA 1987.

——, *Autonomy and Solidarity: Interviews with Jürgen Habermas*, P. DEWS, ed., London 1986, 1992[2].

——, «Transcendence from Within, Transcendence in this World», in D. BROWNING, – F.S. FIORENZA, ed., *Habermas, Modernity and Public Theology*, New York 1992, 226-50.

——, *Vergangenheit als Zukunft*, ed. M. Heller, Munich 1993[2]; English trans., *The Past as Future*, tr. M. Pensky, Cambridge 1994.

——, *Faktizität und Geltung*, Frankfurt 1992; English trans., *Between Facts and Norms*, tr. W. Rehg, Cambridge 1996.

——, «Discourse Ethics», in W. OUTHWAITE, ed., *The Habermas Reader*, Cambridge 1996, 180-192

——, « Relations to the World and Aspects of Rationality in Four Sociological Conceptions of Action», in W. OUTHWAITE, ed., *The Habermas Reader*, Cambridge 1996, 132-150.

——, «The Three Roots of Communicative Action», in W. OUTHWAITE, ed., *The Habermas Reader*, Cambridge 1996, 170-174.

——, «Technology and Science as "Ideology"», in W. OUTHWAITE, ed., *The Habermas Reader*, Cambridge 1996, 53-66.

——, *Religion and Rationality: Essays on Reason, God, and Modernity*, Cambridge 2002.

HABERMAS, J., «Dual-Layered Time: Personal notes on philosopher Theodor W. Adorno in the '50s», *Logos* 2.4 (2003) 52-57.

———, «Public Space and Political Public Sphere: The Biographical Roots of two Motifs in my Thought» (Commemorative Lecture, Kyoto 11/11/2004 Unpublished).

HANCHER, M., «Performative Utterance, the Word of God, and the Death of the Author», *Semeia* 41 (1988) 27-40.

HARRÉ, R., «Persuasion and Manipulation», in T.A. van DIJK, ed., *Discourse and Communication: New Approaches to the Analysis of Mass Media Discourse and Communication*, Berlin 1985, 126-42.

HEATHER, N., «Socio-cognitive Structures: The "Invisible Noticeboard" and Church Text as Social Practice», *Theology* 108 (2004) 105-16.

HELFMEYER, F.J., «אות *'ôth*», in G.J. BOTTERWECK – H. RINGGREN, ed., *Theological Dictionary of the Old Testament*, I, Grand Rapids 1974, 167-88.

HELLER, A., «Habermas and Marxism», in B. THOMPSON – D. HELD, ed., *Habermas: Critical Debates*, 21-41.

HERITAGE, J., «Analyzing News Interviews: Aspects of the Production of Talk for an Overhearing Audience», in T.A. van DIJK, ed., *Handbook of Discourse Analysis*, III, London 1985, 95-119.

HOLMES, U.T., «Liminality and Liturgy», *Worship* 47 (1973) 386-99.

———, «Ritual and the Social Drama», *Worship* 51 (1977) 197-213.

HOUSTON, W., «What did the Prophets Think they were Doing? Speech Acts and Prophetic Discourse in the Old Testament», *BiI* 1 (1993) 167-88.

HUSSERL, E., *Die Idee der Phänomenologie* 1907; English trans., *The Idea of Phenomenology*, tr. L. Hardy, Dordrecht 1999.

———, *Ideen zu einer reinen Phänomenologie und phänomenologischen Philosophie* 1913; English trans., *Ideas: General Introduction to Pure Phenomenology*, tr. W.R. Boyce Gibson, London 1931.

INGRAM, D., *Habermas and the Dialectic of Reason*, New Haven 1987.

IRWIN, K.W., «Liturgical Actio – Sacramentality, Eschatology and Ecology», in L. BOEVE – L. LEIJSSEN, ed., *Contemporary Sacramental Contours of a God Incarnate*, Leuven 2001, 111-23.

———, «A Sacramental World – Sacramentality as the Primary Language for Sacraments», *Worship* 76 (2002) 197-211.

ISAMBERT, F., *Rite et Efficacité Symbolique: Essai d'anthropologie sociologique*, Paris 1979.

ISER, W., *The Act of Reading: A Theory of Aesthetic Response*, Baltimore 1978.

JARRETT, C.E., «Philosophy of Language in the Service of Religious Studies», *Semeia* 41 (1988) 143-59.

JARVIE, I.C., *Concepts and Society*, London 1972.

———, «Popper, Karl Raimund», in *REP*, VII, 533-40.

KEENER, C.S., «Family and Household», in C. EVANS – S. PORTER, ed., *Dictionary of the New Testament Background*, Downers Grove IL 2000, 353-68.

KOHLBERG, L., *Essays on Moral Development*. I. *The Philosophy of Moral Development*. II. *The Psychology of Moral Development*, New York 1981, 1984.

KROGER, J., «Prophetic-Critical and Practical-Strategic Tasks of Theology: Habermas and Liberation Theology», *TS* 46 (1985) 3-20.

LADRIÈRE, J., «The Performativity of Liturgical Language», *Concilium* 2.9 (1973) 50-62.

———, *L'Articulation du Sens*. I. *Discours scientifique et parole de la foi*. II. *Les langages de la foi*, Paris 1984.

LAKELAND, P., *Postmodernity: Christian Identity in a Fragmented Age*, Minneapolis 1997.

LANSER, S.S., «(Feminist) Criticism in the Garden: Inferring Genesis 2-3», *Semeia* 41 (1988) 67-84.

LAWLER, M.G., *Symbol and Sacrament: A Contemporary Sacramental Theology*, New York 1987.

LEVINE, M., «God Speak», *RelS* 34 (1998) 1-16.

LOISKANDL, H., «Data, Facts and Appresentation: The Phenomenological Approach and the Concept of Fact in the Social Sciences», in R. SMALL, ed., *A Hundred Years of Phenomenology: Perspectives on a Philosophical Tradition*, Aldershot 2001, 149-57.

LONERGAN, B., *Method in Theology*, London 1972.

LUKÁCS, L., «Communication – Symbols - Sacraments», in L. BOEVE – L. LEIJSSEN, ed., *Contemporary Sacramental Contours of a God Incarnate*, Leuven 2001, 137-53.

LYALL, F., «Roman Law in the Writings of Paul – Adoption», *JBL* 88 (1969) 458-66.

MARCEL, G., *Présence et Immortalité*, Paris 1959.

MARTINEZ, G., *Signs of Freedom: Theology of the Christian Sacraments*, New York 2003.

MARTINICH, A.P., «Sacraments and Speech Acts», *HeyJ* 16 (1975) 289-303, 405-17.

MAUSS, M., *Sociologie et anthropologie*, Paris 1968[4].

————, *Essai sur le don, forme archaïque de l'échange*, Paris 1934; English trans., *The Gift: Forms and Functions of Exchange in Archaic Societies*, tr. I. Cunnison, London 1980.

MCCABE, H., *God Matters*, London 1987.

MEAD, G.H., *Mind, Self, and Society*, Chicago 1934.

MEIER, J.P., *Mentor, Message, and Miracles: A Marginal Jew: Rethinking the Historical Jesus*, II, New York 1994.

MILLER, V.J., «An Abyss at the Heart of Mediation: Louis-Marie Chauvet's Fundamental Theology of Sacramentality», *Horizons* 24 (1997) 230-47.

MOORE, G, «The Forgiveness of Sins: A Ritual History», *ACR* 77 (2000) 10-19.

MORRIS, C.W., *Foundations of the Theory of Signs*, Chicago 1938.

MUERS, R., «Silence and the Patience of God», *MTh* 17 (2001), 85-98.

NDIONE, E.S., *Le Don et le Recours: Ressorts de l'économie urbaine*, Dakar 1992.

NEUFELD, D., «Acts of Admonition and Rebuke: A Speech Act Approach to 1 Corinthians 6:1-11», *BiI* 8 (2000) 375-99.

NODET, É. – TAYLOR, J., *The Origins of Christianity: An Exploration*, Collegeville MN 1998.

O'COLLINS, G., *Fundamental Theology*, New York 1981.

————, «Believing in the Risen Christ», in *Gottes Zukunft-Zukunft der Welt*, Fs. J. Moltmann, München 1986, 68-77.

————, *Christology: A Biblical, Historical, and Systematic Study of Jesus*, Oxford 1995.

O'COLLINS, G., – KENDALL, D., *Focus on Jesus: Essays in Christology and Soteriology*, Leominster 1996.

O'COLLINS, G., – FARRUGIA, M., *Catholicism: The Story of Catholic Christianity*, Oxford 2003.

OHMANN, R., «Speech Acts and the Definition of Literature», *PhRh* 4 (1971) 1-19.

OSBORNE, K.B., *Christian Sacraments in a Postmodern World: A Theology for the Third Millennium*, New York 1999.

OUTHWAITE, W., ed., *The Habermas Reader*, Cambridge 1996.

OWENS, J., «Dissenting from Reality: The Denials of Evil» *Logos: A Journal of Catholic Thought and Culture* 7 (2004) 133-49.

PARSONS, T., *The Social System*, Glencoe IL 1951.

PATTE, D., «Speech Act Theory and Biblical Exegesis», *Semeia* 41 (1988) 85-102.

PIAGET, J., *L'épistémologie génétique*, Paris 1970; English trans., *The Principles of Genetic Epistemology*, tr. W. Mays, New York 1972.

PILARIO, F., «"Gift-Exchange" in Sacramentology: A Critical Assessment from the Perspective of Pierre Bourdieu», in L. BOEVE – L. LEIJSSEN, ed., *Contemporary Sacramental Contours of a God Incarnate*, Leuven 2001, 85-101.

POPPER, K.R., *Logik der Forschung*, Tübingen 1935, 1982[7].

———, *The Poverty of Historicism*, Boston 1957.

———, *The Open Society and Its Enemies*, London 1945, 1962[4].

———, *Objective Knowledge: An Evolutionary Approach*, Oxford 1972.

POPPER, K. – ECCLES, J., *The Self and Its Brain: An Argument for Interactionism*, Berlin 1977.

POSTMAN, N., *Amusing Ourselves to Death: Public Discourse in the Age of Show Business*, New York 1985.

PRATT, M.L., *Towards a Speech Act Theory of Literary Discourse*, Bloomington 1977.

RAHNER, K., «The Theology of the Symbol» in *TI* 4 (1959) 221-252.

RASMUSSEN, D.M., *Reading Habermas*, Oxford 1990.

REBOUL, A., «Semantic Transparency, Semantic Opacity, States of Affairs, Mental States and Speech Acts», in L. ANOLLI – R. CICERI – G. RIVA, ed., *Say not to Say: New perspectives on miscommunication*, Burke, VA 2001, 46-71.

RÉCANATI, F., *Les Énoncés Performatifs: Contribution à la Pragmatique*, Paris 1981.

———, «Pragmatics» in *REP*, VII, 620-33.

RENGSTORF, K.H., «σημεῖον», *TDNT*, VII, 200-69.

RICOEUR, P., *The Conflict of Interpretations: Essays in Hermeneutics*, Evanston 1974.

RIES, J.C., «Facets of Sacramentology: Introduction», in L. BOEVE – L. LEIJSSEN, ed., *Contemporary Sacramental Contours of a God Incarnate*, Leuven 2001, 105-09.

ROBERTS, P., «Habermas' Varieties of Communicative Action: Controversy Without Combat», *JAC* 11.2 (1991) 121-42.

RORTY, R., ed., *The Linguistic Turn: Recent Essays in Philosophical Method*, Chicago 1967.

ROSATO, P.J., «The Prophetic Acts of Jesus: The Sacraments and the King-dom», in *Gottes Zukunft-Zukunft der Welt*, Fs. J. Moltmann, München 1986, 59-67.

ROSE, G., *Hegel Contra Sociology*, London 1981, 1995².

ROUET, A., «Vers une théologie du diaconat», *Études* 400 (2004) 789-800.

SBISÀ, M., «The room for negotiation in apologizing: evidence from the Ital-ian speech act of *scusarsi*», provisional version of the unpublished paper read at the International Conference Pragma99, «Pragmatics and Negotiation», Tel Aviv and Jerusalem, 13-16 June 1999.

——, «Communicating citizenship in verbal interaction: Principles of a speech act oriented discourse analysis», unpublished notes for the workshop «Communicating Citizenship in Decision-Making Proce-dures», Bielefeld, 28-30 June 2001.

SCHERER, K.R., «Analysis of Nonverbal Behaviour», in T.A. van DIJK, ed., *Handbook of Discourse Analysis*, II, London 1985, 199-212.

SCHILLEBEECKX, E., *Christus Sacrament van de Gosontmoeting*, Bilthoven 1960; English trans., *Christ the Sacrament of the Encounter with God*, tr. P. Barrett, New York 1963.

SCOLA, A., «Human Freedom and Truth According to the Encyclical *Fides et Ratio*», *Communio* 26 (1999) 486-509.

SEARLE, J.R., *Speech Acts: An Essay in the Philosophy of Language*, Cam-bridge 1969.

——, «Reiterating the Differences: A Reply to Derrida», *Glyph* 1 (1977) 198-208.

——, *Intentionality: An Essay in the Philosophy of Mind*, Cambridge 1983.

——, *The Construction of Social Reality*, New York 1995.

SHERZER, J., «Puns and Jokes», in T.A. van DIJK, ed., *Handbook of Discourse Analysis*, III, London 1985, 213-21.

SMITH, B., «Towards a History of Speech Act Theory», in A. BURKHARDT, ed., *Speech Acts, Meanings and Intentions: Critical Approaches to the Philosophy of John R. Searle*, Berlin 1990, 29-61.

SMITH, J.M. – MCCLENDON, J.W., «Religious Language After J.L. Austin», *RelS* 8 (1972) 55-63.

STACEY, W.D., «The Lord's Supper as Prophetic Drama», in *The Signs of a Prophet. The Prophetic Actions of Jesus*, London 1997, 80-95.

STEPHENS, M., «Theologian of Talk», *Los Angeles Times Magazine* 23 Octo-ber 1994, 11-18.

TANNER, N., ed., *Decrees of the Ecumenical Councils*, London 1990.

TANNER, N., *The Councils of the Church: A Short History*, New York 2001.

———, *Is the Church Too Asian? Reflections on the Ecumenical Councils*, Rome 2002.

———, *Was the Church too Democratic? Councils, Collegiality and the Church's Future*, Bangalore 2003.

TAYLOR, J., «Why were the Disciples First called "Christians" at Antioch? (Acts 11,26)», *RB* 101 (1994) 75-94.

THISELTON, A.C., «The Parables as Language-event: Some Comments on Fuchs' Hermeneutics in the Light of Linguistic Philosophy», *SJT* 23 (1970) 437-68.

———, «The Supposed Power of Words in the Biblical Writings», *JTS* 25 (1974) 283-99.

———, «Speech-Act Theory and the Claim that God Speaks: Nicholas Wolterstorff's *Divine Discourse*», *SJT* 50 (1997) 97-110.

THOMPSON, J.B. – HELD, D., ed., *Habermas: Critical Debates*, Cambridge MA 1982.

TOULMIN, S., *The Uses of Argument*, Cambridge 1958.

TRACY, D., *The Analogical Imagination: Christian Theology and the Culture of Pluralism*, New York 1981.

TURNER, V.W., *The Forest of Symbols: Aspects of Ndembu Ritual*, New York 1967.

———, *The Drums of Affliction: A Study of Religious Processes among the Ndembu of Zambia*, Oxford 1968.

———, *The Ritual Process: Structure and Anti-Structure*, London 1969.

URMSON, J.O., «J.L. AUSTIN» *JP* 62 (1965) 499-508.

———, «Austin's Philosophy», in K.T. FANN, ed., *Symposium on J.L. Austin*, London 1969, 22-32.

———, «Austin, John Langshaw (1911-60)», in *REP*, I, 1998, 571-74.

VANHOOZER, K.J., «The Hermeneutics of I-Witness Testimony: John 21.20-24 and the "Death" of the "Author"», in A.G. AULD, ed., *Understanding Poets and Prophets*, Fs. G.W. Anderson, Sheffield 1993 366-87.

———, *Is There a Meaning in this Text? The Bible, The Reader and the Morality of Literary Knowledge*, Grand Rapids 1998.

VAN ROO, W.A., «Symbol According to Cassirer and Langer», *Gr.* 53 (1972) 487-530; 615-73.

———, *The Christian Sacrament*, AnGr 262, Rome 1992.

WALSH, T.G., «Religion and Communicative Action», *Thought* 62 (1987) 111–25.

WARNOCK, G.J., *English Philosophy Since 1900,* London 1958, 1969².

———, «John Langshaw Austin, A Brief Biographical Sketch», in K.T. FANN, ed., *Symposium on J.L. Austin,* London 1969, 3-21.

WEBER, M., *The Protestant Ethic and the Spirit of Capitalism,* New York 1958.

WHITE, H.C., «Introduction: Speech Act Theory and Literary Criticism», *Semeia* 41 (1988) 1-25.

———, «The Value of Speech Act Theory for Old Testament Hermeneutics», *Semeia* 41 (1988) 41-63.

WHITE, S., *The Cambridge Companion to Habermas,* Cambridge 1995.

WHITEHEAD, A.N., – RUSSELL, B., *Principia Mathematica,* London 1910, 1925².

WIGGERSHAUS, R., *Die Frankfurter Schule,* München 1986; English trans., *The Frankfurt School: Its History, Theories and Political Significance,* tr. M. Robertson, Cambridge 1994.

WILKEN, R.L., «Tutoring the Affections: Liturgy and Christian Formation in the Early Church», *Antiphon* 8 (2003) 21-7.

WISDOM, J., *Other Minds,* Oxford 1952.

———, *Philosophy and Psycho-analysis,* Oxford 1953.

———, *Paradox and Discovery,* Oxford 1965.

WOJTYLA, K., «O metafizycznej i fenomenologicznej podstawie normy moralnej (w oparciu o koncepje sw. Tomasza z Akwinu oraz Maksa Schelera)», *Roczniki Teologiczno-Kanoniczne* 6 (1959) 99-124; English trans., «On the Metaphysical and Phenomenological Basis of the Moral Norm: In the Philosophy of Thomas Aquinas and Max Scheler», tr. T. Sandok, in K. WOJTYLA, *Person and Community: Selected Essays,* New York 1993, 73-94.

———, «Podmiotowocsi i "to, co nieredukowalne" w czlowieku», *Ethos* 1 (1988) 21-28; a paper sent to an international conference in Paris (13-14 June 1975); English trans., «Subjectivity and the Irreducible in the Human Being», tr. T. Sandok, in K. WOJTYLA, *Person and Community: Selected Essays,* New York 1993, 209-17.

WOLTERSTORFF, N., *Divine Discourse: Philosophical reflections on the claim that God speaks,* Cambridge 1995.

———, «Reply to Levine», *RelS* 34 (1998) 17-23.

WORGUL, G.S., «Root Metaphors and Sacramental Presence in a Postmodern Age», in L. BOEVE – L. LEIJSSEN, ed., *Contemporary Sacramental Contours of a God Incarnate*, Leuven 2001, 124-36.

YOUNG, R.A., «Speech Act Theory and Conditional Sentences in the Greek New Testament», *Theological Research Exchange Network: Conference Papers* 1988, 1-18.

INDEX OF NAMES

Abendoth: 85
Adorno, M.: 82
Adorno, T.: 82, 83, 85, 91, 128
Alexander of Alexandria: 215
Apel: 86, 91
Aquinas: 10, 75, 141-143, 149-151, 153, 154, 157, 216
Aristotle: 106, 151, 165, 237
Athanasius: 215
Atkinson: 67
Auer: 207
Augustine: 9, 10, 151, 153-157, 198, 215, 216, 219, 220, 226-228
Austin: 12-14, 16, 21-79, 86, 89, 90, 103, 115, 118-120, 122, 137, 139, 140, 147, 158-169, 171, 172, 174, 186, 203, 211, 215, 222, 224, 230, 236, 237, 240, 248
Ayer: 22, 23
Baldovin: 140
Bartali: 80
Bauerschmidt: 133
Baxter: 205
Bellah: 152
Benjamin: 82, 89, 91, 133

Benveniste: 141
Berg: 82, 83
Best: 182
Bloch: 82, 83
Botha: 73, 74, 240
Bourdieu: 140, 163-167, 169, 179, 180
Brecht: 82, 83
Briggs: 72, 171
Brinkmann: 75, 76, 240
Carnap: 19, 110
Chauvet: 14-17, 139-147, 149-164, 167-171, 174-180, 184-200, 203, 213, 230, 231, 233, 236, 237, 244, 248
Chomsky: 90
Cohen: 124
Damascene: 141
Dawkins: 27
Derrida: 43, 63, 157, 215
Descartes: 87
Donne: 69
Drew: 67
Dulles: 239
Dutschke: 80
Eisler: 82, 83
Eliade: 178

Elias: 82, 83
Embree: 25
Evans: 14, 70, 71, 168-173, 175
Farrelly: 136
Fenn: 230, 241, 242
Finney: 29
Fish: 69
Frege: 22
Frere: 206
Freud: 82, 91
Fromm: 82, 91
Fuchs: 71
Gadamer: 85, 112
Gehlen: 128
Gödel: 21, 53
Gorman: 140
Gray: 142
Grey: 182
Grice: 65, 66, 68, 73, 162, 215,
    217, 218
Grimes: 47, 67, 165
Habermas: 13-15, 17, 79-133, 135-
    137, 139, 141, 157, 163-165,
    167, 170, 176, 189, 203, 204,
    207, 210, 211, 214, 223, 225,
    231, 249
Heidegger: 84, 87, 128, 141, 153,
    197
Herder: 128
Heritage: 67
Hermes: 235
Hobson: 222, 223, 247
Holmes: 241
Horkheimer: 81-83, 85, 87
Houston: 72
Hugh of St Victor: 5, 10, 216
Husserl: 25, 94, 95
Isambert: 163, 168-170, 179, 180
Jarvie: 91

John Paul II (see Wojtyla): 16,
    199, 228, 243
Joseph: 22
Joyce: 68
Kant: 87, 132
Kirchheimer: 82
Klingelhöfer: 81
Kohlberg: 91, 133
Kracauer: 82, 83
Ladrière: 14, 74, 75, 169, 171-175,
    241
Lang: 82, 83
Lanser: 66
Lea: 231
Lenya: 82, 83
Linnaeus: 26
Lombard: 10, 235
Löwenthal: 82
Löwith: 85
Lukács: 82, 83
Luther: 64, 70
Mann, E.: 82, 83
Mann, T.: 82, 83
Mao: 80
Marcion: 244
Marcuse: 80, 82
Martinich: 75, 76
Marx: 80-82, 87, 88, 135
Mauss: 180-184, 248
McClendon: 70, 71
Mead, G.: 90, 129
Mead, M.: 241
Melancthon: 64
Ménard: 140
Moore: 20, 71
Morris: 65, 90, 110
Natorp: 124
Neumann: 82
Neurath: 19

Nietzsche: 87, 128
Nodet: 238, 246
O'Brien: 233
O'Collins: 142, 213, 249
Ohmann: 68
Osborne: 231, 235, 236
Owens: 218
Parsons: 91
Piaget: 91, 111, 133
Plato: 149
Popper: 89, 91-93, 98-101, 128
Postman: 219
Praepositinus: 216
Pratt: 68, 69
Prosper of Aquitaine: 194
Rahner: 75
Ranaipiri: 182
Ratzinger: 87
Reboul: 35
Récanati: 73
Rickert: 124
Ricoeur: 14, 199
Rorty: 88
Rose: 124
Rufinus: 215
Russell: 20, 34, 60
Ryan: 182
Sbisà: 65
Schelling: 84
Schillebeeckx: 248
Schlick: 19
Scholem: 82
Schönberg: 82, 83

Schuller: 87
Searle: 62-65, 68-70, 72, 75, 90,
    94, 99, 112, 114, 118, 119, 129,
    161, 214, 215, 232, 234
Sherzer: 67
Smith: 70, 71
Socrates: 149
Sohn-Rethel: 82, 83
Stephens: 84
Swift: 30
Taylor: 238, 246
Thiselton: 71, 72
Tokoahu: 182
Toulmin: 132
Turner: 177
Twain: 27
Urmson: 23, 47, 61
van Dijk: 67
Van Eyck: 133
Vanhoozer: 64, 69, 70
Victoria (Queen): 222, 223
Warnock: 21
Weber: 90, 124
White: 136
Whitehead: 20, 34, 60
Wiggershaus: 80, 81, 83
Williams: 182
Windelbrand: 124
Wisdom: 36
Wittgenstein: 20, 21, 57, 71, 172,
    174
Wojtyla (see John Paul II): 199
Wolterstorff: 72, 73, 221, 223, 226

INDEX OF FIGURES

1: J.L. Austin, 1951 18
2: The Code Model of Communication 35
3: Initial Constative-Performative Relationship 42
4: The Types of Infelicity 47
5: Phones, Phemes and Rhemes 49
6: A Hexagon? 54
7: Final Constative-Performative Relationship 59
8: Jürgen Habermas, 1995 78
9: Popper's Three Worlds 93
10: Maps of the World 98
11: Habermas's Three Worlds 103
12: Domains of Reality 104
13: World-Relations of Communicative Acts 105
14: Analysis of Actions 113
15: Pure Types of Interaction 116
16: «I warn you, smoke a pipe» 121
17: Locating systematically distorted communication 123
18: Parallel between assertoric and normative statements 130
19: Progressive Rationalization of Society 134
20: Louise-Marie Chauvet, 2004 138
21: Paschal Mystery of Christ 143
22: The Structure of Christian Identity 145
23: Structure of Symbol and Sacrament 148
24: Chauvet's "Diagram 1" 190
25: Chauvet's "Diagram 2" 190
26: The "Revealing" Cycle 191
27: The "Operating" Cycle 192
28: Parallel Structure of Sign Nature and Validity Claims 209

29: Worlds and Sacramental Utterance 212
30: Intention and its Recognition 217
31: Sacrament as double-agency discourse 220
32: Timeline of the Origins of the Sacraments 235

TABLE OF CONTENTS

ACKNOWLEDGEMENTS.. 7

INTRODUCTION 9

1. The Aim and the Limits 11
    1.1 John Austin: Speech Act Theory.. 12
    1.2 Jürgen Habermas: Theory of Communicative Action 13
    1.3 Louis-Marie Chauvet: Symbolic Efficacy................................. 14
    1.4 Sacraments within a Catholic Lifeworld 15
2. Toward a Formal Communicative Theory of Sacraments................. 16

CHAPTER I: *John Austin and Speech Act Theory* 19

1. The Contribution of Communication Theory 19
2. The Turn to Language... 19
3. John Langshaw Austin 21
4. Austin's View of Philosophy 22
5. Austin's Method... 24
    5.1 What is it that we say? 24
    5.2 What can we not say?.. 27
    5.3 Look to the Past 28
    5.4 But Attend to the New 28
    5.5 When «what we say» Fails... 30
    5.6 The Distinctions within Ordinary Language 31
6. Austin's Results 33
    6.1 The Descriptive Fallacy 33
    6.2 Performative Utterances.. 39
    6.3 The Doctrine of Infelicities 42
    6.4 The Parts of Speech 48
    6.5 We Say Things to Influence People 51

6.6 What is Truth? 53
6.7 Emotions and the Inner World 56
6.8 Descriptive Statements are Performative Utterances................. 57
6.9 An Austin-style Analysis 61
7. The Uptake of Austin's Ideas.. 61
   7.1 Philosophy – Speech Act Theory 62
   7.2 Linguistics – Pragmatics 65
   7.3 The Social Sciences – Discourse Analysis............................ 66
      7.3.1 Anthropology – Ritual Criticism.............................. 67
   7.4 Literature – Speech Act Theories of Text 67
      7.4.1 Interpreting Action – A Speech Act Theory of Deeds...... 69
   7.5 Theology.. 70
      7.5.1 Religious Language – Self-Involvement...................... 70
      7.5.2 The Parables as Performative Utterances 71
      7.5.3 Old Testament Prophecy as Speech Acts 72
      7.5.4 A Dialogue in John's Gospel – A Speech Act Reading.... 73
      7.5.5 Liturgy – Performative Language 74
      7.5.6 A Speech Act Approach to Sacramental Causality 75
8. What Austin Offers to This Thesis....................................... 76

CHAPTER II: *Jürgen Habermas and Communicative Action* 79

1. Introduction.. 79
2. The Frankfurt School 80
   2.1 The Institute for Social Research 80
3. A Biographical Sketch of Jürgen Habermas.......................... 83
4. Habermas's View of Philosophy... 87
5. Habermas's Method 90
6. Habermas's Results... 91
   6.1 Three Worlds of Discourse 91
      6.1.1 Lifeworld 94
      6.1.2 The Objective World... 98
      6.1.3 The Subjective World 100
      6.1.4 The Social World... 101
      6.1.5 Lifeworld and Worlds... 102
   6.2 Concepts of Action 106
   6.3 Towards Universal Conditions of Possible Understanding 109
      6.3.1 A General Theory of Speech Acts............................ 111
      6.3.2 Categorising Speech Acts 112
      6.3.3 Categorising Interactions 115

6.3.4 Non-verbal Communicative Actions................................. 117
6.4 The Double Structure of Speech 118
6.5 Systematically Distorted Communication 122
6.6 Validity Claims 124
    6.6.1 Redemption of Validity Claims.......................... 125
    6.6.2 Freedom to Refuse 127
6.7 Success in a Speech Act.. 128
6.8 Reflectivity – Arguing with Yourself.......................... 129
6.9 Discourse Ethics 130
6.10 The Evolution of Societies and the Role of Religion 133
7. Conclusion 136

CHAPTER III: *Louis-Marie Chauvet and Symbolic Efficacy* 139

1. Introduction.. 139
2. Louis-Marie Chauvet 139
    2.1 Some of Chauvet's Theological Presuppositions 141
    2.2 The Structure of Christian Identity....................... 144
3. The Structure of *Symbol and Sacrament* 147
4. Chauvet's critique of Metaphysics 149
    4.1 Being vs. Becoming 149
    4.2 Onto-Theology underrates language 151
        4.2.1 Does Chauvet misrepresent Augustine and Aquinas? 153
5. The Symbolic Order which Mediates Reality 157
6. Chauvet's Use of Speech Act Theory 158
    6.1 Constative and Peformative 159
    6.2 The Springs the Illocution Releases 164
    6.3 Applying Speech Act Theory to Rituals..................... 167
        6.3.1 Rituals are Stagings of Illocutions.................... 167
        6.3.2 The Illocution, the Conventions and the Social Other...... 170
    6.4 Self-Implication 171
        6.4.1 Self-Implication in Liturgy 174
        6.4.2 Self-Implication in Sacraments 175
7. Symbolic Exchange... 180
    7.1 In Traditional Societies 180
    7.2 In Contemporary Western Society 184
8. The Act of Symbolization 187
9. The Corporality and Particularity of Sacraments 189
10. «Vatican II» Model of Sacraments.................................. 190
    10.1 Penance – a good fit to Chauvet's model 194

10.2 Eucharist – a challenge for Chauvet's model 196
11. Conclusion 199

CHAPTER IV: *Sacraments within a Catholic Lifeworld* 203

1. Introduction.. 203
2. The Roman Catholic Communicative Community 203
   2.1 Personality Structures 205
   2.2 Sacraments and the Three Validity Claims 207
   2.3 Liturgy and the Worlds of Discourse 210
   2.4 Sacraments as Institutionally Bound Speech Acts..................... 214
   2.5 The Intention of the Minister of a Sacrament........................... 215
   2.6 The Effect of the Sacrament and the Holiness of the Minister ... 219
   2.7 Sacramental Character 222
   2.8 Subjective Requirements for the Recipient of the Sacraments ... 224
      2.8.1 The Baptism of a Baby... 226
      2.8.2 Anointing *in extremis* 228
   2.9 The Total Sacrament in the Total Sacramental Situation 230
   2.10 Historical Continuity.. 231
   2.11 The Institution of the Sacraments.. 233
3. Performative and Constative 236
   3.1 Revelation as Primarily Performative 237
   3.2 Sacraments as Primarily Performative 240
4. Salvation History as Communicative Action 242
   4.1 Always-Already Speaking 244
   4.2 Novelty 245
5. Conclusion 248

ABBREVIATIONS.. 251

BIBLIOGRAPHY... 253

1. Magisterial Documents 253
2. General works 254

INDEX OF NAMES 269

INDEX OF FIGURES 272

TABLE OF CONTENTS 274

TESI GREGORIANA

Dal 1995, la collana «Tesi Gregoriana» mette a disposizione del pubblico alcune delle migliori tesi elaborate alla Pontificia Università Gregoriana. La composizione per la stampa è realizzata dagli stessi autori, secondo le norme tipografiche definite e controllate dell'Università.

Volumi pubblicati [Serie: Teologia]

Per i volumi pubblicati prima dell'anno 2000 si consulti il sito web dell'Università: *www.unigre.it/TG/teologia.htm*

58. BARRIOCANAL GÓMEZ, José Luis, *La relectura de la tradición del éxodo en el libro de Amós*, 2000, pp. 332.

59. DE LOS SANTOS GARCÍA, Edmundo, *La novedad de la metáfora κεφαλή – σῶμα en la carta a los Efesios*, 2000, pp. 432.

60. RESTREPO SIERRA, Argiro, *La revelación según R. Latourelle*, 2000, pp. 442.

61. DI GIOVAMBATTISTA, Fulvio, *Il giorno dell'espiazione nella Lettera agli Ebrei*, 2000, pp. 232.

62. GIUSTOZZO, Massimo, *Il nesso tra il culto e la grazia eucaristica nella recente lettura teologica del pensiero agostiniano*, 2000, pp. 456.

63. PESARCHICK, Robert A., *The Trinitarian Foundation of Human Sexuality as Revealed by Christ according to Hans Urs von Balthasar. The Revelatory Significance of the Male Christ and the Male Ministerial Priesthood*, 2000, pp. 328.

64. SIMON, László T., *Identity and Identification. An Exegetical Study of 2Sam 21–24*, 2000. pp. 386.

65. TAKAYAMA, Sadami, *Shinran's Conversion in the Light of Paul's Conversion*, 2000, pp. 256.

66. JUAN MORADO, Guillermo, *«También nosotros creemos porque amamos». Tres concepciones del acto de fe: Newman, Blondel, Garrigou-Lagrange. Estudio comparativo desde la perspectiva teológico-fundamental*, 2000, pp. 444.

67. MAREČEK, Petr, *La preghiera di Gesù nel vangelo di Matteo. Uno studio esegetico-teologico*, 2000, pp. 246.

68. WODKA, Andrzej, *Una teologia biblica del dare nel contesto della colletta paolina (2Cor 8–9)*, 2000, pp. 356.

69. LANGELLA, Maria Rigel, *Salvezza come illuminazione. Uno studio comparato di S. Bulgakov, V. Lossky, P. Evdokimov*, 2000, pp. 292.

70. RUDELLI, Paolo, *Matrimonio come scelta di vita: opzione – vocazione – sacramento*, 2000, pp. 424.

71. GAŠPAR, Veronika, *Cristologia pneumatologica in alcuni autori cattolici postconciliari. Status quaestionis e prospettive*, 2000, pp. 440.

72. GJORGJEVSKI, Gjoko, *Enigma degli enigmi. Un contributo allo studio della composizione della raccolta salomonica (Pr 10,1–22,16)*, 2001, pp. 304.

73. LINGAD, Celestino G., Jr., *The Problems of Jewish Christians in the Johannine Community*, 2001, pp. 492.

74. MASALLES, Victor, *La profecía en la asamblea cristiana. Análisis retórico-literario de 1Cor 14,1-25*, 2001, pp. 416.

75. FIGUEIREDO, Anthony J., *The Magisterium-Theology Relationship. Contemporary Theological Conceptions in the Light of Universal Church Teaching since 1835 and the Pronouncements of the Bishops of the United States*, 2001, pp. 536.

76. PARDO IZAL, José Javier, *Pasión por un futuro imposible. Estudio literario-teológico de Jeremías 32*, 2001, pp. 412.

77. HANNA, Kamal Fahim Awad, *La passione di Cristo nell'Apocalisse*, 2001, pp. 480.

78. ALBANESI, Nicola, *«Cur Deus Homo»: la logica della redenzione. Studio sulla teoria della soddisfazione di S. Anselmo arcivescovo di Canterbury*, 2001, pp. 244.

79. ADE, Edouard, *Le temps de l'Eglise. Esquisse d'une théologie de l'histoire selon Hans Urs von Balthasar*, 2002, pp. 368.

80. MENÉNDEZ MARTÍNEZ, Valentín, *La misión de la Iglesia. Un estudio sobre el debate teológico y eclesial en América Latina (1955-1992), con atención al aporte de algunos teólogos de la Compañía de Jesús*, 2002, pp. 346.

81. COSTA, Paulo Cezar, *«Salvatoris Disciplina». Dionísio de Roma e a* Regula fidei *no debate teológico do terceiro século*, 2002, pp. 272.

82. PUTHUSSERY, Johnson, *Days of Man and God's Day. An Exegetico-Theological Study of ἡμέρα in the Book of Revelation*, 2002, pp. 302.

83. BARROS, Paulo César, *«Commendatur vobis in isto pane quomodo unitatem amare debeatis». A eclesiologia eucarística nos* Sermones ad populum *de Agostinho de Hipona e o movimento ecumênico*, 2002, pp. 344.

84. PALACHUVATTIL, Joy, *«He Saw». The Significance of Jesus' Seeing Denoted by the Verb* εἶδεν *in the Gospel of Mark*, 2002, pp. 312.

85. PISANO, Ombretta, *La radice e la stirpe di David. Salmi davidici nel libro dell'Apocalisse*, 2002, pp. 496.

86. KARIUKI, Njiru Paul, *Charisms and the Holy Spirit's Activity in the Body of Christ. An Exegetical-Theological Study of 1Cor 12,4-11 and Rom 12,6-8*, 2002, pp. 372.

87. CORRY, Donal, *«Ministerium Rationis Reddendae». An Approximation to Hilary of Poitiers' Understanding of Theology*, 2002, pp. 328.

88. PIKOR, Wojciech, *La comunicazione profetica alla luce di Ez 2–3*, 2002, pp. 322.

89. NWACHUKWU, Mary Sylvia Chinyere, *Creation–Covenant Scheme and Justification by Faith. A Canonical Study of the God-Human Drama in the Pentateuch and the Letter to the Romans*, 2002, 378 pp.

90. GAGLIARDI, Mauro, *La cristologia adamitica. Tentativo di recupero del suo significato originario*, 2002, pp. 624.

91. CHARAMSA, Krzysztof Olaf, *L'immutabilità di Dio. L'insegnamento di San Tommaso d'Aquino nei suoi sviluppi presso i commentatori scolastici*, 2002, pp. 520.

92. GLOBOKAR, Roman, *Verantwortung für alles, was lebt. Von Albert Schweitzer und Hans Jonas zu einer theologischen Ethik des Lebens*, 2002, pp. 608.

93. AJAYI, James Olaitan, *The HIV/AIDS Epidemic in Nigeria. Some Ethical Considerations*, 2003, pp. 212.

94. PARAMBI, Baby, *The Discipleship of the Women in the Gospel according to Matthew. An Exegetical Theological Study of Matt 27:51b-56, 57-61 and 28: 1-10*, 2003, pp. 276.

95. NIEMIRA, Artur, *Religiosità e moralità. Vita morale come realizzazione della fondazione cristica dell'uomo secondo B. Häring e D. Capone*, 2003, pp. 308.

96. PIZZUTO, Pietro, *La teologia della rivelazione di Jean Daniélou. Influsso su Dei Verbum e valore attuale*, 2003, pp. 630.

97. PAGLIARA, Cosimo, *La figura di Elia nel vangelo di Marco. Aspetti semantici e funzionali*, 2003, pp. 400.

98. O'BOYLE, Aidan, *Towards a Contemporary Wisdom Christology. Some Catholic Christologies in German, English and French 1965-1995*, 2003, pp. 448.

99. BYRNES, Michael J., *Conformation to the Death of Christ and the Hope of Resurrection: An Exegetico-Theological Study of 2 Corinthians 4,7-15 and Philippians 3,7-11*, 2003, p. 328.

100. RIGATO, Maria-Luisa, *Il Titolo della Croce di Gesù. Confronto tra i Vangeli e la Tavoletta-reliquia della Basilica Eleniana a Roma*, II edizione riveduta e corretta, 2005, pp. 392.

101. LA GIOIA, Fabio, *La glorificazione di Gesù Cristo ad opera dei discepoli. Analisi biblico-teologica di Gv 17,10b nell'insieme dei capp. 13–17*, 2003, pp. 346.

102. LÓPEZ-TELLO GARCÍA, Eduardo, *Simbología y Lógica de la Redención: Ireneo de Lyón, Hans Küng y Hans Urs von Balthasar leídos con la ayuda de Paul Ricœur*, 2003, pp. 396.

103. MAZUR, Aleksander, *L'insegnamento di Giovanni Paolo II sulle altre religioni*, 2003, pp. 354.

104. SANECKI, Artur, *Approccio canonico: tra storia e teologia, alla ricerca di un nuovo paradigma post-critico. L'analisi della metodologia canonica di B.S. Childs dal punto di vista cattolico*, 2004, pp. 480.

105. STRZELCZYK, Grzegorz, *«Communicatio idiomatum», lo scambio delle proprietà. Storia, «status quaestionis» e prospettive*, 2004, pp. 324.

106. CHO Hyun-Chul, *An Ecological Vision of the World: Toward a Christian Ecological Theology of Our Age*, 2004, pp. 318.

107. VLKOVÁ, Gabriela Ivana, *Cambiare la luce in tenebre e le tenebre in luce. Uno studio tematico dell'alternarsi tra la luce e le tenebre nel libro di Isaia*, 2004, pp. 316.

108. GHIO, Giorgio, *La deliberazione vitale come origine ultima della certezza applicata a Dio. Indagine sugli elementi d'ignoranza presenti nella certezza*, 2004, pp. 258.

109. MORRA, Stella, *«Pas sans toi». Testo, parola e memoria verso una dinamica della esperienza ecclesiale negli scritti di Michel de Certeau*, 2004, pp. 264.

110. SCORDAMAGLIA, Domenico, *Il Padre nella teologia di Sant'Ireneo*, 2004, pp. 366.

111. PLANELLAS BARNOSELL, Joan, *La recepción del Vaticano II en los manuales de eclesiología españoles. I. Ruidor, J. Collantes, M.M. Garijo-Guembe, S. Pié-Ninot, E. Bueno*, 2004, pp. 598.

112. FILIPPI, Nicola, *Essenza e forma di esercizio del ministero petrino. Il Magistero di Giovanni Paolo II e la riflessione ecclesiologica*, 2004, pp. 298.

113. PEGUERO PÉREZ, Javier, *La figura de Dios en los diálogos de Jesús con las autoridades en el Templo. Lectura de Mc 11,27–12,34 a partir de su instancia comunicativa*, 2004, pp. 426.

114. LÓPEZ BARRIO, Mario, *El tema del «Agape» en la primera carta de San Juan. Estudio de 1Jn 4,7-21: una perspectiva antropológico-social*, 2004, pp. 266.

115. BOREK, Wacław, *Unità e reciprocità delle membra della Chiesa. Studio esegetico-teologico di 1Cor 12,21-26; Rom 12,3-8; Ef 4,24–5,2*, 2004, pp. 352.

116. VIVES PÉREZ, Pedro Luis, *La singularidad de Cristo. Perspectivas convergentes en la cristología católica contemporánea*, 2004, pp. 464.

117. WITEK, Bernard, *Dio e i suoi figli. Analisi retorica della Prima Raccolta Salomonica (Pr 10,1–22,16)*, 2005, pp. 416.

118. BORGHINO, Angelo, *La «Nuova Alleanza» in Is 54. Analisi esegetico-teologica*, 2005, pp. 480.

119. URSO, Filippo, *«Imparò l'obbedienza dalle cose che patì» (Eb 5,8). Il valore educativo della sofferenza in Gesù e nei cristiani nella Lettera agli Ebrei*, 2005, pp. 514.

120. KIM, Jeong Rae, *«...perché io sono mite e umile di cuore» (Mt 11,29). Studio esegetico-teologico sull'umiltà del Messia secondo Matteo. Dimensione cristologica e risvolti ecclesiologici*, 2005, pp. 334.

121. DE VECCHI, Gaia, *L'Etica o* Scito te ipsum *di Pietro Abelardo. Analisi critica di un progetto di teologia morale*, 2005, pp. 208.

122. MENDOZA MAGALLÓN, Pedro, *«Estar crucificado juntamente con Cristo»: el nuevo status del creyente en Cristo. Estudio exegético-teológico de Gal 2,15-21 y Rom 6,5-11*, 2005, pp. 328.

123. DUFFY, Mervyn, *How Language, Ritual and Sacraments Work. According to John Austin, Jürgen Habermas and Louis-Marie Chauvet*, 2005, pp. 282.

STAMPA: Giugno 2005

presso la tipografia
"Giovanni Olivieri" di E. Montefoschi
ROMA • tip.olivieri@libero.it